THE BIG BOOK

OF SMALL BUSINESS

THE BIG BOOK

OF SMALL BUSINESS

YOU DON'T HAVE TO RUN YOUR BUSINESS
BY THE SEAT OF YOUR PANTS

TOM GEGAX

with Phil Bolsta

Previously published as *By the Seat of Your Pants*

Collins

An Imprint of HarperCollinsPublishers

THE BIG BOOK OF SMALL BUSINESS. Copyright © 2005, 2007 by Tom Gegax. All rights reserved. Printed in the United States of America. No part of this book may be used or reproduced in any manner whatsoever without written permission except in the case of brief quotations embodied in critical articles and reviews. For information, address HarperCollins Publishers, 10 East 53rd Street, New York, NY 10022.

Previously published as *By the Seat of Your Pants*

HarperCollins books may be purchased for educational, business, or sales promotional use. For information, please write: Special Markets Department, HarperCollins Publishers, 10 East 53rd Street, New York, NY 10022.

FIRST COLLINS EDITION

Designed by Ellen Cipriano

Library of Congress Cataloging-in-Publication Data

Gegax, Tom
      The big book of small business : you don't have to run your business by the seat of your pants / Tom Gegax with Phil Bolsta.
          p. cm.
      Rev. ed. of: By the seat of your pants. 2004.
      ISBN: 978-0-06-120669-6
      ISBN-10: 0-06-120669-5
      1. Small business—Management. 2. Entrepreneurship. I. Bolsta, Phil. II. Gegax, Tom. By the seat of your pants. III. Title.

HD62.7.G434 2007
658.02'2—dc22

                                                            2006043062

        09 10 11 WBC/RRD 10 9 8 7 6 5 4 3 2

This book is dedicated to my father, Bill, an old soldier who battles every day to overcome a horrendous stroke. He was a model enlightened entrepreneur, a fact that took me years to appreciate. His compassion with his employees and dedication to service inspired me to be a better businessman and a better person. When I was growing up, he liked to say, "Son, the most important word in the English language is 'empathy.'" When I told him I was starting a business, his first words were, "Always treat your employees right." He learned that appreciation the hard way, losing his father at a young age and countless war buddies in the trenches. But his love for God, country, and his fellow citizens never wavered. This one's for you, Dad.

CONTENTS

PART II

Pouring the Foundation:

Laying In Your Mission, Vision, and Values   53

PART III

Snatching Up Stars:

Embracing Your Hire Power   79

PART IV

Growing the Culture:

PART V

Building a Systems-Disciplined Organization:

PART VI

Communicating Clearly:

Sending Static-Free Signals

PART VII

Coaching Others:

Cheering and Steering, Not Domineering

PART VIII

Educating Employees:

PART IX

Coaching Yourself:

PART X

Business Function Dos and Don'ts:

PART XI

Weathering Worst-Case Scenarios:

When Bad Things Happen to Good Companies   379

FOREWORD

By Richard Schulze

Founder and Chairman, Best Buy

I met Tom Gegax at an Entrepreneur of the Year awards ceremony in 1994. I had been aware of Tom and of Tires Plus's success. Before leaving that evening, Tom invited me to lunch. A couple of weeks later, we met at one of my favorite restaurants. During the meal, he asked if I would mentor him. It wouldn't be much of a time commitment, he promised. We would get together for lunch every few months (after all, I had to eat anyway, he said) and he'd ask me questions. I was impressed with his earnestness, so, after thinking about it for a few days, I agreed.

Sure enough, Tom was thoroughly prepared for each lunch. He squeezed every ounce of value out of our time together. He came to every meeting with a carefully thought-through list of questions and a real determination to thoroughly understand every issue. He would keep asking questions until everything was clear. Here was a man who was not going to rest on his laurels. He was tireless in his pursuit of knowledge, and genuine in his attempt to learn from all who had achieved business success. Tom's hunger for insight into business management was insatiable. He frequently brought me members of his management team to engage in our dialogue, to share their discoveries and double-check the facts.

That determination paid off. In a competitive industry dominated by multinational firms, Tom and Tires Plus outexecuted their much larger rivals. He and his team turned Tires Plus into an important industry force with a unique culture, outstanding service, and a commanding market share.

Tom is a consummate team player, dedicated to what I value most in a leader—respect and consideration for everyone in the organization. He knows you win with motivated people supported by efficient business practices. That creates a culture of caring, accountability, and continuous process improvement.

Tom's *Big Book* has all the good stuff and none of the fluff. Let it guide your every step and the decisions of those throughout your organization. Then you, too, can find yourself on the road to undreamed-of business success.

LIVING BY THE SEAT OF MY PANTS

A Journey from Clueless to Cashing In

I had sold my company and the papers were signed. But the payment was two weeks overdue. I stared at the ceiling much of the night wondering how a "guarantee" to buy Tires Plus, my midwestern chain of 150 retail stores, had eroded into a "maybe." Tomorrow—tomorrow!—Bridgestone/Firestone had promised, it would wire the cash by 10:00 AM to seal the deal.

Tension in the office the next morning was thick enough to clobber with a tire iron. My CFO, Jim Bemis, called the bank at a few minutes past ten. No wire. He checked again after lunch. Nope. Finally, at three in the afternoon, Jim stepped into my office with a crooked grin. My cofounder, Don Gullett, and I held our breath. Four words sweeter than cotton candy danced on Jim's lips: "It's in the bank." It was all he had to say. A whoop and a holler later, we were high-fiving and hugging anything that moved.

Bridgestone/Firestone's sputtering had sent me hurtling down the high-stress highway. I didn't understand the holdup—until a week after the sale. That's when the big multinational issued a tire recall that made banner headlines around the globe; it threatened to implode the entire corporation and strip the luster off its trusted name. I figure our deal had been on life support.

I'm sure the only thing that saved it from flatlining was the hefty down payment and signed purchase agreement.

Don and I enjoyed divvying up the spoils. Tires Plus teammates pocketed $10 million in stock options and loyalty bonuses. Houses were remodeled, college plans were made. One teammate and his wife used their windfall to bounce back from a disastrous side enterprise that had plunged them into debt.

After cashing out, I dove headfirst into consulting, writing, and speaking. Of course, fiscal fitness is a hollow victory without the physical fitness to enjoy it. Today, at sixty, according to my doctors at Minnesota's Mayo Clinic, I have the heart of a thirty-year-old. I'm also blessed with the love of my family, friends, and life partner, Mary Wescott, an indispensable source of inspiration and strength.

THE REARVIEW MIRROR

Spinning back the odometer slides you into the front seat of a life running out of control and on fumes. As a nineteen-year-old sophomore at Indiana University, I was stone-cold broke with a pregnant new bride, working the three-to-midnight shift as a janitor at the Ford Motor Company factory. After years of rushing from college classes to the factory, changing into my janitor uniform at stoplights; delivering school newspapers; peddling insurance to fellow students; working in the HR department at Shell Oil in Chicago; transferring to sales fieldwork, at twenty-nine—after all that, I dreamed big and shared my idea for a new business with Don, a sales guy working for me. Thumbs-down at nine banks, thumbs-up at number ten. Tires Plus was born.

By 1989, Tires Plus had become a regional powerhouse with thirty locations. Life was good. Then, virtually overnight, life as I knew it ceased. In the course of six months, my doctor diagnosed me with cancer, my twenty-three-year marriage disintegrated, and my CFO told me the company till was a million bucks short and our credit line was dry.

Boom. Overnight, three critical pillars—health, family, career—turned to dust. And damned if that entire time I hadn't thought I was Mr. Got-It-

Covered. Now zombielike, I came in to work, locked my office door, set my phone to Do Not Disturb, and spent hours curled up on the couch. It was months before I could face myself in the mirror and begin taking responsibility for righting everything that had gone so disastrously wrong.

Inner Yearnings, Higher Earnings

Looking back, I see with equal parts amusement and horror that I had been running my company by the seat of my pants. I was sprinting as fast as I could yet always felt a step behind. It was still some time before I learned high-caliber communication and relationship-building skills. I hadn't implemented essential business management disciplines like strategic planning and budgetary protocols. I wasn't following skill-training and task-follow-up methodologies. I was also a mediocre leader, given that I was blissfully unaware of a basic law of the universe: Life is a card table. A well-balanced life relies on the four legs of healthy intellect, psyche, body, and spirit. Ignore one leg and the table wobbles. Disregard two or three, like I did, and it's going to collapse.

It was time to work and live with balance and discipline. I morphed into a knowledge junkie, devouring books, tapes, and seminars on business management and personal growth. For a know-it-all, I was amazed at how little I knew. I sought out the best and the brightest business mentors (Curt Carlson of Radisson/TGI Fridays, Carl Pohlad of the Minnesota Twins, Dick Schulze of Best Buy). Funny, but I had always prided myself on my knack for recognizing flaws in others. Now I turned the interrogation kliegs on myself and unblinkingly confessed years of denial, defensiveness, and doubt. It was painful but exhilarating work.

One by one, I started connecting the dots. Improving mental clarity and emotional health helped me spot and deal with unhealthy behavior. I was more caring, which inspired more commitment from employees and family. My new systems-disciplined mind-set led to greater efficiencies, smarter decisions, and peace of mind. Then something odd happened. The more I profited on a personal level, the more my company profited. Revenues began doubling every three years, reaching $200 million by 1999. Profits performed even better. I had learned the first lesson in Enlightened Leadership 101—establish protocols that hold people accountable. If you focus on the well-being of your employees and customers—as well as your own—success naturally follows.

MY BOSS JUST DOESN'T GET IT!

Entrepreneurs and managers, you'd be frightened how often I explain this philosophy and hear somebody blurt, "But my boss just doesn't get it!" As decision makers, you're fooling yourself if you think a large swath of working America isn't fed up, run-down, and exasperated from working for seat-of-the-pantsers.

Back in the early days of flying, the phrase "seat of the pants" was used to describe how pilots could guide their planes without complex navigation and control systems. They felt the plane react to every nudge of the stick via the largest point of contact between themselves and the plane: the backside of their trousers. "Flying by the seat of your pants" came to mean that, instead of piloting *proactively,* you're operating *reactively* by constantly changing course in response to feedback. In other words, you were figuring things out on the fly instead of creating and executing a flight plan.

A big part of running a business comes down to gut feelings and reactions. Relying on your intuition is smart—you wouldn't have gotten this far without it. But overreliance on instinct can lead to cutting corners: Why waste time planning and analyzing when you can shoot from the hip? Well, because one hiccup and you can shoot yourself in the foot. Sure, a seat-of-the-pants approach may get the job done in an entrepreneurial start-up . . . for a while. But a hot business has a way of starting a lot of brushfires and, as the flames lick your elbows and denial kicks in, you might not be able to face the possibility that your instincts will not save your neck this time.

Chances are you think you already know some of the stuff in this book. I was cocksure I did. But sometimes it's the lessons we've already mastered that trip us up. I'm reminded of mountain climber Cameron Tague. In 2000, Tague attempted to scale the sheer, one-thousand-foot Diamond Face on Longs Peak in Colorado. The expert climber didn't bother roping up on an easy traverse along the Big Wall's wide, sloping ledge, where five-year-olds and a six-piece band had safely climbed. You can guess what happened. Tague's mind apparently wandered; he pulled on a loose rock, and plunged eight hundred feet to his death. In business, we walk the cliff's edge every day—and none of us can afford to get careless.

Not only was I clueless that I was unenlightened, I didn't have a clue that I didn't have a clue. Even if you're smarter than I was, you're way too time crunched to hunt through hundreds of books, tapes, and seminars for the intelligence you need. No problem. These pages are packed with street-smart tips I collected while growing a start-up into a powerhouse in a fiercely competitive industry. In the seven years since I sold my business, I've applied the same strategies in my consulting work with the same results. These principles will boost your enlightenment quotient (EQ) whether you're just getting ready to launch or are a seasoned vet.

What does "enlightened" mean? Clarity of mind and clarity of vision. Scarce commodities that will make you infinitely more valuable and transform you into a chief *enlightenment* officer or an enlightened entrepreneur: *A tough-minded, warm-hearted, systems-disciplined leader who inspires people to embody the organization's mission, vision, and values.*

What's the Difference?

Your shoes are charred from stomping out brush fires. You have nightmares about UFOs (unreachable financial objectives). All-star interviewees turn into duds. Meetings cause more problems than they solve. Your office is a ghost town at 5:02 PM. Familiar scenarios? You may be a seat-of-the-pantser. The opposite is an enlightened entrepreneur—calm, confident, in control. How to tell them apart:

SEAT-OF-THE-PANTSER	ENLIGHTENED ENTREPRENEUR
His self-centered agenda drives every encounter.	He must take care of himself (intellectually, physically, emotionally, spiritually) before he can take care of employees.
She operates without a strategic plan, or with one that overshoots the future. Either way she's constantly putting out fires.	She recognizes that the high-speed marketplace demands flexibility. She knows how to break a strategic plan into operational steps and parcel assignments to the right people.
He cuts corners whenever possible, in pursuit of a better bottom line.	The high road is the only road. He knows that shortcuts become "longcuts" because they're often undone or redone.
She's a micromanager, oblivious to the toll on employees' creativity and motivation.	She knows how much supervision each team member needs and when to untether talented, motivated employees.
He's ready to unload on anyone who offers constructive criticism.	He solicits ideas for improvement—for his performance *and* the company's—through formal and informal channels.
She assumes that the only reason employees take up air on the planet is to do her bidding.	Her attitude toward employees is, *How can I help them grow and succeed?*
He passes on the best and brightest hires in favor of mediocrity for fear that somebody toiling under his command will outshine him.	He hires the best candidate for every position to elevate everyone's performance.
She's a daydreamer who's oblivious to what's going on around her and views details as distractions.	Her catlike situational awareness leads to empathetic relationships, constant quality upgrades, and competitive advantages.

Wonder if you qualify for enlightened entrepreneur status? To benchmark where you're at before reading *The Big Book,* go to the Business Management Assessment & Prescription™ tool at www.gegax.com. I consider it the Myers-Briggs of management assessments.

SYSTEMS AND ATTITUDE MAKE THE DIFFERENCE

Outsiders started sniffing around for Tires Plus's secret sauce after revenues climbed to $200 million from $40 million in just eight years. From the "brain pickers" who wanted to buy me lunch to the guy who playfully bumped his shoulder against mine at a reception and said, "Rub some of that magic on me," everyone hoped I could reduce it to one miracle-making word—like the tipsy exec in *The Graduate* who pulls aside young Dustin Hoffman and advises simply, "Plastics." Actually, the secret to how we thrived while competing against the world's largest corporations *can* be reduced to a single word—*synergy* (though not the "vertical integration" brand that was trendy in the 1990s).

We didn't take our rocket ride until we hit on just the right blend of organizational ingredients. Our mission guided savvy people in a caring, accountable culture, one supported by efficient processes and clear communication. We added the right mix of inspiration, incentives, and educational enrichment to grow through self-coaching. We also mixed in strategies for seven key business functions. This no-nonsense management system produced EBITDA (earnings before interest, taxes, depreciation, and amortization) so robust that we never had to sell shares to outsiders to fund growth.

WHY *THE BIG BOOK* DELIVERS A RICH ROI (RETURN ON INVESTMENT)

It's packed with proven, practical tips. I'm not proposing drawing-board theories that *might* work. The practices I outline in this book *do* work. I had the freedom to experiment in my workplace laboratory, studying the science— and art—of business management. Reading *The Big Book of Small Business,* you'll learn everything I learned during the day-to-day mess of meeting sales and profit projections, making payroll, and facing the consequences of every decision. The proof is in the puddin': I led a team that turned a $60,000 loan cosigned by my parents into a $200 million business that a multinational corporation paid a lot money for.

It charts a new course in managerial ethics. Most managers and entrepreneurs cut their teeth thinking that they must choose between two managerial philosophies: Put profits before people, or put people before profits. That's a false choice. I present a third way: The enlightened entrepreneur combines hard-nosed accountability and efficiency (putting profits first) with treating people fairly and with care (putting people first). Some leaders can squeeze out good short-term performance with the gruff-and-tough management style. But that doesn't work with businesses that benefit from low turnover; people will lose heart and quit after too long under a heartless leader. Likewise, employees respect and appreciate firm yet caring oversight that sets benchmarks and raises their own performance. It's the leaders who are both tough-minded and warmhearted that wind up with happy people and healthy long-term profits.

It's a step-by-step desk reference. Keep *The Big Book* on your desk. No matter what the challenge is, a quick scan of the table of contents will take you where you need to go. Job candidate coming in? Flip to the hiring section. Ideas slipping through the cracks? You want the section on efficient systems. Sales slacking? Grab a yellow highlighter and make a beeline for the sales chapter. No matter what page you land on, you'll find street-smart tips to help you:

- increase your brand equity (chapter 51)
- run meetings that staffers look forward to (chapter 26)
- establish the foundation for value creation (chapter 10)
- create an energized, ethical culture (chapters 17–21)
- protect your business interests (chapter 6)
- strengthen your supply chain (chapter 50)
- ensure that ideas are well executed (chapter 24)
- boost your market share (chapter 52)
- receive and deliver clear information (chapters 28–33)

- harvest outside advice (chapter 7)
- raise your game—and everyone else's (chapters 43–49)
- find, hire, and keep the best people (chapters 12–15)
- inspire employees to delight customers (chapter 53)
- deal with dysfunctional behavior (chapter 22)
- cut costs and improve your bottom line (chapter 54)
- design and execute strategic and operational plans (chapter 23)
- build good teams (chapter 16)
- manage airtight processes (chapter 27)
- enhance employee performance (chapters 39–42)
- manage the finance function and lender relationships (chapter 54)

HOW TO NAVIGATE *THE BIG BOOK*

People often ask, "What's the first step I should take?" Once you've crafted a top-shelf business plan, and once you trust that your model will produce cash, you'd pour the philosophical foundation—your mission, vision, and values. Then you'd snatch up stars, grow your culture, implement pitch-perfect processes, and communicate via static-free signals. You'd also coach your people to be hungry, teach them that school's always in session, and help them reach their peak personal performance.

There's only one problem: You live in the real world. Business, like life, is messy. So, where to begin? Start by identifying the source of your most acute pain—what's keeping you up at night?—and jump in. Morale tanking? In-effective communication may be the culprit. When your people emotionally check out, that also undermines your best practices and sabotages your mission, vision, and values. Or, start with a department—supply management's failure to negotiate better purchasing deals impairs marketing's ability to promote competitive offerings. That depresses sales, which leaves your best sales-people vulnerable to poachers at more profitable companies. Click. Here's your lightbulb moment: Your entire operation is interrelated, and that's reflected in *The Big Book*. Every element is linked to every other element. If any part of your business falters, the circle gets warped or broken. Ah, but when everything is running efficiently? That's when the magic happens.

Reach first for low-hanging fruit—it's important to chalk up early wins. Some shifts require only simple tweaks in thinking. Others take more dedication and planning. Get your team involved. Brainstorm solutions you can all call your own. As relationships are repaired and strengthened, as people feel respected and valued, change occurs. The synergy snowball keeps rolling, picking up energy, until you see no beginning and no end. Just results.

The business world has two constants—change and accelerating speed. It has one variable—your ability to keep up. Enlightened entrepreneurs do more than keep up; they lead the way.

THE BIG BOOK

OF SMALL BUSINESS

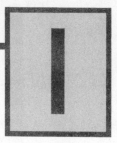

SETTING UP SHOP

What Every Budding Entrepreneur Needs to Know

It was my job as a Shell Oil Company sales manager to organize 1975's gala trade show for our Minnesota service station dealers. Instead of a run-of-the-mill hall, I booked a high-end Minneapolis hotel. What do you know, the upgrade worked: We doubled our sales goal. But my district manager, "John," chewed me out for modestly exceeding the event's budget. I protested that I had still netted a huge profit for Shell. "It doesn't matter," John spit. "You were still over your expense budget!" Hello? On what planet do profits not matter? As John stormed away and left me fuming, I thought, *I can't take this garbage, I've gotta think about starting my own company.*

Shell had planted the seed earlier in the year when execs poured cold water on my entrepreneurial impulse. I had seen a new era dawning for the oil industry when the Minnesota State Legislature legalized self-service gas stations. After researching the market possibilities, I designed a plan that seems obvious today for Shell station owners to convert one of their full-service pump islands over to self-service. Increased volume, I calculated, would more than offset Shell's share of conversion costs. Management yawned and said the self-service concept was probably a flash-in-the-pan trend. It was laughable, they added, to think that self-serve would catch on in the Minnesota tundra. End of discussion. Turns out it wasn't such of a leap to think that Minnesotans, who sit for hours on a frozen lake staring into a fishing hole in the ice, would happily don a parka for cheaper gas.

Two months after the trade show fiasco, my entrepreneurial engine was back in high gear. My boss, John, had scored football tickets to the big December clash between the Minnesota Vikings and the Green Bay Packers. A Packers fan, he asked me to book his hotel room—a presidential suite complete with fresh flowers and champagne—and put it on my expense account. With thousands of rabid Packers fans streaming into the Twin Cities, rooms were scarce. But I had a good relationship with a hotel near the stadium and managed to book precisely what John requested. A few weeks after the game (the Vikes ruled, 24–3), John held a sales meeting and announced a new corporate austerity program. It included a crackdown on expense accounts. After the meeting, I walked up and joked to John that it was a good thing the new policy didn't apply to the football weekend. John looked me in the eye and said, "God, I'm sorry, but it does," and walked away. Nothing more. I was stunned—and wound up paying $750 for John's weekend getaway (that's more than $2,800 in 2007 dollars, a big hit for a young family of four). Strike three; I'm outta there.

A few months later, I resigned to start Tires Plus. To be sure, my eight-year apprenticeship at Shell Oil was invaluable. Met a lot of good people, learned a lot of skills. But the plodding bureaucracy, risk phobia, and office politics were warping my idealism and enthusiasm. I was working in a Dilbert cartoon.

If you're running your own show, you can relate to the urge to ditch the out-of-touch boss, the tone-deaf bureaucracy, corporate America's myopic obsession on quarterly numbers. You and I, we wonder: How do so many people endure soul-draining offices? We're not cut out to work for somebody else. We want more control of our destiny. We're not afraid of hard work. We get excited about valuing entrepreneurship, ingenuity, and fairness—under a shingle that we hang ourselves. Most important, deep down, we possess a certainty—part confidence, part arrogance, part naïveté—that we've got what it takes to make it on our own.

Nodding your head? The next seven chapters describe what the early days need to look like if you want to succeed. There's a swarm of things to anticipate. I'll take you from wannabe entrepreneur to confident, informed start-up chief. Even if you're well underway, think of these chapters like a computerized scope hooked up to your car engine, detecting problems that you can fix now in order to avoid costly breakdowns later.

CHAPTER 1

MAKE UP YOUR MIND

Uncommon Factors to Consider Before Quitting Your Day Job

Call me naïve. It never occurred to me that my new business might fail.

Hey, this was *me* we're talking about. Tom Gegax. Four-sport high-school hotshot. Rising star at Shell Oil—earning promotions like compliments at the prom, tooling around town in a company car, illuminating for service-station managers the finer points of running their businesses. I knew it all.

In reality, I had no idea what I was about to do to myself—and to my family. Oh sure, my wife, Jan, and I had talked it through: Should I stay or should I go? Jan was supportive, telling me that I knew best whether I was up to the challenge. Of course I was. So I took the leap—and landed chest-deep in the proverbial creek, with the rapids rising fast.

Don't get me wrong: I'm glad I went out on my own. I just wish I had better anticipated the toll it would take. If I had been as prepared as you'll be after reading these pages, I would've dealt better with the inevitable crises that flew my way—and dodged many of them altogether.

Entrepreneurial types are apt to jump the starting gun. That pedal-to-the-metal mind-set is one of our greatest strengths. But it can also be our

Achilles' heel. In our zeal to conquer the business world, we may disregard or overlook these critical start-up issues.

Consider the impact on your family. In my acceptance speech for *Inc.* magazine's 1995 Midwest Entrepreneur of the Year Award, I wondered aloud whether the price I'd paid was too steep. In the early years, I was a slave to the business, working miserably long hours. While I did attend most of my kids' activities, and even coached their baseball and basketball teams, it felt as if I was always multitasking, wondering how to replace a key employee who had just resigned or whether I would make the next payroll. My kids, who quickly learned to recognize when I was zoning out, would jar me back into real time by tapping on my shoulder: "Earth to Dad." As the business grew, I had more flexibility for family time, although it took a lot of focus to keep my mind off business when I was off the clock.

Was it all worth it? Would I do it all over again? Yes—under two conditions. First, I'd need to know everything in *The Big Book* so I could escape the straightjacket stress and strain of running a business. That calmer state of mind would fulfill the second condition: a better balance of work and family.

Face the fear. I was twenty-nine years old, my first day off Shell's payroll, and my wife and two sons were at a Dairy Queen in suburban Minneapolis. We ordered Peanut Buster Parfaits and Dilly Bars. As I handed over a five-dollar bill and took the ice cream, ten words ambushed my mind: *Where will the money come from to pay for these?* That thought was more chilling than an Arctic Rush brain freeze. No more checks on the first and fifteenth. No profit sharing, no company car, no expense account. Really, I had no idea if my new business could generate enough revenue to support the four of us. That undercurrent of quiet terror was my constant companion for a long, long time.

When in doubt, gut it out. Tell me I can't do something that I want to do, and I'll work my butt off to prove I can. My junior year of high school, there were fifteen seconds left in the last basketball game of the season. We were trailing by one point against a much larger school that my small town hadn't beaten in twenty years. I had the ball. Dribbling down court, I saw an open teammate streak down the sideline. Misjudging how far to lead him with the ball, I passed it behind him and out of bounds—and threw away our chance to take the final, potentially game-winning shot. I was so embarrassed and guilt-ridden that I didn't show my face in school for two days. The only thing my coach ever said about it was, "Don't bother going out next year; you won't make the team." I loved basketball, so his words lit a bonfire in my belly. I practiced five hours a day, every day, all summer long—with ankle weights. Not only did I make the team, I was leading scorer and all-state honorable mention in Indiana, where basketball is right there next to Mom, God, and country.

That unshakable—and, in hindsight, borderline delusional—belief in myself saved my business bacon countless times. At Shell, my manager said I wasn't tough enough to transfer from HR to the field. After a year, he relented and assigned me to the toughest part of Chicago, the near South Side, Bad Bad Leroy Brown's neighborhood. I helped take South Side dealers from worst to first in tire sales. As soon as I started my own business, before the paint had even dried on my store signs, a competitor told me straight to my face, "You're not going to make it, Tom." Even my equipment supplier had no faith. "I wish you the best," he said, "but it's just not going to happen." Oh, and Michelin initially to supply tires to us because we weren't big enough. Perversely, all that only inspired me to build a team that captured 1.5 percent of the U.S. tire market, selling over a million tires annually.

My post-Shell cluelessness did have a few advantages. Had I known how hard it was to launch a business, price and market products, hire and train people, make payroll, and pay off loans, I might have stayed in my corporate cocoon. But leave I did. Head down and plowing through crisis after crisis, I earned a Ph.D. in business management from the school of hard knocks. I can appreciate Winston Churchill's sentiment when he said, "If you're going through hell, keep going."

Think about partnering up. Remember the buddy system; it works in business, too. Even a motivated overachiever can't always go it alone.

The right partner is a godsend if he's rational, caring, and willing to compromise—on issues, not values. It's hard to come by a partner with integrity, multiple specialties, and the flexibility to deal with change. I did. Don Gullett and I complemented each other like McCartney and Lennon. I was the internal face of Tires Plus (conducting meetings, addressing the troops) and outer face (for business partners, investors, community leaders). Don was in the trenches getting things done—directing operations and making the trains run on time.

Know your would-be partner inside and out (see the interview checklist in chapter 13) before signing anything. If he's a social acquaintance, drill down. How would he handle a financial crisis or a delicate employee matter? Don was a good fit because he had spent eighteen months under me as a sales rep at Shell. Still, from the outset I made it clear—spelled out on paper—that I would be in charge. Fifty-fifty splits are dangerous, in my book. Sure, we'd go with Don's ideas when they were better. But if there was a difference of opinion, the buck stopped with me.

One more reason to team up: It's lonely at the top. Your partner is the only one who can relate to whatever you're going through. It may sound like a negligible benefit, but having a trustworthy peer to commiserate and brainstorm with is like having a close family to endure personal crises with.

Live lean. New businesses gobble up cash, so I looked for every opportunity to save a buck here and make a buck there. Our first real headquarters was a second-rate office park in a third-rate neighborhood and cost $250 for rent. Noticing it lacked vending machines, I asked the building's owner if I could install one myself. That netted $250 a month. Now rent was free.

Labor will likely be your biggest cost. Keep base salaries low by hiring top-notch talent who'll work their tails off for incentive-based payoffs like commissions, bonuses, and stock options. The more hats you wear yourself, the fewer people you'll have to hire. In our first year, Don was a one-man wholesale company—he ordered the products, unloaded them, stocked them, sold them, delivered them, and collected for them.

Initially, anyway, you'll have to pinch pennies more than you'd like. Our family car was a used, eight-year-old Plymouth station wagon with a hatchet hole in the rear, bought at an auction (we imagined that it had been used in some kind of grisly crime). But it got us where we needed to go. I paid myself enough to cover monthly expenses and plowed the rest back into the company.

Why do young companies hoover up so much cash? Other than labor costs, the four main sources of suction are:

- taxes
- start-up loans (with after-tax money)
- inventory (as stock levels increase)
- accounts receivable (even if every customer pays on time, you're still thirty to ninety days behind, depending on the terms you offer)

These greenback gluttons can drain morale along with cash. Let's say you net an annual profit of $400,000. Taxes take $150,000 off the top. Boosted inventory shaves off $75,000. Another $75,000 gets tied up in increased receivables. Oh, and don't forget those loan obligations that take $100,000. For you? That leaves exactly zilch. Now that I'm consulting, I hear it all the time: "I'm working 24/7, sales and profits are increasing, but there's nothing left for me!" That's why entrepreneurs need to keep costs low (chapter 54), ride herd on receivables (chapter 54), and get creative when they're under a cash crunch (chapter 57).

CHAPTER 2

RESEARCH THE MARKET

Analyzing the Data to Determine Your Niche

Before starting Tires Plus, I cased the stores I would compete against. I picked the brain of a tire-distributor friend. I lured five buddies over for beers and a focus group. That was it, that was the extent of my market research. I was somewhat familiar with the industry after working for Shell, but I got lucky. If I tried that nonchalance in today's hyper-competitive marketplace, you'd find me scampering back to Corporate America faster than you could say "going-out-of-business sale." Whether you're starting a retail store, a wholesale operation, a manufacturing business, or a Web-based service, the quality of your market research could spell the difference between fizzling out and rocketing to the top. Research these six areas before you start your own business:

Determine demand. A family friend wanted to open a doggy day care and asked for my advice. The first two things I asked: How crowded is the market, and how profitable is the competition? If they're booked solid for weeks to come, then she could expect some overflow to come her way. If they're hurting, she could expect the same—unless she was offering something dog owners wanted and the competition couldn't deliver. It doesn't matter if you're shampooing schnauzers, designing dream homes, or wholesaling widgets, you'll never repeal the law of supply and demand.

Shop competitors. Back in the day, I flew to strong tire retailers on each coast to check out what worked and what didn't. Mixing in their best ideas with mine got us off to a fast start. Today, scour the competition's Web sites. Google them and explore every link. Track and compare their pricing. If they're retailers, buy something. What are they doing to attract customers? What's their secret sauce? What would you do differently? Where are they vulnerable, and how can you capitalize on that? Rack up some frequent flier miles visiting successful businesses in your space, outside your geographic market. They're less threatened and more open. Buy lunch for owners, and dip into your wallet for consulting fees if need be.

Probe the pros. Draw up a list of questions; then interview ten to fifteen professionals in your industry. Even if you don't personally know them, explain what you're doing and that you'd appreciate their candid comments. Some will blow you off. Most will be happy to give you ten to fifteen minutes. Ask them to poke holes in your plan. The point is to find and plug holes now so pressure down the road doesn't cause a blowout.

Trek to trade shows. Turning up at trade shows is the fastest way to learn industry logistics and build relationships with the movers and shakers you need to be moving and shaking with. Dress smart, find that easy smile. You can't help but literally bump into vendors, manufacturers, and distributors. Now's your chance. Be confident and cordial. Shake hands, build rapport, ask questions, explain your business (in fifteen seconds or less!), collect business cards. Ask everyone you meet to recommend others who're in position to help. When you get home, reconnect with your contacts via phone calls and e-mails as questions arise. Caveat: Treat each contact with care. They're busy people. Undercontact them and they forget you; over-contact them and you're a pest.

Canvass customers. Retailer? Tap into your shoppers' heads. Ask friends and family about their experiences and expectations when they shop for whatever you plan to sell. To go deeper, bust out the chocolates, or beer, and gather a series of focus groups with five or six people (weight for race, age, and gender). That'll net you qualitative research—info that's deep and narrow. For quantitative research—data that's wide and shallow—hire a survey firm and develop some good questions.

Trust the experts. Market-research firms elevate your efforts with both off-the-shelf and customized intel. Don't start your business or expand without a sharp snapshot of the size and demographics of your target market. I'm talking beyond the obvious (age, gender, income, education). You need data points like buyers' occupations, interests, opinions, and habits. Fact-finding missions like this may dent your bank account some, but your data-directed course correction will pay for itself, and then some.

CHAPTER 3

WRITE THE BUSINESS PLAN

Building Your Blueprint for Success

Everybody and their brother, sister, and long-lost cousin has a million-dollar idea—and a ten-cent scheme for making it work. What separates the entrepreneurs from the entrepre-never-wills is the business plan. It's a road map, no doubt, but it's also a ticket to the good graces of investors.

A tight, crisp business plan is more than management bios, marketing tactics, competitive analysis, and crunched numbers. It's a window into who you are, and who you're capable of becoming. It displays your clarity of thought, quality of character, and capacity for problem solving. Lenders and investors don't scratch out monster checks until they're confident that you're capable of executing a smart game plan and multiplying their money many times over.

Writing a business plan is only slightly less demanding than writing a Ph.D. dissertation. It'll take you hiking down every back road and side street in your industry. But it's worth every second. When you're done, your instincts will help you pull untold riches out of undersold niches.

When writing your business plan you should:

- enforce ruthless realism
- sharpen marketing strategies
- anticipate roadblocks
- engage in rigorous risk assessment
- map out contingency plans
- consider resource allocation
- scrub financial assumptions
- fix your target market
- calculate start-up costs
- analyze ongoing cash-flow demands
- appraise the competition
- educate partners on operations and goals
- reassess your management team

These are a few standard features of a business plan:

Executive summary. In three pages, summarize your company's mission, business objectives, target market, points of differentiation, marketing strategy, funding needs, and why it's time to bring your vision to market. Go easy on the details here, and let your enthusiasm shine through, albeit professionally and modestly. Why? If the overview leaves lenders and investors cold—thwack! Your plan hits the recycling bin.

Business breakdown. Begin with your "elevator speech," a one-sentence description of what your business does. Next, detail your products and services, market niches, and what makes you unique. Detail the size and demographics of your target market, the demand for your offering, your expected market share, and the type of legal business entity you plan to operate.

Competitive analysis. List your competitors' locations, estimated revenues, and marketplace history. Report on what they're doing right and wrong, how they're meeting or not meeting their customers' needs, and explain how you intend to neutralize their strengths and exploit their vulnerabilities. Spell out why your offering gives you a competitive advantage. Is it a patented new technology? A better location? Greater convenience? Do your prices, service, or quality give you an edge? How? Most important, how do you convince your rivals' customers to jump over to your side?

Management team. Flying into the fray with an untested squad of rookies? You might as well plan to get by on good looks, because the quality of your management team is what lenders and investors look at first. In three-paragraph CliffsNotes bios, list each exec's skills, education, work history, achievements, and responsibilities. Dip a little deeper into the inkwell for yourself. You have to convince investors that your shoulders are broad enough to carry your team to the Promised Land.

Marketing strategy. Begin with an analysis of the space you're entering: the competitive landscape, the growth opportunities, the niches that make up the market. For good measure, explain how your industry handles the whipsaw of the business cycle. (Trade associations and local industry insiders are excellent sources.) Next, specify the demographics of your target customers, and whether they're local, regional, national, or international. If you're going B2B (business-to-business), identify your potential corporate customers. Who are the decision makers, how will you breach their defenses, why will your product or service be irresistible? If you've already landed some contracts, say so.

Next, explain how you'll position yourself in the marketplace. What methods will expose your offering to potential customers—manufacturer reps, telemarketers, catalogs, online ads? That leads you into promotion. In what media will your ads appear? What about public-relations plans? Will you bring in agency professionals or handle advertising and PR yourself? Follow that with your pricing strategy, and back it up with pinpoint competitive research. Finally, lay out your sales terms and credit policies.

Daily operations. Offer a glimpse into your day-to-day business, starting with the workforce. How will you find, train, and compensate employees and convince them to buy into your vision? Then name the vendor relationships you'll cultivate, and which functions, if any, you'll outsource, and why. Last, describe your accounting plan. Who'll wear the green eyeshades, and what resources will she have?

Risk assessment. Time to remove your rose-colored glasses and assume the role of devil's advocate. Really, quit drinking your own Kool-Aid for a minute and try to prove your assumptions wrong. Every business has vulnerabilities. What are yours, and how could competitors expose and exploit them? Don't try to tap dance around insomnia-inducing issues, drag them to center stage. Explain how you'll avert the preventable crises and deal with the inevitable ones. Investors like to see that you understand—and are prepared for—the risks that lurk for every entrepreneur.

Sales forecast. Lay out conservative and best-case sales scenarios. When in doubt, err on the side of caution. Estimate monthly revenue and units sold for the first year. Do the same, but on an annual basis, for the following four years. Then back up the numbers with detailed underlying assumptions. Where to get the data? Start with competitor and marketplace analysis, field research, trade associations, perhaps focus groups. Pit the numbers against your sales objectives, and account for any discrepancies. Perhaps most important for lenders and investors, spell out your margins and breakeven point, as well as the percentage of the market you need to achieve them.

Financial analysis. Welcome to Hotel Spreadsheet—you can check out any time you like, but you can never leave. All the standard financial statements need room here. Start with the pro forma profit-and-loss (P&L) statement, projecting monthly income and expenses for the first year. Do the same for the next couple of years, but on a quarterly basis. (Develop both conservative-case and best-case scenarios.) Next comes the balance sheet, a snapshot of your company's assets and liabilities on any given day. Again, prepare monthly balance sheet projections for the first year, and quarterly projections for the next two years. Follow the same formula for cash-flow projections. Now that you've set the stage, put a number on how much funding you need, and how you'll spend and repay it. Finally, disclose your own financial circumstances and how much you'll personally contribute to the business. Lenders and investors like to see entrepreneurs with some skin in the game.

Appendix. Attach documentation for your assumptions, analyses, and projections. Include a list of business and personal references, as well as contact info for your bank, lawyer, and accountant. If you're a B2B play, add any letters of intent from future customers. Don't forget to attach copies of your insurance policies!

Okay, that's it. You're done—for now. Later, you'll tighten the nuts-and-bolts portions of your business plan at strategic-planning time (chapter 23). Now thank yourself for that hard work. You're already avoiding the seat-of-the-pants trap and looking more and more like an enlightened entrepreneur. (Helpful hint: For more details and actual business-plan templates, visit www.score.org or www.sba.gov.)

CHAPTER 4

FIND FUNDING

Raising Capital Without Relinquishing Control

This part drove me batty. After eight banks had turned us down, a loan officer at the ninth rejected us because we had no experience running a business. That's when I lost it. "Why do they even need people like you?" I asked. "I thought things like character and credit history meant something. If it's just a matter of not having done it before, why don't you just pop that into your computer and have it spit out, *No experience, no loan*." It wasn't one of my prouder moments, but I was fed up (and it felt good at the time). Luckily, the tenth bank saw what the first nine didn't. They approved our $60,000 loan and we launched.

Scaring up seed capital can be a full-time job. First, of course, calculate how much cash you need (Hint: Check your business plan). Funders expect your financial projections to be detailed and reasonable. Later, if flawed projections cause you to slink back with your hand out, your credibility and competence may be called into question. Twice in our first year we swallowed our pride and went back to our banker to make payroll. Fortunately, the bank president had an entrepreneurial streak. It also didn't hurt that our corporate attorney was on the bank's board.

Start-up funding should cover all the initial one-time costs (corporate I.D., furnishings, equipment, initial inventory, legal fees), working capital (rent, payroll, inventory replacement, accounts receivable, debt service), and reserves. Rare is the business that doesn't burn through 50 percent or more cash than projected.

Why go to a bank for a loan rather than find an investor? Excellent question. A bank is simply a creditor, while an "angel investor" or venture capitalist demands a stake in the company, if not a say in its operation. (I'm proud to say that Tires Plus grew without taking a dollar from investors.)

Here are six funding sources to get you started:

1. Bootstrapping. Funding your company with personal assets is ideal for maintaining control but it can stall growth—and jeopardize your financial future—if your pockets aren't deep. Still, anteing up a nice chunk of change boosts your credibility with prospective lenders and investors—you're a greater risk if you're not willing to put your own money on the line. Together, my partner and I kicked in a third of our $90,000 start-up capital.

You can also self-fund operations with some creativity. Say you cover your start-up costs, and your business is product-based—you might bridge the gap between that first sale and fully funding operations by tapping into your cash flow. How? Do the legwork to find a vendor who has a great product line and inadequate distribution system. Suggest a consignment arrangement, payment via promissory note, or generous terms. If you finagle 120-day terms and turn your inventory every sixty or ninety days, you're operating on the vendor's money, and your pumped-up cash flow can help you stay on top of operating expenses.

In our early years, we approached Bridgestone, not a big name in the United States at the time, though they owned 60 percent of the Japanese market and our research showed their quality was on par with Michelin. It was a perfect match: they had products that other dealers were ignoring; we had stores eager to sell them. Bridgestone embraced us, giving us deep discounts and 120-day terms. We helped each other grow. Years later, an exec from Bridgestone, which had by then merged with Firestone, told me, "You guys were pretty small, but you were young, full of fire and brimstone, and we believed in you."

2. Family and Friends. The initial funding for start-ups is commonly called the "friends and family" round. Tapping loved ones for funding is as common as it is dicey. If it turns out well, life is good. If it doesn't, lifelong relationships can turn sour. Treat these loans like the serious business agreements they are. Present your case as if your relatives were bankers: Quote a competitive interest rate and payback terms, explain the risks. But for heaven's sake, don't let zeal override common sense. If grandma can't afford to lose her entire investment, tell her thank you and politely decline. A shoebox full of twenties isn't the only way to lend support. Both Don's parents and my parents showed faith in us by personally guaranteeing our start-up bank loan.

In addition to family, gather a mix of friends and business folks with vicarious entrepreneurial streaks. In exchange for their money, offer company stock or a better-than-a-municipal-bond interest rate on a five-year promissory note. Now, instead of kowtowing to one sugar daddy, you'll have multiple silent partners—a term that's a little misleading given that they're rarely silent and you may spend hours hand-holding. Still, occasionally fielding phone calls and meeting at Starbucks is a small price to pay for greater financial freedom.

3. Banks. It's all about collateral. Don't expect a bank to hand you a check until enough assets are pledged to cover the full amount of the loan, and then some. We had family guarantees, second positions on our homes, and secured business assets like equipment and inventory. It still took ten banks to find one willing to cut us a check.

4. The Small Business Administration. Turned down by a bank? The U.S. Small Business Administration (SBA), an independent agency of the federal government, also administers loans. Its partners—lenders, community development organizations—make the loans that the SBA guarantees. The agency's loans typically require lower down payments and offer better terms than banks, but the lending criteria is just as demanding. Applicants must pony up personal assets (around 30 percent of the capital loan) and have a healthy debt-to-net-worth ratio and a sparkling credit history. The owner must also be active in day-to-day affairs, put up the same collateral a bank would demand, and prove that cash flow is strong enough to meet his obligations. That said, the SBA is likely to green-light a loan if the only red flag is insufficient collateral, whereas a bank would ding you for it. While SBA loans typically go to existing businesses, well-planned start-ups can also get in on the action.

5. Angel Investors. Yes, there are angels among us, and they usually flutter up after you've gone through your "family and friends" round of financing. But their heavenly cash often comes with a helluva price—and I speak as an angel investor. It's a classic supply-and-demand scenario. In most industries, at most points in the business cycle, there are fewer angel investors than entrepreneurs in need of them (Big exception: the Internet and wireless spaces in the early twenty-first century). Some angels' motives lean more toward mentoring and the joy of business building than simply inflating their net worth. Other angels exploit their leverage by imposing turnip-bleeding terms and draconian exit strategies. An angel may say, "My $100,000 investment would bring the value of your company up to $200,000, so I would own 50 percent of the business. Oh, and by the way, I'll take fifty-one." Just like that, you're answering to somebody else, your dream of working for yourself dashed. (Beware of the dark angel.) Angels will have their attorneys draw up the investment agreements, and typically, he who drafts the document sets the rules. Having said all that, entrepreneurs with no other option may conclude that owning part of a company is better than owning no company at all.

6. Venture Capitalists. After the angels, who often fly solo with smaller bundles of cash under their wings, venture capitalists swoop in with "institutional" money ($1 million and up). Their ranks include former entrepreneurs who offer contacts and expertise ranging from operations to finance to the particulars of the space in which you're planting your flag. VCs, as they're called, try to squeeze even more favorable terms out of new companies than most angels. (That's why you may hear that VC also stands for "vulture capitalists.") Like angels, VCs expect a return on their money in roughly five years. Many start-ups don't interest venture capitalists because they don't meet typical VC criteria—seasoned management, untapped niches in high-risk industries, potential for a financial grand slam.

CHAPTER 5

POSITION YOURSELF

Nailing Your Name, Location, and Differentiation

Nice work. You've poured over market metrics, collected notes on customers and competitors, interviewed industry insiders, shook hundreds of hands at trade shows, and spent some bucks on market research. Once your doors are open, visibility becomes the key to viability. Handled skillfully in advance of D-day, the following three moves make customers sit up and take notice. (Beware of impulse decisions; all three moves are difficult and costly to undo.)

    1. Differentiate Your Offering. Remember Charles Lindbergh's solo transatlantic flight? Roger Bannister's four-minute mile? Creative Carton's perfect record for same-day orders? Missed that last one? It may be the most impressive . . . to manufacturers of corrugated packaging and displays. Minneapolis-based Creative Carton had already carved out its market position as the go-to guys for quick turnarounds. Then a desperate customer shouted four words: "I need it today!"

    After lots of hits and a few misses, CEO Mike Sime possessed the people and procedures to go for same-day gold. Seven years later,

Creative Carton's perfect-delivery winning streak is still unbroken. Same-day service became their marquee differentiator, even though it accounts for just a fraction of orders. "Is it a big deal?" Mike asked. "Well, it is to a customer sitting at his desk with white knuckles and a supervisor breathing down his neck. It's like the old Federal Express commercial—when you absolutely, positively have to have it delivered the same day, what's it worth?" Plenty. Especially in an industry notorious for time-pressured customers. When you offer them something they can't get anywhere else, they can't *not* order from you. Today's need-it-yesterday environment is good news for companies like Mike's, whose core competency is compressing time. "It's great when the world moves faster and faster because that plays right into our business model," he said.

Most differentiation decisions hinge on where you want to land on the price-quality-service continuum. One isn't necessarily better than the other, but ya gotta make a choice. The low-price, bag-your-own-groceries niche is staked out by the likes of Wal-Mart, Southwest Airlines, Home Depot, and Motel 6. Plant your flag in the middle of the spectrum and value-conscious customers will pay a little more to get a little more—think Banana Republic, Applebee's, Holiday Inn, Crate and Barrel. Customers of premium-positioned companies—Mercedes, Neiman Marcus, Ritz-Carlton—will shell out top dollar for superior quality, white-glove service and, perhaps most intoxicatingly of all, cachet.

A hybrid position is "low-price, nicer experience." Look at Target Corp., Best Buy, IKEA, JetBlue, and Kohl's. Early on at Tires Plus, this is how we positioned ourselves against the big boys. Some rivals could match our prices. But nobody else offered upscale stores with clean-cut sales consultants in dress shirts and ties, cappuccino, framed art, movies, and play areas for kids.

Beyond price, quality, and service? Look at subcategories. Creative Carton was already known for speed; same-day delivery added one more point of separation from the pack. It helped the company create a "nested niche"—a niche within a niche. Likewise, FedEx is synonymous with "overnight shipping." But the company knew the only way it could maintain market share was by creating sub-niches—various pricing and delivery options, extended hours, and convenient drop-off locations. Privately owned Enterprise Rent-A-Car has become the largest car rental company in North America, thanks to its differentiator—"We'll pick you up." Geek Squad, a Best Buy–owned "computer support task force," filled a neglected niche by offering personalized security, repair, and technical support to both business types and "civilians." Further distinguishing themselves, Geek Squad "agents" in white dress shirts and skinny black ties make house calls—they'll race to your home in squad-car black-and-white Volkswagen bugs as fast as a pizza delivery man.

Know who you are before you introduce yourself to your customers. Otherwise you'll always be a little hazy to them. Once your doors open, keep asking yourself whether your offering is in tune with what makes your operation unique. To the extent you can, shed your passion for your industry and look at your products and services through your future customers' eyes. Ask yourself, *If I were happy doing business with one of my competitors, what would it take to get me to switch? Price? Speed? Service? Warranty? All of the above?* Once we were underway, I got a kick out of customers ("guests") who came to our stores armed with detailed competitive analyses. It gave us further insight into our guests' motivations.

The best feedback for honing your offering arrives once customers start calling. Software manufacturers have done this for years with "beta" releases that essentially ask customers to give them a hand with working out the kinks. Far from feeling like guinea pigs, most consumers appreciate a closer connection to the businesses in whom they place their trust. Ask the best among your initial customers to test-drive your new product or service and report back on the good, the bad, and the ugly. Budget in free or discounted samples to exchange for their efforts. Whether you're retail or B2B, this sneak-peek strategy also generates advance buzz and stimulates demand.

2. Nail Your Name. Back in 1982, when I decided to shift our focus from wholesale to retail, our three stores were called (City Name) Tire & Auto. Catchy, huh? I knew I needed something better. At a party one evening, I leaned over to my neighbor and said,

"Hey, Bob, I'm starting a chain of tire stores. Gotta tell you the name—Guarantee Tire." Bob scowled as soon as it left my lips. He was ten years my senior, a streetwise ad man from Philly. "Tom," he said, "that's the most screwed-up name I've ever heard" (PG-13 version). Flying dollar signs raced through my head—we already had our logo designed and had given the green light to a sign company. Bob noticed how deflated I was and offered to brainstorm names with me. The next day, I was telling Bob, "My stores will offer tires plus other services." He cut in: "Tires Plus. I like that. Add it to the list." I liked it, too. It conveyed optimism, promised that we had more to offer than our competitors, and left open the door for endless brand extension. Every entrepreneur should be so lucky to have a neighbor like Bob Bechir. (Bob died a few months before I sold Tires Plus in 2000. We invited his two kids to a company party and presented them with a plaque and remuneration to recognize their dad's contribution.)

Convinced you've already got a great name? Don't be afraid to put your identity on the couch. Charles Lukens, cofounder of Planet Salvage, a nationwide, Web-based auction for auto parts, resisted when I challenged him to rename his company. "The name Planet Salvage was like my kid's name to me," Charles said. "Plus, I was hung up on our cool little icon, a planet with a tire around it." The logo was fun, I said, but neither it nor the cartoonish name Planet Salvage fit the company's mission, product, and industry players (conservative insurance companies like State Farm, Safeco, and Nationwide). To his credit, Charles cut his emotional ties. During a staff brainstorming session at the company's Kansas City headquarters, I suggested zeroing in on what they did. We boiled it down to: *We harness the Internet to help companies manage and increase alternative parts utilization* (auto-insurance and body-shop industry jargon). Given that the acronym APU was constantly on the lips of industry execs throughout the business day, the perfect name was a no-brainer—APU Solutions.

With your name in the bank, turn to your slogan. Does it holler why you're different? After Charles settled on the APU Solutions name, I sat in on a meeting with a prospective client, a veep for Farmers Insurance. He wanted a guarantee that the parts he purchased via

APU's Web site would actually be in stock and shipped the same day at locked-in prices. "Look," he said, "I need real steel, real time." The minute we left the building, I said to Charles, "Did you hear that? 'Real steel. Real time.' Isn't that what sets you apart?" He nodded. "There's your slogan. It sums up your business model in four words. It's perfect." So is Best Buy's ("Thousands of Possibilities. Get Yours."), Target's ("Expect More. Pay Less."), and Wal-Mart's ("Always Low Prices. Always.").

Each and every exposure to a strong brand cements your market position and produces free advertising. It's a succinct, powerful name; a memorable slogan; a bold logo (think Nike swoosh). The name Tires Plus told people exactly what we did. Our slogan—"Warehouse Prices. World-Class Service"—told them exactly what to expect. Any time people heard either, our brand message sank deeper into their consciousness. To be sure, a lot of Fortune 500 companies have nondescript names. But odds are it took one heckuva big marketing budget to educate the public about what they sell. If your name doesn't describe what you do, your slogan better. Bottom line: If, after hearing your name and slogan, people on the street still can't say what your company does—and why it does it better than anyone else— you'd better change it. (Heads up: Don't settle on a name until you've secured the corresponding Web address.)

3. Lock in the Right Location. Here's a secret that the big guys don't want mom and pop to learn: Most anyone can afford the best location. Lots of small businesses err by setting up shop in substandard locations to save rent. That's shortsighted, and often has costly consequences. Consumer-oriented businesses are typically better off at an A site, the premium designation in the commercial real estate world. Don't be swayed by promises of lower occupancy costs at a B, C, or D site. Once we started opening stores in A locations, our revenue per store spiked. Our customer surveys showed that despite tons of advertising, the number one reason why they shopped us was "We saw your store and sign."

I shared my story with "Natalie," a consulting client whose annual sales had plateaued at $250,000. The first thing I pointed out was that her women's apparel store was marooned in a D location, a fact she was already painfully aware of. After researching the rental market, we found an A spot for only $4,000 per month more. We did the math and discovered that she needed just six more customers a day to make up the difference—and that was assuming her average sale didn't increase. Despite her partner's resistance, Natalie gulped hard and called the moving van. Three years later, their revenues had quadrupled to a cool million. Customer traffic boomed and her average sale nearly doubled. Not sure how many additional customers you'd see at a premium site? Calculate how many more customers you'd need just to break even, and imagine your business at an A site versus a C site. The number is probably fewer than you think to support an A site.

For office locations, the benefits are less tangible but no less important. Even if your clients never visit, potential clients will see your sign more often and have a better impression of you. In business, as in most of life, perception is reality. It's virtually impossible to run a first-class operation at a low-class location. Bottom line: Don't let higher rent scare you. What Goliaths understand, and most Davids do not, is that it's not what you pay; it's how much you net for what you pay.

Negotiating a low-risk lease is crucial. Locking in a long-term lease can be perilous. You could find yourself in a pickle if business takes off and you outgrow your space, or if you sputter and need to hit "eject." Yet a short-term lease might force you to vacate sooner than you'd like. Best bet? Negotiate a short initial term with as many extension options as you can get. For example, rather than a five-year lease, hammer out a two- or three-year lease with three additional three-year options (adding in rent escalators, typically 2 to 3 percent). Then you'll have the option to stay and the flexibility to leave while hedging against nasty rent hikes.

Enthusiasm alert: Think twice before making enhancements to rented property (aka, leasehold improvements) that are made and paid for by you, the lessee. Legally, it's the property of the lessor once the lease expires. I heard the founder of a retail food business confess that she had sunk $150,000 into building a full kitchen in her rented space. From the very beginning she knew that her landlord could boot her when her five-year lease (without options) expired. She also knew there was talk of condemning her building for road construction. Yet she plowed in the money anyway. You know how this one ends: She lost her lease and the financial hit knocked her so hard that she couldn't recover in time to start over in a new location.

One more location consideration: Countless non-retail start-ups thrive by hitching their wagons to business incubators. An incubator is nothing more than a building divided into offices that are leased— often subsidized—to early-stage outfits. Economic development organizations, government entities, academic institutions, or other nonprofits manage most of North America's one thousand incubators. Most are closely associated with high-tech start-ups, but the concept has expanded into virtually every industry.

The lucky start-ups that are accepted into an incubator typically pay below-market rent and share a common receptionist, copy and fax machines, even bookkeepers. Networking and strategic alliance opportunities abound in these hallways, where potential investors love to loiter. How long does the incubation period last? Till the start-up is financially healthy enough to leave the nest and fly on its own. (For more information, visit the National Business Incubation Association at www.nbia.org.)

CHAPTER 6

LINE UP YOUR LEGAL DUCKS

Protecting Your Business Interests

There's no one on the planet I trust more than Don Gullett. We started our company with a verbal agreement and a handshake—then made it legal with a detailed contract. Life's twists and turns are impossible to anticipate. You and your future business partner can epitomize integrity, then along comes miscommunication or poor planning. Suddenly things spiral out of control. That's when you want a legal safety net. I don't care if you're starting a business with your grandmother, these four words are nonnegotiable: *Get it in writing.*

From the get-go, a primary legal concern was establishing controlling interest. I had asked myself, *What's the worst thing that could happen? And what can I do now to prevent it from happening?* My take was that a partnership disagreement could prove fatal, and that the solution was for me to own a majority interest.

The business idea had been mine, and Don had reported to me at Shell, so it only followed that majority interest should rest with me. It was incumbent upon me, of course, not to misuse that control. A few years later, when the company was gaining in value and Don had a rare misfire on a key assignment, he asked if he should resign. "Are you kidding? Absolutely not," I told him. "You don't mess up any more than I do, and you're too critical to the company." I could have stockpiled more shares had Don left, but it would've felt wrong and it would've been wrong. Besides, Don really was too valuable to lose and we'd been through way too much together.

An employee stock-ownership plan later diluted our fifty-five/forty-five split, but I always retained 51 percent of the voting stock. My unequivocal advice: Do not divide the ownership pie even-Steven. I once served on the board of a fifty-fifty company where the co-owners, after a brief honeymoon, refused to speak to one another. Get this—they required intermediaries to shuttle messages between them. Every company needs a clear, buck-stops-here leader. She's someone who strives for consensus but isn't afraid to stamp a veto when the organization's mission, vision, and values are threatened.

These are steps to ward off legal woes:

Hire the best lawyers. Take the time, do the research. Solicit referrals from your network, and ask prospective attorneys for references. Do what it takes to retain the best legal eagle you can afford, a skilled business analyst who delivers practical solutions, as opposed to theory. Experience, efficiency, and quality count more than hourly rate. If Lawyer A takes three hours to prepare a contract, and Lawyer B takes one hour at twice A's hourly rate—and does it better—well, do the math. Our plan to start our company depended on purchasing the franchise rights to three Shell Oil service stations that we would turn into tire stores that sold gasoline. Well, Shell tried to block approval of our franchise rights in order to keep Don and me in the fold. We looked around for an attorney and found Minnesota's former securities commissioner, who had authored the very laws governing franchises and dealerships that were in play. Case closed.

Read the fine print. Decision makers sign countless contracts. From equipment leases and supplier agreements to strategic alliances and employment pacts, don't just flip to the last page and sign. It's your job to spot the fox in the henhouse. Certainly, legalese induces sleep, kinda like flipping through a medical journal. Power through and read it anyway. Highlight what you don't understand. Ask your attorney to explain (briefly) the mumbo jumbo, but only after you explain to him the business issues involved.

Be thorough. My longtime corporate attorney once reviewed an office lease for another client that allocated $4,500 for tenant improvements. That was one crucial zero less than the $45,000 the client had been promised. Fortunately, the client had thoroughly briefed the attorney on every detail before feeding him the contract. An ounce of prevention saved the guy forty grand in pain. Also, make sure that important contracts address your worst-case scenarios—and comfortable solutions for when (not if) one of them occurs. What happens, for instance, to your volume discount if a supplier runs out of merchandise during your busiest month? What happens if your strategic-alliance partner files to break up with you and claims your technology that they've shared is now theirs? So many agreements are stitched together in the eleventh hour, but even then—especially then—examine it word by word. A few extra hours prior to signature will avoid contentious renegotiations, court, and steep legal fees.

Choose the most favorable business entity status. Most small businesses benefit from selecting Subchapter S Corporation or Limited Liability Company (LLC) status. They offer the owner the liability protection of a C Corporation and the pass-through tax advantages of sole proprietorships and partnerships. That said, state law governs the formation of business entities, so consult a good CPA or corporate attorney to help select what's right for you.

SOLE PROPRIETORSHIP

DEFINITION: Although a sole proprietorship may have employees, it's typically favored by lone wolfs.

ADVANTAGES: It's the simplest, most inexpensive business entity to form and operate. Profits are not double-taxed. Closing the business is easy. No separate tax return is required; simply attach a Schedule C form to your personal tax return.

DISADVANTAGES: The owner is personally responsible for business losses. The business is liable for the owner's personal liabilities. Each member's proportionate share of profits represents taxable income, whether or not profits are distributed. Typically, arrangements are made to distribute a portion of profits to the owner to reimburse him for that year's tax obligations. Taxable income is subject to self-employment tax as well as federal and state income taxes.

C Corporation

DEFINITION: A business entity that pays corporate taxes on its net profit.

ADVANTAGES: Owners are not personally liable for business losses. It's easy to add owners or investors. Transferring ownership is also easy, subject to complying with security laws. Stock sales can raise capital. Takes advantage of employee-benefit tax breaks.

DISADVANTAGES: Double taxation: Net profit is taxed at corporate rates; and if net profit is distributed to shareholders, it's also taxed as a dividend. (The only exception is the payment of salary, bonuses, or other compensation to owner-employees to the extent it's accepted by the IRS as "reasonable compensation.") A separate corporate tax return must be filed. The company is subject to formal requirements like annual reports and board of directors meetings. It's relatively expensive to create and maintain. It can be a headache dealing with federal and state agencies that oversee corporations.

Subchapter S Corporation

DEFINITION: A domestic corporation with only one class of stock and no more than one hundred shareholders. ("Subchapter S" refers to a particular tax status, rather than a type of company.) Ask your tax adviser how to time the filing of the Subchapter S election form.

ADVANTAGES: Owners report corporate profits and losses on their personal tax returns. Early losses can be passed through to the shareholders, giving investors a tax write-off against ordinary income, up to the amount of the investment. Once the corporation turns a profit, the tax liability is passed on to the shareholders—they're insulated from personal liability for business debt—and taxation is eliminated at the corporate level. Avoids double taxation. Withdrawal from Subchapter S status is easy.

DISADVANTAGES: Each member's proportionate share of profits represents taxable income, whether or not profits are distributed. Typically, arrangements are made to distribute a portion of profits to the owner to reimburse him for that year's tax obligations. Stockholders and employees must declare employee benefits such as health insurance as taxable income if they own more than 2 percent of the stock. The company must use the calendar year as its fiscal year. The number of shareholders cannot exceed one hundred. It's relatively expensive to create and maintain. It can be a headache dealing with federal and state agencies that oversee corporations.

LIMITED LIABILITY COMPANY (LLC)

DEFINITION: Similar to a Subchapter S, with the exception that the LLC may offer several classes of ownership (or "membership") interests; does not limit the number of members; permits corporations, partnerships, and trusts, as well as individuals, to become members; and typically imposes fewer formal filing and reporting requirements. For tax purposes, the IRS treats an LLC as though it were a partnership.

ADVANTAGES: Without incorporating, owners are still generally protected from present and future liabilities or judgments against their business. Offers many of the tax benefits of sole proprietorships and partnerships, including pass-through taxation. In general, subject to IRS regulations, LLC entity documents may provide for disproportionately splitting member profits and losses—i.e., in percentages different from ownership percentages.

DISADVANTAGES: Each member's proportionate share of profits represents taxable income, whether or not profits are distributed. Typically, arrangements are made to distribute a portion of profits to the owner to reimburse him for that year's tax obligations. Because it's considered earned income, each member's share of net profit is subject to self-employment tax.

PARTNERSHIPS

DEFINITION: Two types—general partnership and limited partnership. In the first, two or more people agree to start a business and, through the partnership, own the assets, profits, and losses. A limited partnership, on the other hand, consists of a combination of one or more general partners (personally exposed to the partnership's liabilities) and one or more limited partners (liable only in proportion to their ownership in the enterprise). In limited partnerships, the general partners control business decisions, while the limited, or "passive," investors have no votes or say in operational matters. If state statutory requirements are not followed, the law views a limited partnership as a general partnership.

ADVANTAGES: Partnerships can accommodate multiple owners. Avoids double taxation. Structure is easily created, flexible, and maintained with relatively few legal formalities.

DISADVANTAGES: General partners are personally responsible for all of the partnership's liabilities. Each member's proportionate share of profits represents taxable income, whether or not profits are distributed. Typically, arrangements are made to distribute a portion of profits to the owner to reimburse him for that year's tax obligations. General partnerships have largely been superseded by LLCs because an LLC offers the tax benefits of a partnership but without owner-liability issues.

Clarify ownership issues. Great partnerships can run smoothly for decades. Others sputter after a few weeks. A corporate lawyer's job is to assume the latter and think, *What agreements can we write to keep the business going when the starry-eyed shareholders are no longer on speaking terms?* It doesn't matter how long you've been up and running. If you haven't clarified these important issues, complications can crop up if shareholders grow apart. Before it gets nasty, consult an attorney about:

Liability. Most lenders require personal guarantees to secure financing. A contribution agreement among guarantors ensures that responsibility is divided along the same lines as shareholder ownership. This prevents the bank from forcing the guarantor with the deepest pockets to cough up money in default cases. If only one shareholder guarantees the loan, he may ask for a guarantee fee from the company to compensate him for assuming all the risk. Paying a fee ensures guarantors that management is motivated to produce positive results. The fee is higher if the company can't survive without the guarantor's signature, and smaller if a company's higher net worth diminishes the guarantor's risk.

Role of Equity. How many classes of stock, or membership interests, should you have? Do voting rights differ for each? Which is best for you? It's an oversimplification, but let's say one class of stock provides for only equity and financial rights, while another class receives those rights *plus* voting privileges. The former may be fine for passive investors; the latter is the province of players who want a say on strategic decisions.

Value of Contributions. Make sure the executive-compensation program is in writing, whether for common stock awarded in exchange for sweat equity or for stock options granted to key employees. For stock options, calculate the tax implications and make sure they're properly recorded on the company's ledger.

Shareholders' Buy-Sell Agreement. This document addresses the closely held company's valuation, how shareholders must first offer their stock to the company or insiders, and what happens upon the death of a shareholder. In fact, include a life insurance plan here so in the event of a principal shareholder's death, a buyout doesn't break the company bank. Each shareholder should have his or her own attorney eyeball these issues. Details of shareholders' agreements can vary depending on the cause of the cash-out. For instance, if a shareholder voluntarily gets off the bus before it reaches its destination, buyout price and payment terms may be more draconian than if a shareholder dies or is disabled. To protect majority shareholders, include a "drag along" provision that contractually requires all shareholders to participate in a sale at the same price per share (many buyers, especially big private equity firms, only want to buy 100 percent ownership). To protect minority shareholders, include a "tag along" provision that guarantees that all shareholders can participate in a sale at the same price per share should the majority decide to sell.

Exit Strategy. This hot button gets everyone's attention. How will principals cash in their chips? Under what circumstances can shareholders—angels, VCs, Grandma—force the company onto the block to recoup their investment? Beware of somebody inconspicuously slipping in this common yet onerous provision.

Strategic Financial Planning. Long-range objectives may be undermined if the buy-sell agreement, exit strategy, and other aspects of ownership are not seamlessly coordinated with estate and succession planning. Once or twice a year, gather your team (attorney, accountant, estate planner, insurance planner, and others) to make sure all angles are covered. Don't rely on just one expert's opinion. Your attorney may have a brilliant legal mind, but unless he's also tax savvy, he may overlook important IRS ramifications.

Protect your intellectual capital. In our early days, tire dealers in other parts of the country used our brand name and plagiarized our Yellow Pages ads. Sure, imitation is flattering and all that, and the dealers weren't even close to direct competitors. But we had big expansion plans, and we hardly relished the idea of someday competing against our own brand-name. So we mailed cease-and-desist letters to the poachers. Problem solved. Don't wait to trademark your brand name, slogan, and logo; nor should you wait to copyright your ads and marketing materials. Also protect your proprietary products and processes to preserve your competitive advantage (chapter 14). "Protection money" pays for itself by increasing your brand equity. When we sold our 150 retail stores to Bridgestone/Firestone in 2000, the big ol' Fortune 500 corporation actually changed the name of its four hundred existing stores to Tires Plus.

Prevent unwarranted employee claims. You should know this document better than anyone else. It shields you against a variety of claims by unhappy campers. Each time a worker crosses boundaries, document the incident and have him sign a written warning. The more documentation, the better your odds in court if a terminated employee pushes it that far.

Cover your assets. Soon after starting Tires Plus, Don Gullett and I met with an insurance agent. "This is for if your customers sue you," he said, slapping a thick policy on the desk. "This is for if your employees sue you." Plop. "This is in case someone steals from you. This is for somebody running a car into your store. This is in case you get sick and you can't support your family. This is in case a tornado destroys your building." It went on and on, and so did the pile of paper. Don and I looked at each other with wide eyes that said, *What in God's name did we get ourselves into?*

Entrepreneurs are risk takers by nature. Still, take the time to weigh the costs and benefits of various insurance coverage. Not every one applies, but rolling the dice on the whole stack is a gamble you can't afford. It's not just your business that's at risk—your family's financial future may also be on the line. Some coverage may be required by lenders, landlords, licensing entities, or the law.

Property Coverage. Insure the business's real (buildings) and personal (contents, including inventory) property for their *replacement costs,* not depreciated value.

General Liability Coverage. If the owner is found legally liable for injuries occurring on company property (including job sites), this policy pays damages. The business is also protected from claims related to product liability and "completed operations" (providing a service that leads to injury or property damage). Get covered for at least $1 million per incident. Certain businesses (consultants, architects, engineers, financial specialists) may also need *Professional Liability* coverage, which covers "errors and/or omissions" they may make in the course of their day.

Business Auto Coverage. The liability portion protects owners from injuries or property damage caused by company vehicles. Make sure anything with an engine and wheels is titled or leased in the name of the business to maintain "insurable interest." It's also a good idea to include comprehensive and collision coverage for damage to the vehicle itself. Employees use their personal vehicles for business? Add *Hired and Non-Owned* coverage to protect the business against damages above and beyond the driver's personal insurance limit. Sure, employees' personal auto insurance policies offer primary coverage. But if it isn't sufficient for, say, a serious accident, the claim could drag you in, since the employee was operating the vehicle on behalf of your business.

Coverage caveat: Make sure your uninsured and underinsured coverage matches your liability limits. Why? More than 10 percent of drivers are uninsured, and many others hold only minimal coverage. One bad accident could push you to the brink of collapse. Besides, if you're willing to provide coverage for others when you're at fault, it makes sense to get the same level of protection for yourself.

Workers Compensation. Every state enforces workers compensation laws to protect employees against loss of income and to pay medical expenses caused by work-related injuries or health problems. Premiums are based on payroll costs, and coverage isn't mandatory. But you can't afford to be without it, even if you exempt yourself and have just one other employee. Nor should you try to skirt the rules by declaring employees "independent contractors." States have wised up to that trick and instituted qualifying conditions that few employers can meet. If you don't carry workers comp and an employee does get injured, her care will come out of the state fund, and the state will come after you for the money, plus penalties (and it's not a debt dischargeable through bankruptcy).

Umbrella Coverage. General Liability policy limits may not fully protect owners from serious property damage or personal injury claims. An Umbrella excess-liability policy offers additional coverage over and above General Liability, Auto Liability, and the Employers Liability section of the Workers Compensation policy. Umbrellas are available in $1 million layers. Smart owners add enough Umbrella coverage to protect all of their business assets. If your insurer offers it, include matching limits of uninsured and underinsured motorist coverage.

Employers Liability Coverage. Protects the business owner from employment-related suits like sexual harassment, wrongful termination, and age discrimination. General Liability covers none of these claims, which grow more expensive to defend by the day. Without coverage, you have to pop for defense costs and any judgments against you, and pick up the plaintiff's attorney fees. The sad fact is, it's often a matter of when, not if, claims like this hit a business.

"Key Man" Life Insurance. This is simply a life insurance policy written on the life of the owner. The policy pays for costs associated with running the business temporarily should the "key man" die. Tailor it to direct proceeds to another beneficiary (the owner's spouse) should the surviving decision makers choose to dissolve the business.

Disability Insurance. Pays the owner up to 66 percent of his pay (tax free) if he's unable to work. Disability coverage is especially helpful for all those small-business owners who exempt themselves from workers comp coverage. If the owner is disabled, his salary goes to paying somebody else to take the wheel while he recuperates.

Coverage caveat: Make sure your policy is tied to your occupation. That means you'll get paid for as long as you're unable to perform the job you held at the time of injury. Many disability policies pay out for only twenty-four months, after which you're required to get back to work doing just about anything productive.

Sit down annually with your commercial insurance agent to confirm that your coverage in key areas is keeping pace with your growth. It's especially important for small businesses susceptible to swamping by the tiniest of waves.

Avoid litigation at (almost) all costs. Lawsuits are like accidents—they're impossible to predict. Fifteen years after "Jeff" purchased a Tires Plus franchise in St. Paul, a better location developed near a major shopping mall. Jeff declined to relocate or open a second store, so we built a company store there. Even though it was outside of Jeff's exclusivity radius, he sued us. As it happened, our company-wide franchisee meeting fell during the dispute. At the meeting, I walked over to Jeff. "Wanna stand up for a minute, Jeff?" I said, turning with him to face the other franchisees. "I wanted to let you all know," I said, "for those who hadn't heard, Jeff and I have different perspectives on an issue and we're letting the judicial system determine the outcome." I put my arm around him. "I still care a lot about Jeff," I said. "He believes he's right, we believe we're right. Regardless of how it's decided, we're going to remain friends." A few weeks later, Jeff settled for the rights to develop another franchise in a different area.

Legal hot zones must be top-of-mind for new business owners. The justice system wasn't designed by the Founders to resolve business issues. As Jeff's story illustrates, winning a case on the merits is beside the point. Legal fees run far beyond what you pay your attorney.

Consider the time spent by the executive team on pretrial discovery, document review, general trial preparation, and the trial itself. Even when you win, you lose.

Still, litigation happens. When it does, show respect for the people on the other side of the courtroom. More often than not, an aggressive yet empathetic approach saves you money and produces a mutually beneficial outcome. Vengeful legal battles tend to end with a thud.

CHAPTER 7

BUILD A STRONG BOARD

Getting Help, Not Headaches, from Outside Advisers

Galloping into the mid-seventies marketplace with six-shooters blazing, my pardner and I were looking to make a name for ourselves with hard work, chutzpah, and hustle. We barged ahead and did what the smart money said we couldn't do, until we skidded to a halt in front of the furthest reaches of our know-how. Fortunately, in the mid-eighties we wised up and found our commercial Holy Trinity—CPA John Berg, attorney Tom Macintosh, and business consultant Dean Bachelor.

These guys saved our hides. They'd been in the trenches with hundreds of companies in dozens of industries. Their "been there, done that" insight stood in stark contrast to our "going there, dreamed that" naïveté. Still, we didn't accept their advice without grilling them first. While we couldn't match their sophistication and expertise, neither could they look through our eyes and see our vision. Tires Plus was our dream, not theirs, and we had an innate sense of what was best. We just didn't know how to fill in every blank. That's where our first informal board—John, Tom, and Dean—stepped in.

Set high standards for your board of advisers. Mixing with mediocre minds or big egos is a waste of time. In addition to the three outsiders, our board included six members of our senior management. (I regret that I didn't formalize our board sooner, though we still received great value from our early ad hoc arrangement.)

Landing the ideal board member can provide that mystery check-and-balance. In early 2000, the country's runaway-stagecoach economy was lurching but still rolling along. A packaging company purchased five months earlier by National City Equity Partners, a Cleveland private equity firm, was planning to build a fourth manufacturing plant. That made Carl Baldassarre nervous. A new board member (and National City's general partner), Carl looked down the road and saw potholes. "I didn't know if the wheels were going to fall off," Carl recalled. "But knowing that the packaging industry closely follows the economy, clearly it was time to pull back the reins."

But how hard? A new board member can't just ride into town on a white horse, grab the longtime sheriff by his vest, and lay down the law. Carl had to persuade the packaging firm's successful CEO to abort his expansion plan without alienating him. (Taming hyenas is easier than "advising" a successful CEO.) The CEO acknowledged it could take two years to build enough volume for the new plant to become profitable. He reasoned that the other plants were humming along at full capacity and could offload business to the new facility. On behalf of the board, Carl asked the entrepreneurial CEO's team to war-game how various revenue-softening scenarios would impact the existing plants. At the same time, Carl requested, lay over the cash output for the new facility's lease, capital equipment, labor, and other one-time expenses.

Snapping the CEO out of his passion and into objective analysis had a sobering effect. He recognized that even a 10 percent drop in top-line revenues, combined with the new facility's start-up costs, would jeopardize the company's liquidity and bank covenants. If that happened, abandoning construction would alarm customers, employees, and the marketplace. Not good. "Asking the CEO's team to run the numbers," Carl said, "moved them out of a defensive posture and helped achieve consensus. In the end, the CEO strongly recommended that we not pursue the expansion." Given the recession that followed the dot-com bust that March, canceling the expansion proved a wise choice.

Fill your board seats with Carl Baldassarres. His firm manages a billion-dollar investment portfolio with stakes in over sixty companies, three-quarters of which generate $25 million to $150 million in revenue. Carl, who serves on seven boards (I've been fortunate to join him on one), is the perfect blend of caring and fairness. He's tough, but not rough, smart, and understands the value of relationships.

Follow these board benchmarks to pull the most value out of your wise men and women. While it may take awhile to work your way toward formal meetings, these tips can help you get there faster.

THE DYNAMICS

Compensate fairly. Board members command increasingly higher stipends. They're also taking on greater risk. The 2002 Sarbanes-Oxley Act—the congressional response to scandals at Tyco, Enron, and Adelphia Communications—cuffed all public companies with tough new requirements. Now officers and directors are held even more accountable. That raised the bar for privately held companies, too. Higher expectations, heavier workloads, and a greater threat of litigation have turned board members into cold-eyed realists—*My time is valuable. I'm assuming more risk. Pay me what I'm worth.*

Still interested in tapping their wisdom? Here's what you do. First, write a check for directors' and officers' liability insurance—"D and O insurance." (Board candidates may still beg off, citing potential coverage holes.) Second, small-to-midsize companies can expect to shell out anywhere from $12,000 to $30,000 annually to each director. Granted, that's too rich for most start-ups—start if you must by inviting some trusted graybeards out to dinner every few months with the promise of a more lucrative and formal arrangement as your business grows. Third, consider throwing equity into the mix in the form of stock options and purchase programs. Give everybody their own oar and a part of what's on shore, and they'll row like mad regardless of the tide. (Caveat: The Financial Accounting Standards Board ruled that stock options must be expensed in a company's P&L, somewhat dulling the allure of stock options.)

Looking for a budget-conscious alternative? In contrast to a statutory "board of directors," there's no legal exposure for members who serve on a "board of advisers." It's not just semantics. In the former, executive management must implement the board's decisions; the latter is a less formal advisory relationship in which the CEO calls the shots. Private companies tend toward boards of advisers, especially if the CEO has a controlling interest. The advantages: avoiding D&O insurance expense, less difficulty finding board members, and no obligation to accept the board's advice. A board of directors, on the other hand, typically sprouts when a company has multiple investors, none of whom has controlling ownership. It's the best way to maintain checks and balances on entrepreneurs like us and our management teams.

Diversify. A board typically has five to nine members. Pick people from both inside and outside your industry whose talent doesn't duplicate your own. Complementary skills—finance, marketing, operations—among members is good. A lot of boards reserve a chair for the retired sage. Certainly, there's a role for wisdom, but depending on the industry, contemporary knowledge can be even more valuable. The best directors have been through the wars of growing, building value, and exiting a company. They've already done what you want to do, on a larger scale. Yet they're still in touch with day-to-day operations.

Select straight shooters. The board is your last line of defense (other than your spouse and kids) against fooling yourself. That means that members must say exactly what's on their minds. Avoid the types who play politics and try to curry favor with management. They can cripple you. When I joined the board of a manufacturing company, I was shocked to discover that a lot of critical operational disciplines—org chart, budgets, board financial-statement reviews, accountability timelines—were either nonexistent or rubber-stamped. When I spoke up, an old-timer on the board went postal and scolded me for disrespecting management. Once his rant sputtered, the company's chairman chimed in. "Tom is 100 percent right," he said. "These are not radical ideas. They need to be implemented and we're going to do them. Period." Leaders who hire yes-people do little more than bore holes in their own hull.

Prescribe protocols. Boards of privately held companies need to spell out how they do their work, lest conflicts creep in. Then everybody should stay out of each other's way. An audit committee composed of outside board members should review financial statements and deal directly with the company's outside accountants. Determine executive compensation with a committee composed of at least two outside board members—and the CEO if he or she is majority shareholder. Each committee elects a chair, who reports to the board of directors—not the CEO. Make sure each committee's protocol and responsibilities are clearly defined. Also, translate the board's principles into simple procedures that dictate things like implementing strategy, evaluating executive officers, and keeping tabs on company performance. Best-practice boards evaluate not only their own performance but also that of their committees and individual directors.

Disclose rules. In the interest of transparency, good boards post their principles on corporate Web sites (standards vary for publicly held and private companies). They may include how a board relates to management, how stakeholders access the board, and why the board does or does not separate the roles of chairman and CEO.

Make the board a planning partner. We expect them to think strategically, yet some companies strand board members on the sidelines during strategic-planning marathons. Strategy isn't a spectator sport. Pull members into the game. Ask them to help identify the company's SWOTs (strengths, weaknesses, opportunities, threats). Or, go all the way and invite them to every single planning session. At the very least, tap them during the final review phase—and deputize them to help track and analyze results.

Get the soft stuff right. It used to be that board members were concerned only with strategic planning, financial health, and picking executive officers. That is *so* twentieth century. Now boards decide standards of ethics and help weave them into the cultural fabric. That requires aligning everyone's values—the board's, individual board members', and the organization's.

Manage the board. Like every collection of people, a board has its own agendas, egos, frailties, and conflicts. Be mindful of a board's needs and personalities. A good entrepreneur works his board, which isn't manipulation. Build the board into your consciousness. Occasionally do quick one-on-ones over coffee. Besides rapport building, you'll learn a ton. Share information—e-brief members regularly. Solicit input, not for consent or assent, but to stay connected and keep everyone in sync.

THE MEETING

Start spreadin' the news. Distribute the "board book" (agenda, financials, meeting minutes, updates on issues and external relationships) digitally or via hard copy three days before the big board meeting. Do it any earlier, and the info goes stale. Any later, and members lose precious processing time. Everyone should be up to speed by the opening bell.

Balance the tell/ask ratio. These meetings have two halves: management (typically the CEO, CFO, and VP of operations) presents information about various agenda items; then the board members earn their fee by providing feedback and counsel. I've watched too many executives spend more than two-thirds of the meeting presenting and less than a third soliciting feedback. Flip that ratio. Some people mistakenly consider it a sign of weakness to ask for help. They view board meetings primarily as stages on which to trumpet their team's feats.

Lead with the numbers. Companies on the move like to crow about the numbers early and often. In down times, the financials magically slide to the bottom of the agenda. Imagine which meeting has people beating a path to the coffeemaker. Avoid frustration—now and at future meetings—by getting to the financials early. It keeps the clock on your side, adds clarity and realism to the agenda, and presents tough, hidden issues when everyone is fresh.

A good board walks a tightrope between coaching and challenging. A good board straddles two constituencies during meetings— shareholders (which it represents) and management (which represents the interests of the workers). A good board advises your management team on strategic plans and grills your execs on the spot to make sure strategies are credible, in everyone's best interests, and well executed.

The board doesn't run the company, management does. Seasoned management needs space during meetings. That's why good board members generally don't overstep. They ask questions until the truth reveals itself. But you want the gloves to come off if execs are dishonest or in deep denial—then a direct challenge is in everyone's best interest. Good board members can and should look over management's shoulder by asking simple questions like, *Is the company meeting its goals and performing well compared to industry benchmarks and committed timelines?* If yes, the board should stick to strategy. A no is your invitation to venture into operations.

Maintain an "action item" list. After digesting the financials, review the status of actionable, management-level items generated at the last meeting—what was to be done, by whom, and by when? Update the list as the meeting progresses. Without this discipline, key initiatives can slip through the cracks of faulty memory and neglect.

Keep it short. The longest a meeting should run is four hours. Any longer, and it's not a board meeting so much as an unfocused-company-in-trouble meeting. Marathon meetings can devolve into dysfunction, with advisers, even when they're sated with a pricey dinner, growing restless. Do not waste the board's time. Keep things moving with good preparation and agenda restrictions that limit the number of critical issues. Appoint a watchdog to (judiciously) keep an eye on the clock.

KEY POINTS

SETTING UP SHOP

➤ **Think things through.** Before quitting your day job, consider the impact that starting a business will have on your family and finances. Expect to make constant companions of fear and rejection. Investigate leasing options, partnering up, and covering your assets with insurance.

➤ **Do your due diligence.** Market research is a must. How will you know how to position your offering? Shop competitors, canvass customers, attend trade shows, probe industry insiders, and gather the best demographics money can buy.

➤ **Write a knockout business plan.** It's your road map to success and your entrée to lenders and investors. Writing your plan is a valuable exercise. It forces you to anticipate roadblocks, assess risks, sharpen strategies, analyze competitors, and calculate start-up costs.

➤ **Scare up seed capital.** Can't self-fund your company? Start with family, friends, and business contacts. Need more cash? Banks and the SBA are your next-best bets. Approach "angels" and venture capitalists only if you're willing to give up some equity.

➤ **Create visibility.** Position your new company so customers can't avoid you. Differentiation is the key. Find the perfect niche along the price-quality-service continuum. Make sure you've nailed your name and slogan. Before signing a lease, remember: It's not what you pay, it's how much you net for what you pay.

➤ **Protect yourself legally.** Choose the right type of operating entity. Hire a top-notch attorney. Don't sign contracts unless every word makes sense. Take steps now to protect your intellectual capital.

Head off employee defections and bogus claims. And for Pete's sake, get every last ownership agreement in writing.

➤ **Build a great board.** Hold hands with savvy, sophisticated outsiders who will share their expertise (for a reasonable fee). Look for complementary skills, encourage frank feedback, and keep everyone on the board current and connected.

POURING THE FOUNDATION

Laying In Your Mission, Vision, and Values

Picture a general addressing his nervous troops on the eve of a decisive battle. He implores them to fight fiercely for the honor of everything and everyone they hold dear. He stresses that the safety of their loved ones rests on how courageously they perform on the midnight battlefield. Then the general strides over to a second company of troops and orders them to conquer the enemy or die trying. The objective, he thunders, is to earn him that elusive fifth star and a heftier pension. It's a safe bet the first group will hit the battlefield with a steely resolve and accept nothing short of total victory. It's just as certain the second bunch would rather smash rocks in the hot sun than put their leader's selfish objectives ahead of their own self-interest.

The do-or-die spirit of an army or marine unit is the essence of what an enlightened entrepreneur must instill in the men and women under his command. That lofty goal is within reach, but only if the answers to three fundamental questions are clearly articulated, strategically spread, and consistently reinforced:

1. Why does the organization exist?
2. Where is it going?
3. How does it need to act to get there?

The answers must be precisely expressed—in a mission statement, vision statement, and statement of operating values—and held with conviction throughout the culture. "Conviction" is the operative word. If a company's mission, vision, and values aren't genuinely believed and championed by you and your management team, they're just words on paper. Ah, but when conviction is convincing, the organization rises above the sum of its parts and produces an inspired team. The change is palpable. It's also contagious. Writing your mission statement, vision statement, and statement of operating values amounts to nothing short of pouring the foundation of your business.

The Mission Statement. Sure, it's Business 101—something most companies have (gathering dust next to some plaques in a forgotten storeroom). But is it working? In seat-of-the-pants outfits, it's often just slapped together, a generic, white-bread substitute devoid of motivational nutrients. Or, tons of time has been invested in it only to produce something more complicated than memorable. Even if a mission statement clears those hurdles, it often hasn't been integrated into the culture. Take a look at yours. Is it in the front or back of people's minds? Or, is it pulled out only occasionally, like the what-were-they-thinking wedding gift that makes an appearance when the in-laws visit?

A mission statement is fundamentally immutable. Carve it in granite and display it behind glass. Market forces, business strategies, and senior management shift all the time. But a good company's core purpose is timeless. Through boom and bust, 3M's mission will always be *To solve unsolved problems innovatively.* Even when aggressive competition impacts Sony's marketing tactics, its mission remains *To experience the joy of advancing and applying technology for the benefit of the public.* These missions don't reference profits or shareholder value, and they ain't poetry. They give employees permission to throw themselves into the work they love and make a difference in the world.

Now imagine you've just received an advance copy of *BusinessWeek.* Emphasis here is on the word "advance"—the publication date is ten years in the future. The cover story features your very own business. Before you riffle through the pages, pause for a moment. What would you like that article to say about your company—its image, its culture, its values, its accomplishments?

What can you do right now to turn those dream headlines into scrapbook clippings? Now that everyone's on board the mission train, how do you keep from derailing into complacency or chaos? How can they pick up a head of steam while they're at it? Hitch up to the ol' Double-V—vision and values. Unlike your mission, which states your purpose, a vision statement asserts where your company is headed. A statement of operating values spells out the traits you and your employees must possess in order to live up to the company's mission and get them to their vision. Are the pieces in place but not breaking through to the surface? Get them going until every employee catches the wave.

CHAPTER 8

MISSION CRITICAL

Embodying Your Mission Statement

To help restore people to full life."

That's the essence of Minneapolis-based Medtronic's six-part, 171-word mission. It's also the mantra Ann Krzmarzick heard in each of the eight interviews she endured to become a communications specialist at the renowned medical technology company. It was a test of sorts. If Medtronic's mission didn't resonate, the human resources manager told her, she should look for employment elsewhere. Ann smiled and nodded. It was a catchy sound bite, but she figured it would have about as much impact as a bumper sticker on her day-to-day duties.

She figured wrong. Ann quickly discovered that those seven words were the beating heart of Medtronic's corporate body. "I didn't realize," she said, "that the light of that mission would shine so brightly on the everyday work in communications, given that we're fairly removed from direct patient care." The mission was consistently—almost reverently—referenced in every meeting and memo. It informed every decision at every level. It even reached all the way to the annual holiday party, where six bona fide patients share their stories of heartache, hope, and renewal. There's never a dry eye in the house.

Surveys reveal that nearly every one of Medtronic's twenty-six thousand employees knows the company's mission statement and how it applies to their job. They're inspired because they know their work makes a big difference in people's lives. Is it any wonder that Medtronic always appears on *Fortune* magazine's list of "100 Best Companies to Work For"?

At Tires Plus, we expressed our company's guiding principle through our thirteen-word mission: *"Deliver caring, world-class service to our guests, our community, and to each other."* A noble sense of purpose was essential for attracting quality employees. Most people consider working in the tire business to be only a little more appealing than getting a root canal. The industry is often thought of as dirty, unprofessional, and sometimes even dishonest. So why would people come work for us? Not to sell tires, but to improve the lives of customers, employees, and the world at large. It's people, not tires, that make the world go round.

I was a human billboard for our mission statement. Take the time my cofounder, Don Gullett, and I chartered a four-seater to visit four stores in North Dakota. Along with a contractor and a real estate agent, we landed in Fargo and rented a car. "As we were driving into the parking lot of our store," Don recalled, "Tom jumped out while the car was still rolling, ran over, and started talking to two people. The three of us just looked at each other."

I had spotted the couple coming out of the store and sensed by their expressions that they weren't happy. I asked if there was a problem. There shouldn't have been, because a big part of our mission was empowering store employees to resolve customer complaints. I found out what they were upset about, got them to walk back inside, resolved it, and turned them into happy customers. "It would have been very easy for someone in Tom's position to remain in the car until we had finished parking," Don noted. "But by the time we had gotten out of the car and into the store, those people would have driven off. So Tom went out of his way to introduce himself and correct the situation. I'm sure he left a lasting impression on that store's personnel, not to mention those customers."

Our corporate commandment—*Thou shalt be caring*—was like a global-positioning satellite that helped our people navigate the choppy waters of day-to-day decision making. More important, it helped managers identify and capitalize on "coachable moments"—instances when an employee's actions conflicted with our mission. For instance, our follow-up system required us to contact customers not more than forty-eight hours after providing a price quote. On a regular systems-review visit to a suburban Minneapolis store, I checked the phone log and saw that a teammate was skipping the follow-up call. Turns out he hadn't been properly trained and wasn't sure how to do it. So I spent some time teaching him the ropes via the Confucius Checklist (chapter 41).

I listened in when it was time for him to make an actual call. The woman he called told him she had opted to buy new tires from Firestone. "Oh, that's too bad," he said, "you really missed out." After he hung up, I said, "Wow, you basically told her she made a bad decision. How do you think that made her feel? Do you remember what our mission is?" He stammered, "To give caring, world-class service to our guests?" I asked if that phone call was consistent with the mission. He acknowledged it wasn't. "If somebody tells us their needs were taken care of," I said, "our reply should be, 'I'm glad you got what you needed. Your car is safer and will handle better now, and that's what's most important. Next time you're in the market, we'd love to have another opportunity to serve you.'" I stressed that alienating a potential customer today means we're also slamming the door shut on future sales. But that's not why people should be treated with respect. When you genuinely care about somebody's well-being, the good-will benefits everyone.

We upheld our mission's integrity just as vigilantly for "internal customers." If an employee treated a colleague rudely, I challenged him. I wanted amends made and behavior corrected immediately. "How would you feel if somebody treated you that way?" I'd ask. "How would you react?" I'd remind the offender in no uncertain terms that our mission called for everyone in the company to deliver caring service, and that also applied to one another.

Emphasizing worker civility isn't just the right thing to do. It's also practical. The average Fortune 1000 boss spends 13 percent of his time refereeing his staff, according to a study by the Marshall School of Business at the University of Southern California. Do the math. That's seven squandered weeks every year, a crippling price for neglecting to put your manners where your mission is.

RETOOLING YOUR MISSION

Is your company's mission in mothballs? Two words: huge opportunity. Re-igniting your mission can set off sparks that fire up the whole team. Stir things up at the next executive-team meeting. Ask if anyone knows the mission from memory, or at least its essence. If they can't, chances are no one can. That means your mission registers a big fat zero on the inspiration scale.

That's time for an update. First, convene a brainstorming session with top brass. The leaders should have an innate sense of the company's purpose. (Hint: A management consultant can smooth the process if her focus is fixed on facilitating; however, the question of purpose requires an insider's insight.) How to begin? Start by describing your offering. Ask, "Why is that important?" Challenge what the group comes up with, asking again and again, "How does that help our customer?" Go deeper until you finally punch through the brick wall of logic and tap into people's hearts. After five or six iterations—the whole thing could take two or three sessions—odds are you'll nail the essence of why you're in business.

Now it's tweak time. Create opportunities for every employee to pitch in. Reach out to resident wordsmiths and deep thinkers by posting drafts of the mission wherever people will see it—elevators, bathrooms, paycheck envelopes. Send it out in an e-mail blast. Call a company-wide meeting. Tell people how to submit their ideas. Getting everyone involved—and assuring them that all suggestions will be valued—builds trust and teamwork. Before you know it, a well-scrubbed mission statement will be hanging in everyone's office and cubicle.

SOWING SEEDS

Your responsibility as CEO (chief enlightenment officer) is to champion the company's mission until it guides every member of your team like the North Star. A leader breathes life into a mission statement by consistently modeling it. Then it evolves into a force that shapes employee behavior. It's like Johnny Appleseed, only with words, sowing seeds that take root in minds, hearts, and souls. Feature your mission everywhere—in orientation seminars, employee manuals, visual reminders, promotional materials, staff meetings, performance reviews, one-on-one coaching sessions, special functions, ceremonies.

To promote awareness of your mission:

- Use it as a **litmus test** in one-on-one and group meetings: "Is this in sync with our mission?"
- Ask people to **commit it to memory**. At team meetings, randomly call on someone to recite it. Reward a correct answer with a gift certificate.
- Hold an annual **team meeting** to make everyone aware of the company's mission and how it meshes with their daily routine.
- Try an **essay contest** with a topic like, *How our mission helped me make an important decision*. Or, *How our mission inspires me to give my best*. Or, simply, *What our mission means to me*. Post the entries on your intranet or bulletin board and award a prize to everyone who enters.
- Start a "Mission Mentions" section in the **company newsletter** to officially recognize employees for embodying the mission through words and deeds. At smaller shops, low-tech bulletin boards work just as well as high-speed e-letters.
- Post a **suggestion box** for comments about how the company can follow through on its mission.
- **Encourage employees to speak up** if they see circumstances that clash with the mission. Make various reporting channels available. The energy spent on this will pay huge dividends directly and indirectly throughout your business.

VISION CHECK

Composing Your Vision Statement

Think of your vision statement as a list of dreams committed to paper. It's a collection of shooting stars that inspire people to reach for the heavens. Not only did I share our vision with new hires, I reinforced it every quarter at regular team meetings. I never missed an opportunity to plug it. Our people worked harder when they were excited about where we were headed. More important, they'd give blood when they understood how our arrival would affect them personally.

I saw the fire in their eyes when I'd single one of them out and say, "Joe, how old are you going to be in ten years? Forty, huh? Well, if we grow 15 percent every year for ten years and turn our vision into reality, how will our performance incentives affect your salary? What kind of opportunities do you see for yourself in a $1.7 billion company? With your help, and the help of everyone in this room, we can make it happen."

People crave a clear sense of purpose (mission) but they also love to be on a winning team (vision). Show them the way by painting idealistic, yet reachable, targets. Help them plug into the high-voltage current of your company's vision. Here's the six-part vision statement we came up with at Tires Plus:

1. Become a national player with $1.7 billion in revenues and eleven hundred stores by 2010.
2. Become the marquee tire company in the U.S.
3. Become the number-one or number-two market-share leader in every market we serve while creating a fair return for our efforts.
4. Serve guests so well that 99 percent recommend us to family and friends.
5. Develop the strengths of a big company while maintaining the agility of a small one.
6. Provide a nurturing and healthy environment that establishes us among America's most desirable companies to work for.

Unlike a mission statement, you can tinker with a vision statement. At the close of each year, determine whether your objectives need to be modified in light of unexpected events. But don't tarnish them with the rust of lower expectations unless you have a compelling reason.

Need to update your vision statement? Follow the steps you took to retool your mission (chapter 8), keeping in mind two distinctions:

"Bold" and "Fearless" are the Operative Words. Shoot for the moon, like JFK in a 1961 speech to Congress: "I believe that this nation should commit itself to achieving the goal, before this decade is out, of landing a man on the moon and returning him safely to the earth."

Telescope Out Seven to Ten Years. Peering that far requires visionary thinking and a willingness to look beyond current capabilities and market conditions.

CHAPTER 10

CHAMPION CORE VALUES

The Link Between Character and Higher Profits

If a scientist extracted your company's DNA and placed it under a microscope, the image she would see is your operating values. It's the cultural backbone of your organization, a list of valued traits and deeds expected from all employees. Your vision statement shows employees where you want to go; your operating values spell out what they need to do to get there.

These core values should run so deep through your culture that the hurricane winds of markets, disruptive technologies, and economic conditions can't uproot them. If you can imagine any circumstances that would force one of these values off the list, then it's not a core value and should never have been identified as one. Like your mission statement, these values must be championed and modeled by management. Otherwise, employees will shrug off a "Values We Value" campaign as just another sleepwalking initiative.

Promoting its values helps an organization avoid hiring and harboring people who don't measure up. For instance, if your talent scouts look for new hires based on attention to detail, world-class service skills, and innovative thinking, it's unlikely that a lazy conformist will sneak past the front gate. Those who do will soon either run for the door or have it shown to them.

The ideal Tires Plus employee possessed six qualities. Scott McPhee, our retail operations veep, coined the acronym COPPSS to make these attributes easy to remember: Caring, Optimistic, Passionate, Persistent, Systems-disciplined, and Spirit-filled. We snapped up everyone we could who embodied these six qualities:

1. Caring. Twenty-four years in my workplace laboratory convinced me there are two kinds of employees—those who are deflated by mixing with the public and those who are energized by it. The distinction may initially be difficult to discern. Nineteen out of twenty applicants for client-service jobs will assure you, "I love working with people!" Yet six months into the job, the self-proclaimed "people person" is bellowing, "These people are driving me nuts!" We sought out employees who loved to make someone's day. Every business, regardless of its offering, is in the business of helping people. Every employee, no matter how removed from customers and colleagues, contributes to the organization's CQ (caring quotient). The higher the CQ, the more harmony in the workplace. That means a happier, more productive hive.

Stress and losing ourselves in our work are just two of the factors that can push aside "the better angels of our nature." Several years ago, I found myself hunched over my laptop on a flight from Minneapolis to San Diego. I was trying to nail a deadline under less than ideal conditions, made worse by the oaf in front of me who fully cranked his seat into my lap. Agitated over this guy's boxing in my six-foot two-inch frame, I sank my knees, already pressed into his seat, a little deeper to send a message. Forty-five minutes later, a woman in her eighties rose in front of me and used a walker to reach the restroom. I was horrified. I had zinged an elderly lady, of all people, with my knee-jerk reaction.

To this day I draw upon that woman when I'm in a rush. It reminds me to always recognize the humanity of other people. The Sanskrit greeting Namaste expresses this intent: "The divine in me bows to the divine in you."

2. Optimistic. In the Optimism Olympics, Eddie Haskell would be barred from the stadium. At best, Eddie's oily brand of optimism on *Leave It to Beaver* was annoying ("Mrs. Cleaver, I know your dinner party is going to be a big success!"). So is the modern corporate yes-man equivalent ("That's an awesome report, Boss; it's going to double our revenues!"). At worst, it perpetuates dishonest behavior.

On the opposite end, overt negativism kills initiative and deadens spirits. It's also contagious. I've seen one employee with a rotten attitude seductively infect his colleagues until a black cloud hovered over an entire department. Grousing about coworkers is especially toxic. It sows dissention and doubt throughout your shop. Pessimism becomes self-fulfilling. Once your people lock themselves into it, they wind up spending more energy justifying their negativity than in searching for solutions.

Once I got steamed during a biannual operating-plan review. Dan, one of our regional managers, had unilaterally reversed our formula of devoting 10 percent of a plan analysis to identifying obstacles and 90 percent on how to hurdle them. His presentation turned into one long excuse for why he hadn't met his profit goals. Typically, I'm gentle with underperformers, especially in front of their peers. But Dan had worn my patience thin. I asked him point-blank why he hadn't told us about his problems earlier so they could've been solved by now. He mumbled something about not being able to get people's attention. It was clear he still didn't get it. A few months later we had to "free up his future." Not caring on our part? Not excising a cancerous attitude like that would have been uncaring to our team.

Does this attitude sound familiar? *The glass isn't just half empty, it's cracked down the middle and smudged with ChapStick.* Yeah? Here's hoping you can convince your people there's a more pleasant—and productive—way to look at the world. It ain't easy, that's for sure, especially if they've been counterprogrammed since childhood. But help someone change their mind-set and you change their life.

The healthy middle ground between mind-numbing positivism and Doomsday Dan is a place I call authentic optimism. It welcomes thoughtful dissent, inspires the confidence to hurdle any obstacle, and reframes roadblocks as opportunities. For instance: "Yeah, landing that account is a challenge. But if we study the offering our competitor submitted and put Sue on this, we can do it." As the placebo effect proves, optimism can create ideal outcomes. It's also a basic law of the office that people will scale the tallest filing cabinet to help cheerful colleagues succeed. Art Linkletter summed it up perfectly:

> *Things turn out best for the people who*
> *make the best of the way things turn out.*

Optimism poured out of our phones daily: "It's a great day at Tires Plus. This is Tom. How can I help you?" You should have heard the reaction when I first proposed that greeting. Groans all around. But I insisted, and soon it became second nature. Eventually, a number of Fortune 500 companies appropriated our greeting. That's great. The world needs all the optimism it can get.

3. Passionate. Selling a new idea to colleagues is like a district attorney trying to persuade a jury to lock up the bad guy: Conviction equals success. More precisely, success hinges on the *passion* of your convictions. In its purest form, passion is the combustible mixture of meaning and purpose. A passionate pitch is more likely to get a warm reception. But check yourself, don't get volcanic. Quiet, controlled passion also packs influence. Besides, erupting too often raises eyebrows. People are more apt to help someone who maintains an even keel and hollers, "Man overboard!" only after a really loud splash.

A passion deficit is a deal breaker whether you're introducing a new initiative, coaching an employee, or apologizing to a customer. Tone and body language speak louder than your words ever will. The B.S. Detector goes berserk when verbal and nonverbal cues don't jibe. With phony passion running rampant nowadays, don't be surprised if people put up their guard or search for ulterior motives if they sense your passion isn't genuine. The cynicism will fade once they see consistency, or if an authority vouches for you. Dave Wilhelmi, our vice president of marketing, ran into skeptics all the time. "A lot of people thought Tom's passion was fake or somewhat calculated at first," Dave said, "but the more they got to know him, the more they saw it was real." Dave recalled a party we threw in 1998 to celebrate winning U.S. Tire Dealer of the Year. "Tom gave one of his heartfelt addresses, thanking all the people who were such a big part of our success," Dave said. In the hallway afterward, Dave ran into a new vendor-partner who asked whether Tom was always so passionate. "It's as if you can feel everything he's saying," the guy said. "I just smiled," Dave recalled, "and said, 'What you see is what you get.'"

4. Persistent. Our first three tire stores were small converted service stations that also sold gasoline. With the late-'70s energy crisis in full swing, my gasoline allocation was grossly inadequate and I struggled to meet payroll. So I wrote an appeal letter to the federal government for more gas. Denied. I called the Department of Energy's Midwest office in Chicago to request a meeting with the director, Ray Fiene. Denied. I was told in no uncertain terms that Mr. Fiene was unavailable. Undaunted, I hopped a plane to Chicago and tried to sweet-talk his receptionist. Denied. Now, I had seen his picture once, so I plopped down, scanned the lobby, and waited. And waited. A few hours later, there he was, shuffling past me on his way to the men's room. Golden opportunity. I followed right behind. There, at the urinal, I sidled up beside Mr. Fiene, apologized for the intrusion, and launched into my pitch. He shot me a look of disbelief. Then he laughed and zipped up. "Okay, kid," he said, "get into my office!" I did. He heard me out and upped my allocation. That's how my company survived its earliest, darkest days.

A persistence deficit will derail even the most talented professional. Murphy's Law—*Whatever can go wrong will go wrong*—will never be repealed. But that doesn't mean you can't hurdle or dodge Murphy through dogged persistence. When employees bounce off obstacles, educate and inspire them to find another route. Remind them that a corollary of Murphy's Law is *Whatever's worth doing will be more difficult and time-consuming than you expected*. Yet if the juice is worth the squeeze, keep the pressure on.

Calvin Coolidge's "Law of Persistence," dated though it may be, has been on my wall ever since I started my business:

Nothing in the world can take the place of persistence.
Talent will not; nothing is more common than unsuccessful men with talent.
Genius will not; unrewarded genius is almost a proverb.
Education will not; the world is full of educated derelicts.
Persistence and determination alone are omnipotent.

It's unbelievable the number of people I've seen limp away after stumbling over a roadblock or two. Little did they know that success was just around the bend.

5. Systems-disciplined. In my younger, ego-drenched days, I often challenged authority—professionally and privately—and relished every opportunity to beat the system. Hindsight is humbling. It's now clear that playing by the rules produces less chaos and honors others more.

Choosing to ignore even a minor procedure can be costly, a point I liked to dramatize at store-manager meetings. I'd stand in front of the room and ask what a phone call from a potential customer was worth. I'd say, "When we don't do the things we're supposed to do when they call, you might as well do this," and I'd take a $100 bill out of my wallet and slowly rip it in half. "Tom's point," said Dave Urspringer, a manager whose Coon Rapids, Minnesota, store always excelled, "was that if a prospect called and you didn't use the script to determine their needs—then ask to reserve the tires that filled those needs—you're losing a chance to help a guest and basically throwing $100 out the window. Because that's what the profit on an average sale was worth. That really made an impression."

Does this mean every rule should be slavishly obeyed? Of course not. Veering onto the dirt shoulder and roaring past law-abiding traffic may be necessary in emergencies. Just keep an eye on your rearview mirror to make sure the dust you're kicking up doesn't cause a fender bender or pileup. (For more on systems, see chapters 23–27.)

6. Spirit-filled. On a Paris business trip in 1998, I had the honor of meeting François Michelin, then seventy-three years old and head of the company bearing his name. Impressed with his vitality, I asked how he stayed in great shape. "Spirit!" he told me. "When translated into Greek, *pneu*, the French word for 'tire,' means spirit. Air is to the tire as spirit is to the human body." He emphasized the point by giving me a big hug. *Wow*, I thought, *I hadn't realized I was in such a spirit-filled business.*

"Spirit-filled" evokes the image of pumping your tank full of air at a metaphysical service station. I believe spirit is an inherent part of who we are—something to be released rather than created. Spirit flows from seeking meaning and purpose in life. It does not mean espousing religious beliefs around the watercooler. It means having the courage to hold fast to your cherished values and be authentic. When you're connected to spirit, you're unconsciously modeling a better way to live and work.

This wisdom is implicit in "May the Force be with you," Obi-Wan Kenobi's benediction to Luke Skywalker in *Star Wars*. Call it what you will—spirit, God, the Force. It's the omnipresent intelligence that governs everything. Align yourself with it, with the pure intention of benefiting the world, and you'll emerge from the shadows of self-absorption into the sunshine of selfless service and synchronicity. Doors will open, obstacles will vanish, people will appear—meaningful coincidences that nudge you closer to your goals.

Connecting with spirit is a primal need. Mythologist Joseph Campbell spoke of our innate desire to "feel the rapture of being alive." I felt this euphoria of living more intensely the more I avoided spiritual tranquilizers—unhealthy food, booze, no exercise, denial, guilt, inappropriate anger. Russian philosopher P. D. Ouspensky explained that most of us move through life in a waking sleep that prevents us from tapping into our spirit. If that sounds familiar, stop hitting the snooze button. It's time to wake up.

CHAPTER 11

ACCOUNTABLE ETHICS

The Four Pillars of Ethical Leadership

Good leaders watch like a hawk for decisions that fail to uphold the company's mission, advance its vision, and express its core values. This may sound like some utopian B-school dogma, but compelling evidence points to a direct link between ethical leadership and higher profits. That's according to the Center for Ethical Business Cultures (disclosure: I'm a board member) in its 2001 study, *The Ethical Advantage: Why Ethical Leadership Is Good Business.* Certainly, ethical leadership offers no protection against a badly flawed business model or strategy. But a fundamentally ethical organization stands to gain an advantage by developing four traits:

1. Balanced Stakeholder Interests. Look around. You aren't operating in a vacuum. Your company fits into a larger community. Its relationships—with employees, customers, business partners—are intertwined. Tending the till in an enlightened social context drives superior financial performance. A firm generates this virtuous circle when it honors employees, who then turn around and produce a high-quality product on service. Ultimately, customers are so pleased that they become pied pipers leading everyone else in town to your door.

Whenever our executive team voted on a big issue, we first mulled over its effect on all our constituencies. Our three-word litmus test—*Is it fair?*—exposed flawed analysis and produced better decisions.

2. Leadership Integrity. From the start, Tires Plus stores were upscale, with cappuccino machines, prints on the walls, TV and movies, toys for kids, and shiny, clean floors for them to play on (did I mention these were tire stores?). The industry was tagged as unprofessional, so I wanted to set Tires Plus apart by presenting a clean-cut, professional image. Some team members thought we went too far. An internal survey showed that 60 percent of our sales staff hated wearing white shirts and ties. The issue came to a vote at an executive-team meeting. I voted yes. Everyone else voted no. I vetoed the team's decision, one of only a handful of times I overruled everyone.

Conflict like this will certainly produce blowback. But enlightened entrepreneurs tune out the grumbling. They're purpose pleasers, not people pleasers. They're less concerned about who is right than what is right. Base your decisions on what's best for all stakeholders, in the broadest sense of the word. Long-term benefits are worth the short-term price. Set the ethical tone by modeling West Point's "Cadet Prayer":

> *Make us to choose the harder right instead of*
> *the easier wrong, and never to be content with*
> *a half truth when the whole can be won.*

3. Process Integrity. Otherwise known as institutional integrity, process integrity is a reflection of how deeply a company's ethics are ingrained in its core processes. Every element must be held to the same high standard. People, as well as procedures, are accountable for results. In an environment like this, employees feel free, and perhaps obligated, to report individual and organizational breaches of conduct. They follow their scruples, even at the cost of profits.

It's a principle that guides Reell Precision Manufacturing Corporation, a thirty-seven-year-old manufacturer of electromechanical components such as clutches and hinges. When fears of a recession plunged orders and revenue in 2001, Reell executives asked employees to take a temporary pay cut to avoid layoffs. Employees readily accepted the proposal because the dozen senior execs had already stepped up and slashed 16 percent off their own pay. Reell saved half a million dollars—and dozens of jobs.

That's business as usual for this Vadnais Heights, Minnesota, company, awarded the 2002 Minnesota Business Ethics Award. Reell's institutional integrity is strengthened by its *teach/equip/trust* style of management—as opposed to *command/direct/control*. The results show up on the assembly line. Workers are typically hired with no particular skills, but they learn every stop on the line, from scheduling and assembly to quality checks and failure analysis. Product is shipped only after the line worker signs off—without backup inspection (other than periodic audits).

The goodwill between Reell's management and labor propels the company's virtuous circle. "Turnover is almost zero," said Reell cofounder, Bob Wahlstedt. "The most important reason for enriching the production jobs is to benefit the workers—they're happier and more fulfilled. But from the company's standpoint, encouraging and educating employees to develop mastery in their work, and to take pride in it, makes for a consistently better product." Reell's faith in its people and processes produces stratospheric quality achievements. Of the roughly half a million units Reell shipped annually to Xerox, not one was rejected during a four-year span.

Ironically, times of crisis magnify a firm's ethical advantage. When everyone—employees, customers, business partners—categorically trusts a firm, they're more likely to pitch in to help it weather a storm. Six months after Reell's pay cut, the company restored salaries and returned to profitability.

4. Environmental Stewardship. It's a good bet that Buddha wasn't contemplating the relationship between commerce and the environment when he said, "Do no harm." But who knows? The fact is, protecting our natural resources is a business's moral responsibility. Every Tires Plus store recycled paper and plastic. In our hydraulic lifts for vehicles, we used biodegradable vegetable oil instead of petroleum-based oil whenever possible. Spent tires were chopped into hockey puck–size chips and burned for fuel in EPA-approved facilities. We even teamed up with the U.S. Department of Transportation to produce guidelines that showed drivers how to tread easier on the environment.

Why all the fuss? Because a healthy earth is good business. It's a lesson that smog-clogged China is quickly learning as its population falls in love with the automobile. My friend Terry Tamminen, a fellow board member for the International Waterkeeper Alliance, which he cofounded, was so persuasive with this argument that California governor Arnold Schwarzenegger tapped him for a cabinet secretary post. "The numbers on the bottom of the balance sheet will grow in direct proportion to the balance of clean air, clean water, and healthy landscapes we bequeath to our kids," said Terry, who served as the secretary of the California Environmental Protection Agency. "For example, installing energy-efficient lighting and electrical equipment pays for itself in as little as eighteen months and reduces the need to burn fossil fuels. How many business decisions do you make that are good for both the soul and the cash register?"

For guidance on environmental sustainability, check out:

- Alliance for Sustainability (www.allianceforsustainability.net)
- Rocky Mountain Institute (www.rmi.org)
- Business for Social Responsibility (www.bsr.org)
- Business Alliance for Local Living Economies (www .ballenetwork .org)
- Sustainable Business.com (www.sustainablebusiness.com)

Care to shore up your company's ethical infrastructure? First step: Assess your organizational climate with the CEBC Integrity Measurement Program(SM), created by the Center for Ethical Business Cultures and Gantz Wiley Research. It provides credible, unbiased feedback and helps you develop principled practices. For more information, visit www.cebcglobal.org.

NO SHORTCUTS

Unethical behavior is a seductive narcotic for both Corporate America and Small Business U.S.A. It can produce a quick high, but it inevitably—and insidiously—rots the tapestry of both your company and your life's work. Do not treat this as a taboo subject around your people. Describe how they'll feel invincible until that hopeless, horrifying day when their reputation and aspirations unravel before their eyes. It begins with that first puff. Pocket a few pens from the supply room here. Slide personal mail through the postage meter there. It's easy to rationalize minor transgressions: *Nobody will notice. It's just a few bucks. They don't pay me enough anyway.*

But a tiny crack in the glass gradually expands until you can't see out the windshield. That is, one dishonest action, no matter how slight, can compromise our sense of right and wrong and leave us vulnerable to the allure of more dangerous temptations. Especially when people are under pressure to make those high mortgage payments, get the kids into the best schools, and own a luxury automobile.

We never intended to cross the line. But that's what we do when we cut corners on quality to save a few cents per unit. Or when we dodge environmental regulations. Or cook the books. Smart business decisions, we tell ourselves. Before we know it, security is escorting us out of the building. Or, worse, we trade in pinstripes for prison orange. Feel yourself edging up to a slippery slope? Take an ethics check. Ask yourself how you'd feel if your behavior were broadcast on the local news. Would you make the same decision if your family were standing at your side? Some may consider this litmus test naïve and overly simplistic. They'll argue that situational ethics are too complex to be boiled down to shirtsleeves decision making. I disagree.

Corporate responsibility demands that leaders recognize a common interest beyond their own self-interest. In 1776, the American Revolution coincided with the publication of Adam Smith's *Wealth of Nations,* which revolutionized economic thinking. The Scottish philosopher and economist theorized that the "invisible hand" of the market transmutes the individual pursuit of self-interest into a public benefit. Two hundred eighteen years later in Switzerland, the Caux Round Table took a more practical view. In recognition of the complexities of the modern world, this annual gathering of business leaders from Europe (Alfredo Ambrosetti, chairman of the Ambrosetti Group), Japan (Ryuzaburo Kaku, chairman of Canon), and the United States (Winston Wallin, chairman of Medtronic) endorsed a set of ethical practices. These seven "Principles for Business" are rooted in the Western ideal of respect for human dignity and the Japanese ideal of *kyosei,* which asserts that human beings should strive to live and work together in harmony for the common good. In other words, self-interest alone doesn't cut it.

Don't get me wrong. I'm a staunch defender of economic and intellectual liberty. I agree with philosopher Ayn Rand that a free mind and a free market go hand in glove. But as the implosions of Enron, WorldCom, and Tyco clearly illustrate, our capitalist system is riddled with loopholes. The rash of corporate scandals in the early 2000s angered large swaths of America, to say nothing of the millions of ethical businesspeople who felt tainted by association. It's incumbent upon each of us to act, at all times and in all ways, ethically, responsibly, and with the common good in mind. A heroic effort is required to earn back the respect of employees, the confidence of shareholders, and the trust of the public. I'm confident we can answer the call.

KEY POINTS

POURING THE FOUNDATION

- ➤ **A well-crafted mission statement is the foundation of an enlightened organization.** Revisit your company's purpose for being and, if necessary, revitalize it with inspiration. A mission is the polestar that corrects and directs employees. But if team leaders don't embody it, it's just one more empty piece of paper pushed by a wannabe titan.
- ➤ **Re-craft your vision statement with boldness and idealism.** Look at least seven to ten years out, well beyond organizational capabilities. Declare a destination, rally the troops, and the road map will begin to take shape.

➤ **Spell out your core operating values.** Defining "success behavior" for employees weeds out the wrong people and keeps the right ones on track. Through the collective power of employees' deeds, these fundamental principles define your firm's character.

➤ **Revisit your vision statement occasionally, but preserve your mission and core values.** Update your vision statement when market forces or company performance render it irrelevant. Operating values, however, are organizational DNA and off-limits to tampering.

➤ **Enlightened entrepreneurs base decisions on more than self-interest.** Healthy pursuit of self-interest often leads to parallel public benefit. But as the Enron and WorldCom scandals demonstrate, lax ethical principles and social concerns can topple corporate giants, ruin lives, and cause enormous economic damage.

➤ **Ethical leadership and sound business practices increase profits.** A company gains an ethical advantage, which translates into a competitive advantage, when it demands integrity from its leaders, processes, stakeholder relationships, and environmental stewardship.

SNATCHING UP STARS

Embracing Your Hire Power

The hiring process, a romantic dinner, walking a tightrope—what do they all have in common? A rush job can produce disastrous results. Hiring after one interview—no probing, no references, no work-history review—is like hopping a red-eye to Vegas to get married after one date. It's impulsive and expensive, and the chances for long-term harmony are abysmal.

The more time invested on the front end, the less likely the chance of getting bitten on the back end. Shortcuts are tempting, especially when a candidate's personality, résumé, and references are intoxicating. The swoon is like puppy love, as if the person has been delivered by divine decree.

Seat-of-the-pantsers typically put mediocre employees in charge of hiring. Big mistake. It takes a sharp person to recognize a fellow thoroughbred—and to be delighted, not intimidated, by their star power. Leverage the street smarts of some elite performers by placing them in the interviewer's chair.

Beware of the fear factor. Some managers don't *want* their socks knocked off. Sure, it's only human nature to feel threatened by someone who could do your job better than you. But the only way to build a strong team is to hire the best people you can find. Sharper people challenge you to grow *and* make your business more productive. Guess who looks smarter then? If you hire only people you feel intellectually superior to, you'll wind up holding yourself hostage to a bunch of deadwood subordinates who need approval to sharpen a pencil. That sets the dominos in motion. Inevitably, the really good people leave, the really bad people are fired, and all that's left is a hot, steaming pile of mind-numbing mediocrity.

CHAPTER 12

TALENT SCOUTING

Finding the Best People

Tom Greenwade's Oldsmobile must have been caked with dust by the time he pulled up to the bleachers in Baxter Springs, Oklahoma. The baseball scout was there to bird-dog the third baseman for the Whiz Kids, a local semipro team. But it was the young shortstop that caught Greenwade's eye by belting two monstrous home runs into the river well past the fences. Since the phenom was only a high school sophomore, Greenwade vowed to return bearing a contract on the young slugger's graduation day. True to his word, two years later, Greenwade attended commencement ceremonies for the Commerce High School Class of '49. That's how Mickey Mantle signed his first New York Yankees contract.

Business is a lot like baseball. Get the right talent and your company can be a champion. It's unlikely, however, that a few tiny lines in a classified ad are going to reel in a big home-run hitter. Finding the best people requires the diligence and resourcefulness of Tom Greenwade.

To attract and find top-notch talent:

Turn your workforce into an army of bounty hunters. Dangling a cash reward in front of employees is a good way to get their attention. Ninety days after a candidate was hired, we added a bonus of up to $500 to the referrer's paycheck. (We also gave finder's fees to suppliers and vendors.) One caveat: Employees can be your best recruiters—or your worst. In an enlightened environment they'll deliver a steady stream of quality candidates. Unhappy employees, however, tend to bring in unhappy prospects.

Pluck prospects from your web of business partners. When we needed a new CFO, the first thing I did was contact our accounting firm. I asked the partner in charge of our account if he knew anyone who might fit. He recommended a financial wizard named Jim Bemis who had just resigned from a troubled company. Snapping up Jim was critical to taking our company to the next level. Word travels fast in professional circles, so don't be shy about mining business contacts for referrals.

Crank up your visibility. The real estate mantra "Location, location, location" doesn't apply just to land valuation. It also helps land valuable employees. Ask yourself, *Where are the people we want to hire?* Go there, and start schmoozing. Join the chamber of commerce. Attend all the business, community, and charitable events you can. The hand you shake may be your next superstar.

Keep your radar on high alert. Wayne Shimer, who headed up our recruiting and retention, was in Omaha in 1998 to guide some store openings. Standing at an ATM machine, of all places, he met a guy who was wearing a shirt, tie, and name tag. "I asked him, 'How are you doing?'" Wayne recalled. "'I'm doing *great*!' he said." Impressed, Wayne struck up a conversation and discovered that the guy was bored with his sales job at a hat shop in the mall. They exchanged cards and Wayne returned later to scout him out. "The guy was fantastic," Wayne said. "I hired him on the spot and he's still with the company today. And doing very well, thank you."

Radar is important because you bump into tomorrow's stars all day long—the cheerful, efficient waitress who clearly enjoys working with people; the friendly clerk who makes you feel like you're his favorite customer. When I saw a smile on someone's face and a sparkle in his eyes, I told him he gave great service. "How long have you worked here?" I'd ask, and follow up with a couple more: "Do you like what you're doing?" and "Is there a good career path for you here?" If the answer to the last two were yes, I'd thank him and be on my way. But nine times out of ten he'd say it was only a temporary job. I'd tell him I was always looking for good people like him. If he showed interest, I handed him my card. I've hired dozens of people like that.

Draw quality like a magnet. Attracting quality employees is a lot easier when you're a quality employer. Talented people seek organizations with exceptional standards and sparkling reputations. To paraphrase the Center for Ethical Business Cultures, the most valuable employees want to contribute to their customers and to society, and to learn and grow themselves in the process. In the war for talent, an ethical edge can hook the best people.

Don't take no for an answer. We didn't mess around when somebody was right for us. We took him to dinner, introduced him to the team, and did whatever it took to persuade him to sign. One of my recruiting execs once said we should ding a candidate because he wasn't pursuing us vigorously enough. "Heck no!" I said. "The stars don't have to go hard after companies. We're the ones who need to pursue *them*." Some twenty years ago, we were searching for a specialized sales rep. I knew Tom DuPont was the guy for the job by the end of our first interview. But he had just left a similar job at a competing firm and nursed doubts about staying in the business.

Over two weeks, I bought him lunch, brought him back to the office, and called him three or four times. "Tom just kept coming at me and coming at me until I finally relented," DuPont recalled. "He kept telling me, 'You've got to join the team!' He was very persistent. That really made me feel great because it's always nice to feel wanted." DuPont took the job and stayed with us for ten years until he left to start his own company. Moral of the story? Don't let the good ones get away. They can't see the other side of the mountain like you can.

Explore the jungles of guerrilla recruiting. Recall bank robber Willie Sutton's famous line? Asked why he robbed banks, he quipped, "Because that's where the money is." Apply Willie's logic to the office—your competitors' payroll is an obvious place to find the skill players you need. As a fast-growing company with an insatiable appetite for talent, we sometimes marched right into a competitor's store and told the staff we just wanted to say hello to our neighbors. Oh, and by the way, we'd say, we're always looking for help. Did we mention our $500 referral fee? Invariably, we heard one of three responses: (1) "Don't let the door hit you on the way out," (2) "Five hundred bucks? Sure, I'll keep my eyes open," or (3) "I'm not happy here, can I schedule an interview?" Of course, we never tried to "steal" employees who were content. But we felt good about providing opportunities to anyone who felt underappreciated.

Look under your nose. The lowest person on the totem pole often carries the tribe on his shoulders. I always put that theory to test in the field. When I walked in the front door of one of our stores, I greeted the guys in sales and management, then headed right for the service bays. I was searching for sleeping stars the manager had squirreled away. In Cedar Rapids, Iowa, I hit the jackpot in a technician so gregarious and sharp that I ran to the sales floor and told our personnel guru, Wayne Shimer, "You've gotta meet this tire tech. He's really something." We spent forty-five minutes talking to the guy. Within days, we moved him to the sales floor. A year later he was managing his own store.

Fall in love with internal promotion—it'll return the favor in spades. Career Awareness Day was the linchpin of our retention success. Once a year in our support center, employees who were considering career changes walked among booths representing every department. "You've got to find that diamond in the rough who's already drawing a paycheck," Wayne said, "and help him further his career." Tire techs, for instance, discovered opportunities in the warehouse. Sales staff combing the want ads found openings in, say, customer service. "Every department had somebody who was working toward a business degree," Wayne recalled. "We discovered people's hopes and dreams, but just as important was what their hopes and dreams were not." It's like the guy who sold his home to travel the world in search of fortune only to hear later that one of the world's largest diamond mines was discovered on his old property. "We cultivated our field all the time," Wayne said. "We knew if we didn't, we'd lose 'em. We'd just be a stopover point instead of a career destination."

Don't forget schools, agencies, and trade shows. Forget the buried treasure. Network at universities and vocational schools, consistent sources of leads. Search firms and employment agencies produced some three hires for us at every job fair we attended. Trade shows and industry meet-and-greets are full of hungry job seekers. Subscribe to newsletters. Scour the business section. Whatever you choose, be quick and efficient. Your competitors may read *The Big Book,* too.

CHAPTER 13

INTERVIEW ESSENTIALS

Stripping the Guesswork Out of Hiring

Interviewing a job candidate is like asking your kid what he did at school. You won't find out what's worth knowing until you ask just the right questions in just the right way. In the Hiring Game, it's crucial to arm yourself with probing, open-ended questions. Most job seekers know the drill inside and out. They're skilled at telling you what they think you want to hear and, more important, suppressing details they *don't* want you to hear. But that, my friend, is exactly the information you need to know.

Who should be there? The candidate's quality and the importance of the job determine who sits in on the initial interview and how many cycles it will take. Lots of companies pinball a candidate from one manager's office to the next to face the same predictable litany in an endless circuit. That wastes the applicant's time and nets canned responses. I typically arranged a panel of three to five teammates for key positions. Granted, "six against one" can be intimidating, but it also provides insight into how an applicant performs under gentle pressure. No matter how many "suits" are in the room, create a relaxed, welcoming environment.

Before launching into a friendly grilling, level the playing field a bit and ease into the conversation. I'd thank a prospect for considering us and acknowledge that she was interviewing us as much as we were interviewing her. I'd emphasize that we'd each benefit from total candor, noting that important details that didn't surface could come back to haunt us. I'd promise not to oversell my offer and ask her to return the favor.

After going over our mission, vision, and values, I'd pepper her with thought-provoking questions arranged under nine themes. I'd do my best to come across as both caring and curious, probing but not prosecutorial. Through tone and body language, I'd lob up even the most challenging questions like softballs. I'd encourage her to go with the first response that came to mind and let her do 70 percent of the talking.

The interview checklist:

Mission, vision, and values. If you can't establish congruence with the Big Three, there's no point continuing the interview.

- *How does our mission statement sound to you? What do you like about it? How do you feel when you think about it?*
- *How could you help us reach our vision-statement goals?*
- *Which of our values resonate with you and why? Which of our values are you uncomfortable with?*
- *Can you give me two examples of the role these values play in your life?*

Job history. Start with the basics and add a twist. To understand a prospect's experience, ask about her last three jobs.

- *What was your job description, and what did you actually do?*
- *What did you love about the job, and what did you hate?*
- *How would you rate your boss, and why?*
- *Did you leave the job or did the job leave you? What exactly happened?*

The kicker? Don't ask what her last supervisor thought about the quality of her work. Instead, ask, *What will your supervisor say about you when I call?* Odds are you'll get a more honest, revealing answer because she's probably thinking, *Uh-oh, I better come clean.*

Rethinking references: If the applicant worked at a smaller business, you might squeeze some candid impressions out of her supervisor. It can't hurt to try. Larger companies refer questions like that to a tight-lipped HR rep who will only confirm dates of employment and positions held. For serious intel, ask the applicant for names of former colleagues. Later, follow through: "Bill? Hi, this is Tom over at Tires Plus. Your name came up during an interview with Jane Doe and I wanted to know if you could tell me anything about her. What? Terminated for tardiness?"

Drive and ingenuity. These questions determine a job seeker's capacity to work hard *and* smart.

- *Walk me through a typical day at your most recent job (or the one most relevant to the position under discussion). How did you feel about each part?*
- *What were your biggest contributions to your last employer?*
- *What are some on-the-job examples of your going beyond the call of duty?*
- *Tell me about the times you underperformed. What did you do about it?*
- *What is your understanding of what this job requires?*
- *How many hours did you work at your last job, and how many do you expect to work at this job?*

Integrity. Don't pass up the opportunity to stress zero tolerance for bad ethics. People with integrity deficits assume that everyone else shares their twisted concept of right and wrong. That's how they rationalize ethical shortcuts. Pick out the bad apples with these questions:

- *Everyone has bent or broken a rule at one time or another. What was one of your recent transgressions, and what did you learn from it?*

- *Are all rules valid?*
- *If you felt a rule was unfair, what would you do about it?*
- *Have you ever broken a rule to satisfy a customer? If so, how?*
- *Which is more important, customer service or making a profit? Why?*

Judgment. These four questions help judge the candidate's maturity and the quality of her decision making.

- *Tell me about a few good decisions you made recently.*
- *What was the toughest work-related decision you've made?*
- *Describe the result of the biggest calculated risk you've ever taken.*
- *Why would this be a good place for you to work?*

Ambition. My eyebrows rise when a prospect makes even a modest attempt to define her career dreams. It makes me more confident that she's selective about the job she wants. Suddenly, an image of a hard-working, productive employee snaps into focus. These questions help you glimpse a candidate's career vision.

- *What are your short-term and long-term career goals, and why?*
- *How are you going to accomplish them?*
- *What alternative careers are you pondering, and why?*
- *Why did you apply for this position?*
- *How does this job help you meet your career goals?*

Personality. My hiring philosophy is simple—avoid surprises. With the interview now more than halfway through, remind her that the more you know about each other the better. Agreement secured, ask a series of tough, unorthodox questions to gauge her emotional and psychological maturity.

- *What's the happiest you've ever been, and why?*
- *What makes you sad?*
- *What scares you?*

- *What makes you laugh?*
- *What really made you mad at your last job? What did you do about it?*
- *Describe a poorly handled encounter with a colleague. What would you do differently?*
- *How would you react if a colleague or customer yelled at you?*
- *How well do you work under pressure and deadlines?*
- *When do you find you are not a team player?*
- *What is your greatest accomplishment?*
- *Tell me about your most spectacular failure.*
- *Tell me about three big changes you've made in your life and what you learned from each.*

A touchy issue to keep in mind: I'm a big proponent of standardized psychological testing for high-level managerial positions. Even though there are legal risks to consider, it's a good way to make sure a candidate's personality, worldview, temperament, and work ethic match the rest of the team's. If a prospect was a square peg that would fit snugly into our square hole, I knew we could train and integrate her.

Self-analysis. You need clarity about a candidate's strengths and vulnerabilities to know if she's a magical match. Generic, open-ended questions like *What are your greatest strengths?* yield only marginally useful information. Instead, list a dozen or so topics—organizational skills, software and web proficiency, time management, customer service, reaction to change, work ethic, teamwork—relevant to the open position. Begin with the first subject and ask her to rate her skill from one to ten. Follow up with, *What will it take to get you to a ten?*

Compensation. With two questions, you'll zero in on a salary you'll both be comfortable with. First, ask, *What would you like to make?* After she gives a figure, ask, *What's the minimum you'd feel good about?* It's a question rarely asked. She'll hesitate. Be patient while she does some quick math in her head: *If the number's too low, I'll cheat myself. If it's too high, he'll lose interest in me.* I call it the "Goldilocks Strategy"— people feel compelled to shoot you a number that's *juuust* right.

It's worth noting that we never hemmed in people with strict salary guidelines. If we settled on above-market pay, we told new hires we expected above-market productivity. After all, it's not what you pay that's important, it's what you get for the pay. Do the math. Which would you rather have—nine highly productive self-starters earning 11 percent more than average, or ten average performers earning an average salary?

By this point, I'd have a sense of whether I wanted to shift the interview into higher gear or hit the brakes. If the light was green, I'd give her the hard sell on the career opportunities *we could offer her*. Why? A star candidate has likely wowed other suitors. If you're impressed, throttle up to make sure she's just as impressed with you. First, repeat your company's mission, vision, and values. Then connect the dots from that corporate DNA to information gleaned from the interview: "You said you had a passion for serving customers. That's great, because it's an important part of our mission."

Finally, if the candidate has potential, say so, and invite her back for a second interview. More questions will arise from the post-interview panel discussion, reference checks, and personal reflection. Welcoming somebody into your workplace family is a life-changing commitment. I often conducted a third interview to ward off the old college sin of "wishing 'em beautiful and willing 'em brilliant."

ADVANCED INTERVIEW STRATEGIES

Inquiring about past jobs and money, let alone poking around under the psychic hood, are not enough. Sometimes, candidates hide behind pat answers and the impulse is to move on to a new question. Instead, soldier on. The greater the resistance to answering a question, the more important it is to question the answer. Keep going deeper. Here are two techniques to squeeze even more information out of an interview:

Funnel Down Technique: If she hesitates, whether from pondering the question or not wanting to share the answer, it might be tempting to fill in the silence. Don't. An awkward pause (I've seen them go on for an eternity) usually gives way to valuable outpouring. Thanks to the Funnel Technique, I quickly terminated an interview with "Janet" and saved both of us valuable time.

ME: How did you like your last position, Janet?

JANET: Oh, it was okay.

ME: Was there anything about it you didn't like?

JANET: No, I liked it all right. It was pretty good.

ME: There was nothing at all you didn't like?

JANET: Well, maybe my boss.

ME: Well, bosses can be that way. What didn't you like about him?

JANET: He was too requiring.

ME: What do you mean, "too requiring"?

JANET: Oh, he really worked me hard.

ME: Yeah, sometimes bosses can do that. How many hours a week did he want you to work?

JANET: Forty!

ME: Forty, huh? *(Red light. After a few more questions, it's a wrap.)* Well, it's been good talking to you, Janet. I wish you luck in your job search.

Get real with role-playing. Can you imagine a director casting an actress in a starring role based solely on how well she talked about how talented she is? He needs to see her in character. That's why our hiring honchos asked candidates to act out theoretical—but real-world—situations. For a customer-service job, for instance, the interviewer assumed the role of an angry customer. Trying to crack management? We thrust him into an employee conflict or budget dilemma. Sales? We asked him to sell us a tire or chrome-plated valve stem. We weren't looking for the next De Niro; we just wanted to toss it back and forth for a few minutes.

Some applicants I interviewed were tentative: "Well, in that situation, I guess I'd say . . ." I'd stop him and say, "No, I'm the customer and you're the salesman. Let's get in character." After a pause, he'd start again, "Okay, here's how I would handle it . . ." Again I'd interrupt. "No, I don't want you to *tell* me how you'd handle it, I want you to *show* me how you'd handle it." Nobody ever walked out on me, but some found it difficult to get into the spirit of the exercise. I paid attention to that. Unwillingness to project into a different mind-set spoke volumes about a prospect's comfort zone, creativity, and ability to think on his feet. No matter, every "audition" yielded valuable information.

Closing the Deal

Offers and counteroffers. Convinced it's a magical match? Be ready to pop the question as the second or third interview winds down. First, gauge his interest. Ask, "Do you think this position is a good fit for you?" Follow up with, "Are you interested in pursuing it?" If yes, say, "Great. We think it's a good match, too."

Next, confirm his compensation expectations. "What I heard earlier is that you'd be comfortable with a salary range of $X to $X. Is that right?" Now that you're both on the same page, close the sale. "So, if we offered you this position for $X with a start date of month/day, would you accept it?" If so, say, "Then that's what we'd like to do. You'll start on month/day with a salary of $X."

There's one more crucial piece of business to take care of before shaking hands and directing your new teammate to HR for orientation. If your new hire is as good as you think he is, you may have to fight a counteroffer from a jealous employer in the throes of re-falling in love. This sample script can help prep the prospect and get a stronger seal on the deal.

YOU: John, just curious, how would you react if your company
   promised you the moon to keep you?
JOHN: Oh, I don't think anything could change my mind.
YOU: John, I have to advise other candidates for this position that
   we've filled it. So, I have to ask: Is there any possibility you could
   be influenced by new promises? Because if you tell me later
   you've reconsidered, that puts me in a very tough position. I
   would have to call back my second choice—and nobody wants
   to be second choice.

JOHN: No, Tom, this is firm.

YOU: *(Extend your hand)* Great, I'm really glad to have you on the team.

It takes only a minute. Don't pass up the opportunity to cement the commitment with a verbal agreement. Finish up by giving him a tour and introducing him to people he might call teammates someday. Helping him feel at home will reduce the stress of a career move.

Solicit feedback. Refine your hiring process by gleaning info from:

The Candidate. After the interview, ask him what he liked and disliked about the process at other companies he's interviewed with. Simply posing the question is flattering. Most people will be happy to share their experiences.

Your Employees. Ask them to grade your hiring process. Now that they're in the fold, they'll fill you in on what surprised them and what made them sweat.

The Ones That Got Away. Respectfully ask decliners for their reasons. Chances are you'll get some worthwhile feedback.

CHAPTER 14

LABOR LEGALITIES

The Dos and Don'ts of Employment Law

Y ou shake hands with an applicant and ease into the interview. "So, married? Kids? Great. My son's ten. How old's yours?" Just small talk, right? Not if you ask the federal government. It's up to you to know where they draw that legal line in the sand. Knowing what you can and can't ask in a job interview is in many ways the epicenter of employment law.

It's pretty simple, actually. There are seven factors that cannot affect your hiring decisions: age, sex, race, religion, physical handicap, nationality, or sexual orientation. Juries routinely award lost wages and punitive damages to victims of any type of discrimination. You may not have a discriminating bone in your body, but phrase a question wrong or make an improper comment, and you may wind up forced into writing a check with lots of zeroes.

Before interviewing candidates, create job descriptions that lay out duties, responsibilities, hours, and reporting relationships. Decide in advance how much schooling and experience is required for each position. It's also crucial to maintain detailed records after the interview to explain why each applicant was rejected or selected.

Steer clear of any question that's unrelated to job qualifications or could be viewed as discriminatory. That goes for qualifications you list on job notices, advertisements, and other recruitment efforts. It's easier to avoid the minefield completely than to tiptoe your way through it. Remember, what you write during a job interview can be just as self-incriminating as what you say. Don't take any notes about the job-seeker's age, race, appearance, health issues, or other such observations. If he or she offers such information, don't jot it down or even respond to it. Sure, it all sounds a bit paranoid. But this is exactly the kind of stuff that subpoenas root out and use against you.

Personal History, Ethnicity, and Preferences

Ask:
- What is your educational background?
- Do you speak any foreign languages [only if the job requires it]?
- What is your address?
- What is your contact information?
- How long have you lived in this city?
- Are you a citizen of this country?
- Have you ever been convicted of a felony [if duties include handling money or confidential info, you may ask related questions]?

Don't Ask:
- Are you a native-born or naturalized citizen?
- When were you (or any family members) granted citizenship?
- Where did you grow up?
- What country do you come from?
- What is your ancestry?
- What is your native language?
- How long have you lived in this country?
- Have you ever legally or otherwise changed your name?
- What's your maiden name? [Exception: if applicant's name is different on education or employment records.]
- What clubs, associations, or organizations do you belong to?
- Do you consider yourself a feminist?

- What religion do you practice?
- What church do you attend?
- What religious holidays do you observe?
- What is your sexual orientation?
- Do you have any friends or family members working here?
- Do you rent or own your home?
- Have you ever been arrested?
- Have you ever pleaded guilty to a crime?

Age

Ask:
- Do you have a driver's license [only for driving-related jobs]?
- Are you of legal age [only for jobs handling tobacco, alcohol, or other restricted substances]?
- If you're younger than eighteen or older than sixty-five, what is your age?

Don't Ask:
- How old are you?
- When's your birthday?
- When did you graduate from high school?

Family

Ask:
- Is there any reason you cannot work the hours of the position as explained to you [only if asked of all applicants]?
- Is there any reason that you couldn't travel for work?

Don't Ask:
- Are you married?
- Are you divorced, separated, widowed?
- Should I call you Miss, Mrs., or Ms.?
- Do you have a live-in romantic relationship?

- Do you plan to get married?
- Do you have children?
- How old are your children?
- Do you plan to start a family?
- Do you have a child-care provider?
- If you have any children in the future, who will provide for them while you work?
- What's your spouse's name?
- Is your spouse covered by health insurance?
- What kind of work does your husband/wife/son/daughter do?
- Are you the chief wage earner?
- Where are your family members employed?
- How does your spouse feel about your out-of-town travel?

Work History and Requirements

Ask:
- What experiences qualify you for this job?
- Do you have the required certification (or licensure) for this job?
- Can you provide documents proving that you can legally work in this country?
- Is any of your employment history under a different name?
- Do you belong to any organizations related to this field?
- Are you willing to travel?
- Are you available for overtime?

Don't Ask:
- Have you ever filed a workers compensation claim?
- Have you ever had a work-related injury?

Disability and Health

Ask:
- Is there any reason why you could not carry out the responsibilities of this job?

- A company physical is required for this position—is there any reason why you wouldn't agree to that?

Don't Ask:
- Do you have (a specific disease)?
- Have you ever been treated for (a specific disease)?
- Do you have any physical limitations that will prevent you from handling this position?
- Will your disability compromise your ability to do this job?
- How many days were you sick last year?
- Are you taking any prescription drugs?
- What conditions, if any, have you been hospitalized for?
- Have you ever been treated for alcoholism or drug addiction?
- Do any of your family members have disabilities?
- What conditions, if any, have required treatment by a psychiatrist or psychologist?

PREVENTION AND PROTECTION

Don't fear employment law. Keep the compliance cops at bay by leading the charge on key issues. Here's how to keep your legal safety net in perfect position:

Make sure your employment-law attorney knows her stuff. A good labor-law expert is an extension of management. She irons out wrinkles when your corporate culture clashes with state or federal requirements.

Post these posters. The U.S. Department of Labor Occupational Safety and Health Administration (OSHA) requires employers to post the OSHA "Job Safety and Health Protection Poster" (downloadable at www.osha.gov). OSHA's Web site also helps you determine which additional posters (minimum wage, equal employment opportunity, and the Family and Medical Leave Act) should be displayed.

Partner with a full-service insurance broker. Don't let paperwork and protocols distract you from your core business. Large insurance firms often have HR specialists to manage claims, update policy manuals, and provide benefits resources (on-site seminars, administration of 401(k)s, disability). They also administer risk-management services, such as OSHA compliance, on-site safety meetings, and training. For further questions, consult a reputable labor-law or HR attorney.

Guard against defecting employees. We insisted that all our managers and top salespeople ink non-compete agreements. Why? Given their access to our playbook (the recipe to our secret sauce), we felt it was only fair for them to sit on the sidelines for a year after leaving. Non-competes typically state that the employee agrees not to join a direct competitor or start a competing business for an established time in a specific geographic area. The shorter the time period and the more restrictive the geographic area, the better your chance of enforcing the agreement in court. A non-compete is also a psychological impediment for the rare mercenary employee who wouldn't think twice about jumping to a rival and taking your classified info with him, regardless of its impact on his teammates (can you say "Benedict Arnold"?). It will also give pause to rivals eyeing your people. Nobody wants the cash drain and PR hit that comes with contractual conflagrations.

Inform the employee during the interview process that a non-compete is required for the position. Then get his John Hancock on it by his first day on the job. After that day, demanding a signature may jeopardize the non-compete's enforceability due to the lack of "consideration" (something of value given to the employee in exchange for a contractual commitment not to compete). Potentially, the non-compete could be enforceable against a current employee if, at the time of signing, the employer gives the employee "new consideration," such as a bonus or a right to buy stock. Check with an employment-law attorney to confirm the adequacy of "consideration" and to ensure that the agreement is worded precisely. The law regarding enforceability of non-competes—addressing geographical coverage, duration, the definition of what is and is not "competition," and the timing and adequacy of consideration—varies from state to state.

Keep your trade secrets secret. Fired up about your breakthrough software? Or your cutting-edge widget design? Protect your competitive edge from corporate espionage with nondisclosure agreements (aka, NDA, confidentiality agreement, trade-secret agreement). NDAs prohibit employees who sign them from disclosing or profiting from trade secrets or proprietary info gleaned in your office. The agreements also provide for business partners—you need their signatures, too. Even if the horse is already out of the barn, a court order can zip loose lips to prevent further leaks. You can also sue for damages or press criminal charges.

NDAs function as both stand-alone contracts and clauses within non-compete agreements. Like the non-compete, get the NDA signed, sealed, and delivered before the newbie clocks in on his first day. Go as far as attaching an NDA to the front of your business plan or strategic plan before circulating it. It's a warning shot to ethically challenged readers. Do not, however, expect everyone to sign the agreements, although that does force a risk-reward decision.

Stay up-to-date. Business and Legal Reports (www.blr.com) offers HR news, white papers, and federal and state info on employment law. For online training, check out www.skillsoft.com and www.hrclassroom.com. The U.S. Equal Employment Opportunity Commission (www.eeoc.gov) provides the scoop on legal issues, from age, sex, and religious discrimination to litigation stats and education programs. The U.S. Department of Labor (www.dol.gov) lists state-specific information.

HIT THE GROUND RUNNING

Welcoming New Hires

Like proud parents welcoming a new daughter-in-law, we warmly, if methodically, welcomed new employees into the fold. New hires acquired a "buddy" who gave them a tour of their new home along with the lowdown on the people and culture. We introduced new associates with a group e-mail detailing their career history, family background, hobbies, and interests. It helped break the ice with new teammates: "Hey, I love softball, too. What position do you play?" Those efforts built camaraderie, trimmed learning curves, and minimized unproductive, profit-draining downtime.

We assimilated new hires into our coaching culture as quickly as possible. Their department head asked open-ended questions to draw them out, build rapport, and establish healthy communication: "What do you see as the biggest challenges in your new position?" "What new skills would you like to develop?" "What can I do now to help?" Orientation sessions briefed new hires on what was expected of them—and what they could expect from us—regarding attitude, ethics, and behavior.

Making new teammates feel valued from day one produced a big competitive edge. As a service outfit, our success hinged on hiring and keeping great personalities. We understood that the first week is crucial—that's when people decide whether they see a future with a new company. The time and money you'll spend welcoming new hires is a pittance compared to the revolving-door cost of constantly hiring and training new employees to replace those who were unhappy and unproductive.

THE LAW OF DIMINISHING DEDICATION

Ever been so fired up at a leadership seminar that you were champing at the bit to race back to the office to test things out? You were still pumped up when you got back to your desk. Then the regular stuff began crowding out your time. The days rolled by. Enthusiasm for what you learned began to wane, and finally, what was once so fresh in your mind had faded into a dusty memory.

So it goes with a new job. Most people show up for their first day all gung ho and eager to contribute. With luck, a wise team leader and a healthy culture will greet them. Otherwise, bureaucratic roadblocks, turf wars, inefficient systems, and the hypnotic comfort of daily routines will blunt their passion and lull them into mediocrity. It's as quiet and insidious as radon poisoning.

To avoid the Big Sleep, I personally talked to new recruits during weeklong orientation courses at the company school. New employees are open. I set aside six hours to distill for them our mission, vision, and values. I urged them to keep up their guard should they happen across a rebel teammate. Even though we were vigilant about sustaining a positive, enlightened culture, I occasionally saw a new hire sabotaged by a negative colleague.

How do you combat that? I stressed there are best practices for everything, from heart surgery to piloting a plane, and that sticking to our system was the fastest route to success. I cautioned that they might get ribbed for following procedures so closely: "Aw, look at the rookie. Here, kid, lemme show you how we do it around here." Call me obsessive, but we also role-played a way to handle those encounters. I suggested something like, "Thanks. Sounds like that works for you, but I'm going to go by the book so I can catch up to your level someday." Reaching new heights—and staying excited about the journey—is what the rest of *The Big Book* is about.

KEY POINTS

SNATCHING UP STARS

- ➤ **Think of yourself as a top talent scout.** Landing the hot hire requires diligence and resourcefulness. Keep a lot of balls in the air—work your business contacts, offer referral bonuses, hit schools and hiring fairs, consider search firms. Make sure your culture attracts and retains good people.
- ➤ **Don't let stars in your eyes cloud your vision.** Don't assume that heavy hitters on other teams have more expertise or will fit seamlessly into your culture. Do your homework—and don't make exceptions to your standard hiring process.
- ➤ **Develop a good game plan.** Job interviews are like hide-and-seek. Candidates try to hide their faults—you seek to discover them. Ask probing questions that reveal a candidate's personality, maturity, strengths, and vulnerabilities. The greater the resistance to answering a question, the more important it is to question the answer. Established drills like role-playing help avoid the irritation of watching new hires turn into misfires.
- ➤ **Make it mutual.** It's just as important to impress applicants as it is for them to impress you. If she knocks your socks off, chances are she's wowed other employers, too. A perfect fit? Get an offer on the table ASAP (after her references check out).
- ➤ **Follow the law.** Know what you can and can't ask in a job interview. Guard against ill-advised comments that a candidate could misinterpret. Display mandatory posters and keep detailed records to explain why each applicant was rejected or selected. Require new hires to sign nondisclosure and non-compete agreements so your trade secrets stay secret.

➤ **Welcome new hires.** Make employees feel comfortable from day one. Assign them a "buddy," introduce them to colleagues, build rapport with management, and brief them on what's expected from all sides. A healthy, team-oriented, systems-disciplined culture prevents newbies from drifting into mediocrity.

GROWING THE CULTURE

Seeding an Enlightened Environment

Employees are like plants. To thrive and bloom, they need to be rooted in the rich soil of a nurturing environment. They need to be watered with care, and warmed by the sunlight of appreciation. Yet too many leaders, all thumbs in the art of human horticulture, treat their people like cactus. They expect them to flourish in an arid, remote atmosphere.

By design or default, every business has a corporate culture. But I suspect most business folks would be hard-pressed to describe theirs in any detail. By my lights, "culture" (some prefer "climate") is an umbrella term encompassing

- the conditions and standards that define the office environment
- employees' shared understanding of team dynamics and how they fit in
- the "tribe's" behavior, dress, appearance, and rituals
- the team's collective personality and identity

Whether or not you can put your finger on what makes it so, you sure as heck know a good culture when you see it. It's one where people

- look forward to coming to work
- feel pride in being on the team
- consider their coworkers friends
- get excited by the organization's vision
- gladly go beyond the call of duty when required
- enjoy personal satisfaction when the team does well
- feel in sync with the organization's operating values
- believe their work contributes to the team's success

The leader who neglects to grow his organization's culture does so at his peril. Sure, changing an existing culture is difficult. But it's doable. The pressure of running a company can siphon your attention away from employees. That it's difficult to stay focused on their satisfaction, however, makes it no less necessary. The less attention paid to people's basic desire to offer value and feel valued, the faster spins the revolving door of turnover. (Of course, to an enlightened entrepreneur without a healthy bottom line, morale is a moot point.) While good morale helps grow a healthy bottom line, beware justifying most anything for employees in the name of morale. That can hurt the bottom line.

The best people—productive, creative, passionate—won't settle for less than an energized, ethical shop abuzz with a spirited team attitude. John Lasseter, executive vice president of Pixar Animation Studios, would agree. Under his direction, the studio's animated blockbusters (*Monsters, Inc.; A Bug's Life;* the *Toy Story* films; *Finding Nemo; The Incredibles*) have generated worldwide grosses of more than $3.2 billion. As *Newsweek* noted:

> *With such success, you might think all the competing studios would have plundered Pixar like an unguarded vault—which, technically, it is, since unlike at every other studio nobody besides Lasseter works under contract. So far everyone is staying put. "A piece of paper won't keep them here," Lasseter says. "You want their heart here. So you make them creatively satisfied."*

CHAPTER 16

THE CAMARADERIE CREDO

Developing Team Spirit

The esprit de corps at Tires Plus was impossible for visitors to ignore. During one of my talks at a company gathering, a tire vendor whispered to Brad Burley, a regional manager, "Does Tom make you all drink the same punch, or what?" Brad laughed as the vendor went on. "You guys all talk the same. You don't have 'problems,' you have 'opportunities.'" Brad took it as a compliment. "It was recognition that the tone of a culture is set from the top down," Brad recalled. "That attitude bled into everything we did, from executive-team meetings to the way customers were treated." A lot of business owners prattle on about teamwork, but few walk their talk. Yes, individual expression is prized and indispensable, but getting everyone on the same page is equally important. A half-dozen team-building measures can transform a collection of individuals into a collective "team ego."

1. Saturate the Environment. Our offices pulsated with teamwork. Anyone in a position to coach preached that our success depended on the sum of our parts. Egomaniacs stuck out like cutoffs at a cocktail party. Now, that doesn't mean we wanted everyone to think alike. In fact, it's important they don't. As General George S. Patton said, "If everybody's thinking alike, somebody isn't thinking."

2. Talk the Walk. Talk isn't *always* cheap. We asked our people to call their colleagues "teammates." It reinforced the Three Musketeers motto, "One for all and all for one." It also made a world of difference when our managers told their people, "Here's what the team needs," rather than, "Here's what I need." When an outsider knocked the company, everyone took it personally—and took personal responsibility if fixes were in order. A company isn't a corporate seal on a piece of paper, it's a team of people. All those people have a common goal—making the organization better than it was yesterday.

3. Hire Team Players. We asked job candidates questions like, "Where do you rank as a team player on a scale of one to ten?" and "When do you find you are *not* a team player?" Invariably, they would leave the interview with our mission statement plastered on the billboard of their mind—*Deliver caring, world-class service to our guests, our community, and to each other.* We drew special attention to the last four words. The message was plain—lone wolves need not apply.

4. Recognize and Reward It. If you don't actively promote teamwork, you may as well endorse selfishness. Toss out a "Way to go!" whenever you catch someone team-building. Good moves won kudos—and occasionally cash awards—at staff meetings. That was just the tip of our incentive iceberg. A big portion of our bonuses rode on achieving team goals. We even built a baseball-style "farm system" to reward skilled coaches. For instance, if Store A needed an assistant manager and was eyeballing a promising sales staffer over at Store B, then Store A had to "draft" the up-and-comer. The manager who had tutored the hot prospect got something in return. Store A had to pay $3,000 to Store B for the honor of picking up the future assistant manager. That fee in turn pumped up Store B's profits, added to the bonus kitty split among staff, and encouraged the team to continue to develop strong talent.

5. Embody It. You can hold a pep rally seven days a week, but it's merely platitudes and pom-poms unless biz owners themselves exhibit the highest standards of teamwork. Early on, I'm embarrassed to admit, it was always about me, me, me instead of we, we, we. As I shed my seat-of-the-pants ways, I came to my senses, and John Hyduke, a vice president, noticed. Our executive committee had been deliberating about strategic timing for planting our flag in an array of new markets. "Tires Plus was a private company, and Tom had majority interest," John recalled. "He had every right to make decisions while shaving in front of the mirror." John appreciated that I weighed my opinions against those of the rest of the committee, and rarely exercised a veto. "We all shared a sense of ownership in the decisions," John said. "So, whether or not a store was successful, morale was never a problem. We didn't stand around second-guessing; we just moved on."

6. Celebrate Achievement. We celebrated all the time. "Tom was a stern taskmaster," Brad Burley recalled. "But he wanted us to feel good about what we accomplished." Establish traditions to mark hard-earned victories and bolts from the blue—hand out cigars, pop the cork on some Dom, give the team the afternoon off. Announce triumphs—a successful product launch, blowing past projections, landing the huge account—while blasting Queen's "We Are the Champions."

CHAPTER 17

LEAD THE CHARGE

The Twenty-one Laws of Cultural Leadership

Break these laws and your culture surveys will be graded D for *dreadful.*

Be authentic. Regrettably, employees view bosses through a distorted lens. Bosses are nonhuman, devoid of feelings, android, plug in at night. It gives employees an excuse to downplay their boss's good side and exaggerate his bad. Then, when job frustration hits critical mass, they can justifiably check out emotionally. Unfair as it is, there's a reason: Too many business owners perpetuate the stereotype. Forget the notion that signs of emotion or fallibility are unprofessional. My relationships with employees grew healthier when I started admitting mistakes, revealing more of the real me, and being more caring. Never doubt the paradoxical power of vulnerability.

Hand out all-access passes. Imagine you're a kid again. Somebody treats you like dirt, yet your parents won't listen to your grievance. Now you're frustrated and resentful. Well, as a boss, you've got to recognize that you're a surrogate parent for a lot of the people around you. Make yourself available *when they need you*. Give them your full attention, and their appreciation will show up in the simple metrics of productivity and turnover. "Anybody in the company, from a store manager to a tire technician, could meet with Tom about anything," recalled Dave Urspringer, one of our top managers. I did have two stipulations. Employees had to first address the issue with their superiors (assuming it didn't involve family or health troubles). Second, they had to bring me at least one solution. "It was an ironclad rule," Dave said. Knowing we'd be listened to at the highest level, that we'd be treated like our ideas really mattered, was one of the biggest secrets to our success."

Project a positive image. An egomaniac inspires a lot of feelings, but loyalty and passion aren't among them. If he's followed, it's only reluctantly. Ditto negative, insecure leaders. An enlightened entrepreneur projects the right mix of confidence and humility. She's serious about life and work but doesn't take herself too seriously. "Tom carries a pretty good-size ego," observed Trent Stoner, our director of public relations and marketing. "But at the same time, he's so giving and caring that it doesn't put people off in any way. Tom leads with his mind *and* his heart."

Beware your impact. I still remember the huge crush I had on Linda Harness in high school. No clue was too minor to crack the case on whether she liked me or, you know, *liked* me. Did she smile? Was she looking over my shoulder when we talked? Like it or not, that's how your employees think of bosses (minus the romantic part, I hope). It's not fair, and it may even be a bit odd, but that's reality—one wrong look from the boss can ruin someone's day. It's a fault line to keep an eye on, but there are limits to your vigilance. Take the time I forgot to bring my eyeglasses to a sales meeting. The next day, I learned that a young sales associate was smarting because he had nodded and smiled at me from across the room and I failed to respond. I called him right away and joked that without my glasses I could only make out blurry outlines of people. He laughed and accepted my apology, and I never forgot my glasses again.

Snoop like Columbo. Enlightened entrepreneurs root out the truth like a gumshoe. If key details are missing, you can't make the right choice, solve the big problem, launch the stinger strategy. When employees told me things were fine, I dug deeper: "Anything I can help you with?" "If *you* ran things, what would you do differently?" Sooner or later, the answers spilled out. "When Tom hit the field, we'd do everything in our power to make sure the stores were firing on all cylinders," said Jim Pascale, a regional manager in Iowa. Before one of my visits, Jim asked all his store personnel—over and over—the questions I typically asked. "Sure enough," Jim recalled, "Tom ended up asking many of the same questions I had. But he got twenty new answers!"

Be relentless. It's instinctive to withhold bad news from the boss. Some try to protect underperforming colleagues, or hide embarrassing details. Other times, the truth remains elusive because no one's connected the dots between problem and root cause. I methodically drill like a west Texas derrick to the core problem. Beware, though. I sometimes hit nerves instead of veins. "There were times," recalled Wayne Shimer, head of retail operations, "when I wanted to reach out and say, 'Stop!' But ultimately, Tom was right, because everything was out on the table all the time. And I don't care what anybody says, that's a healthy culture to work in."

Practice the accordion. The best decisions emerge from a process that's neither exclusively top-down (leader calling the shots) nor bottom-up (rank-and-file referendum). It's gotta be a collaborative effort I call "the accordion." You can argue that top-down decisions are smarter because upper management commands a broader view of economic, cultural, and mission-related facts. Yet management is too often out to lunch on the down and dirty details, if only because employees hate delivering bad news. The remedy: raw intel, gathered from as many sources as possible. I'd tell people, "If something needs to be said, don't minimize it or dramatize it. Just flat-out say it."

In too many shops, input from the floor is either ignored or discounted. The rationale is predictable—*Hey, if my employees were smarter than me, I'd be reporting to them.* Perhaps a common military axiom will shed some light: "Battle plans never survive contact with the enemy." Without a constant feedback loop from the front, plans hatched by the commanders can be comically naïve or fatally flawed. That's why Wayne Shimer's store inspections started in the service bays. Why did he talk to the guys with grease under their fingernails first? In high school, Wayne had worked construction for a family friend named Mel. Every morning, Mel pulled up in his station wagon and headed straight for the welders. One day Wayne asked him why he spoke to the foreman last. "Wayne," Mel said, "after talking to the guys, I knew if the walls were going up at the right pace, I knew if the sand was being delivered, and I knew if the cement guy had been by. So by the time I got to the foreman, he couldn't snow me."

Eliminate obstacles. My first day at Shell Oil in Chicago was electrifying. I was twenty-one and ready to take on the world. I wanted just one word to come to mind when my boss thought of my performance: *spectacular*. I never lost the desire to do great work, but, bit by bit, a bloated bureaucracy and stifling daily routines blunted my gung-ho edge. Naïve as I was, it was obvious to me that a company's procedures and systems have gotta be user-friendly. I also learned not to jerk people from one can't-wait-another-minute project to the next, and not to call a meeting unless I absolutely had to. People can't soar when they're bogged down in systemic sludge.

Keep 'em in the loop. One reason I left Shell Oil was I didn't know whether I was making a difference. Every nugget of information was closely held. That didn't make sense to me. Leaders at all levels need real numbers to make smart decisions and inspire people to hit their targets. Information sharing is also a valuable insurance policy. Take Al, one of our veeps, who felt alienated by his old employer's top-secret culture, where strategic initiatives and financial results were rarely shared. At Tires Plus, all department heads knew the revenue and expense flow of every unit, and everyone cross-advised everyone else's departments. (All personnel knew the nitty-gritty of their store's profit-and-loss statement.) "Without that culturally ingrained information sharing, we would've been badly hurt if we lost a key manager," Al said. "We may not have been able to step in seamlessly to run their division, but it wouldn't have floundered either."

All employees should be briefed on the enterprise's performance and plans. Keep them up to speed with the company intranet, group e-mails, internal newsletters, and team meetings. Transparency inspires loyalty. As Sam Walton pointed out:

> *Communicate everything you possibly can*
> *to your [employees]. The more they know,*
> *the more they'll understand. The more*
> *they understand, the more they'll care.*
> *Once they care, there's no stopping them.*

Face the facts. My passion for a project has been known to derail my common sense. I'd just want the darn thing done, the heck with the details. As *New York Times* film critic A. H. Weiler quipped, "Nothing is impossible for the man who doesn't have to do it himself." Sometimes it took me months to realize a project was doomed. Once I told Wayne Shimer to get popcorn into all our stores. He scratched his head, duly priced out the machines and supplies, and researched popping big-quantity corn. He also took every opportunity to tell me that popcorn wouldn't lure customers, never mind that managers had better things to do. "Tom kept hounding me for six months to finish the popcorn project," Wayne remembered. "One day I dug in deep enough to get him to understand we'd need a food license, which meant regular city food inspections and plastic gloves for the sales staff. Finally, he threw up his hands and said, 'Fine, I give up.'" A year later, I recognized a familiar look on Wayne's face when I handed him a new project. "This is another popcorn project, isn't it?" I laughed. That became our inside joke.

Talk it through. Larry, a consulting client, wanted to thaw the tension at his small Minneapolis packaging firm. "I just don't understand why people here don't get it," he told me. "I tell them what to do, but they don't seem capable of following simple instructions."

After talking to his employees, I broke it to Larry that *he* was the one who didn't get it. I was told that Larry often snapped, "Because I said so," or "Just do it, okay?" when employees questioned his methods. That just doesn't fly with people, I told Larry. They'll tune you out and do things their own way. Be direct. Ask the employee what she would do differently when she disagrees with your decision. If her suggestion makes sense, tell her you'll consider it and get back to her. If it's impractical, explain why. If she's still upset, say something like, "I know you don't agree, but I think it's the right thing, so I hope you'll support it for the good of the company." Even if she doesn't agree with you, it's more likely she'll accept your decision if you weigh her input and explain your rationale.

Look with fresh eyes. The status quo is a work in progress. One question always on the tip of my tongue was, *What did you learn?* "If you didn't have a good answer," recalled regional manager Brad Burley, "you got a little tough love. Tom and I would visit stores together, and knowing he was going to ask me that question at the end of the day kept me very focused." Another question that yanks people out of their daily grind: *Let's assume there are flaws in our customer service procedure (or ad-approval process or flextime policy). If we were starting from scratch, how could we make it more effective?* The question often lit the fuse to innovation.

It's up to you to lead the fresh-eyes charge. Unfortunately, leaders are conditioned to project a know-it-all facade. Escape that trap. Admit when you're stumped. Listen *to* new ideas, not *against* them. It'll influence your people more than any lecture. Remember, the more you say, "I don't know," the more you'll hear back, "Let's find out."

View mistakes as opportunities. In the heat of frustration, it may be tempting to rub employees' noses in their mistakes. I used to do that. It should be obvious, but there's a whiff of sadism in shaming somebody who is already beating herself up. Besides, morale and confidence spiral when the boss chews you out, especially if it's mean-spirited. Enlightened entrepreneurs pose thoughtful questions until the light of understanding flicks on. Here's how to use question-based coaching to convert a miscue into a teachable moment:

YOU: So, John, how'd you feel when you heard we lost that order because the form was filled out wrong?

EMPLOYEE: Pretty lousy.

YOU: Yeah, it's tough. This has happened before, hasn't it?

EMPLOYEE: Yeah, a few weeks ago.

YOU: What happened then?

EMPLOYEE: I dunno. I guess I was just rushing and got a little careless.

YOU: Same thing this time?

EMPLOYEE: I guess so.

YOU: Well, let's look at this a minute. If you find yourself rushing again, what will you do differently?

EMPLOYEE: I guess I'd tell myself to slow down and get every detail right because one wrong digit can really screw things up.

YOU: Yeah, your job demands dotting all the *i*'s and crossing all the *t*'s, doesn't it? Do me a favor and grade yourself on attention to detail.

EMPLOYEE: Probably C-minus.

YOU: Okay, that's honest. And where would you put your desire to get better? Low, medium, high?

EMPLOYEE: High, definitely high.

YOU: That's what I was hoping. Now, are you willing to put in the effort to upgrade your skills and get organized?

EMPLOYEE: Absolutely.

YOU: Excellent. Let's put our heads together on an action plan to make it happen.

Partnering with an employee creates solutions both parties own, as opposed to one side getting a lecture. It takes a little extra time, but also winds up saving lots of time. It preserves dignity and helps lessons sink in. When employees use their own noggins to find solutions, they're more likely to execute them with gusto. It's human nature. People *want* to expand their capacities. They *want* those "Ah-ha!" moments.

Of course, sometimes action speaks for itself. The story goes that Thomas Edison and his crew worked twenty-four hours straight to build the first commercial lightbulb. Exhausted, Edison placed the precious orb in the hands of his young assistant to carry upstairs. Due to the gravity of the moment, the nervous boy was shaking so badly that he dropped the bulb on the way up. The team spent another twenty-four hours making a second bulb. Come time to carry it upstairs, Edison smiled and again handed it to the boy. Confidence restored, the kid ferried the bulb upstairs without incident. The simple gesture of trust earned Edison the boy's loyalty for a lifetime.

Be tough, not rough. One day, a shipment of high-performance tires arrived at one of our stores instead of its true destination—our chief competitor. Dave, the manager, quietly accepted delivery, only to get busted later during a routine audit. Pressed for details, Dave confessed that Jerry, his district manager, advised him to hang on to the $700 tires. I happened to be visiting my mother in Indiana, and was patched into a hastily called teleconference. Deliberations were rough. My heads of HR and loss prevention urged termination for both Dave and Jerry. It was as if they had broken into a rival's shop and stolen the tires, they reasoned. Two other execs argued for suspension because Dave and Jerry had clean records and years of exceptional service.

I broke in with a challenge: "I want the person who's never accepted too much change at the bank or grocery store to speak up, please." Silence. "Is what they did wrong?" I asked. "Absolutely. Should there be consequences? Of course. But it *isn't* just like breaking into another company's store. And don't tell me this is worth trashing the careers of two decent men. That's overreacting. Who among us has never needed a second chance?" We returned the tires to UPS and slapped Dave and Jerry with two-week suspensions. Both men literally broke down when they learned we had spared their jobs. My management team also learned a lesson—big decisions that impact the lives of our people shouldn't be made in the heat of the moment.

Slip on those moccasins. A few months after launching the company, we moved our "headquarters" out of the back room of a gas station and into a small suburban office building. As I mentioned in chapter 1, cash was tight, so I persuaded the building owner to let me install a vending machine in the community break room to help defray rent. I filled the machine with granola bars, nuts, and fruit, expecting to offset the rent. It soon became clear that I was the only one dropping coins. Puzzled, I asked the other tenants if they knew about the vending machine. Sure, they said, but it wasn't stocked with anything decent like Snickers, Hershey bars, or chips. Click went the lightbulb. Wasn't there a touch of arrogance to my assumption that if I wanted healthy snacks, everybody else did, too? Gee, what a concept: *Not everybody likes what I like.* Suddenly, my "me-ism" and lack of empathy were grimly comical.

Huddle up. We were getting ready for the grand opening of our first store in Minneapolis's trendy Uptown district. Flanked by a couple of key execs and the store manager, I saw an opportunity. "Hey, everybody," I said, "let's huddle up on the marketing plan." Gathered around a stack of tires, we ping-ponged ideas. In twenty minutes, we produced a grassroots marketing campaign complete with a dozen action steps.

Lesson: Seize opportunities for spontaneous brainstorming. When I was talking to a store sales team about a big issue, I'd often call a time-out and pull in the mechanics. Everyone stopped work for fifteen minutes to hash things out, then returned to work energized because they had a chance to weigh in on a big decision. Huddle up on everything from marketing and operational issues to personnel conflicts and general malaise, or simply to communicate need-to-know info. If I sensed tension in a department, for instance, I didn't hesitate to pull everyone together and ask what was going on. Often, all it takes to reverse negative momentum is a forum for people to speak their mind. (Caveat: A brainstorming huddle works only if you're truly seeking input, not simply validation for decisions already made.)

Respond rapidly. Back in the day, whenever a subordinate asked me to do something—review a draft, powwow over a big issue—my reflex was the same: *Hey, I'll get back to you when I feel like it, pal. I'm the one* *who calls the shots around here.* Inevitably, deadlines came and went and I got mad. I'd ask people where their reports were, and they'd explain that they were still waiting on me for info. It took awhile, but the message finally sank in. First, these were things I had asked them to do. Second, it's intimidating to ask the boss for something more than once. Last, the faster I got things back to people, the faster things got done. *Man,* I thought, *whenever somebody needs something from me from now on, I'll hit the ball back into their court ASAP.*

Make amends. During an executive-committee meeting, Neil offered a suggestion I didn't like much. I was in a foul mood and jumped all over him. It wasn't one of my best moments. When I returned to my desk, the devil on my right shoulder urged me to forget it. "So you were a little rough on him," he said. "You sign his paychecks. He'll get over it." But the angel on my left shoulder wouldn't let it go. "That was inexcusable," she whispered. "How would you feel if you were treated that way? Go to his office and apologize." Gulping down a big slice of humble pie, I coached myself on the danger of letting my ego—the size of a state fair watermelon—get the better of me. I had to pry myself out of my chair. Swallowing hard, I knocked on Neil's door. "Neil," I said, "I am really sorry for the way I embarrassed you. It was inappropriate, and I promise it won't happen again." Fortunately, Neil accepted my apology.

For some reason, the words "I'm sorry" are kryptonite to entrepreneurs. But they're also two of the most powerful words in the leadership lexicon. They're a tonic for employees who feel wronged and cling fiercely to resentment. Only a heartfelt apology can ease the pain and repair the relationship. We all make mistakes, but not owning up to them ranks among the biggest mistakes of all.

Invite dissent. The Denver expansion was cruising along. My cofounder, Don Gullett, had invested eighteen months in learning the Front Range market and working its commercial realtors. We'd already entered into a number of development agreements. It was a done deal—until Jim Pascale, our VP of franchise operations, piped up at an executive-team meeting. "I don't think we're ready," Jim said. Stunned silence. "We've just gone into Kansas City, Omaha, and Oklahoma City," he continued. "Look at the cash flow and the cash draw in those markets. They haven't matured yet. Going forward with Denver would stretch us too thin."

Nearly everyone around the table disagreed, strongly. I sat back and weighed Jim's argument. No, I said finally, Jim's right. We need to take a harder look at the numbers. I turned to Jim Bemis, our CFO. Was Jim's assessment accurate? Bemis nodded. We slept on it, then decided to press *Pause* on Colorado until our new markets ripened. A year later, we took Denver. There was a time when I crushed opposing views. But that only pours cold water on a hot company. "Tom began encouraging us to be assertive and to share opinions," Jim said, "especially if they differed from his."

Don't play favorites. Signing John Leach to a consulting contract was like the New York Yankees signing A-Rod. John was an all-star with great instincts in the field and a sharp mind for the game. He had been head of Western Auto Supply Company, a division of Sears that owned Tire America and NTW, two of the country's largest tire chains. Soon after John began attending executive-committee meetings, however, two members approached me independently and accused me of knighting John "The Golden Boy." They claimed I valued his advice above theirs. At the next meeting I asked if anyone else felt that way. They all did. I fought off the urge to justify my favoritism. Instead, I bit my tongue and looked at things through their eyes.

Humbled, I pleaded guilty to the charge of poor leadership. Few things are more deadly for morale than a star system. Sure, cashing in on the fresh eyes of new teammates is smart. But I overdid it. Listening to one person at the expense of others pains the entire room. Certainly, you can't treat every idea equally. Nor should you suppress enthusiasm for a great one. But find the healthy middle ground. Avoid consistently valuing one teammate's opinion, or one outside consultant's at the expense of everybody else's.

Express gratitude. Few things are appreciated—or inspire deeper loyalty—like the balm of a heartfelt thank-you for a job well done.

Among the ways I thanked my execs was writing annual birthday notes—like this one to our treasurer, Jim Wolf:

> *Jim, happy birthday. Thanks again for your dedication to our team. Your contribution is very important: lowering interest rates, critical budgets and projections, handling cash, and profit improvement team, among a few biggies. You do all this with a sense of fun as well as discipline and focus—a great combination. Great attitude. Thanks and take care, Tom.*

Little did I know that Jim saved every letter. "A handwritten note like that," Jim recalled, "with specifics about my performance, told me Tom really took the time to think about what he was writing." Eric Randa, our loss-prevention czar, had never worked at a company where the owner handwrote letters of appreciation. "It was one of the best pats on the back I ever had in my life," Eric said. "I now do the same thing at my new company. One of my managers just told me it meant the world to him to read the kind words I had written." The difference between thanking people and taking them for granted is only a minute or two.

Congratulate publicly. Wayne Shimer, a sixteen-year colleague, never complained, never got defensive—he just rolled up his sleeves and blasted away. To Wayne, a job well done was its own reward. In 1992, a grueling but rewarding year, I started handing out a Most Valuable Player Award at our annual convention. It gained instant Oscar-like stature in our little tire universe. I had been riding Wayne hard all year, but we had made a good profit, and I presented him with the inaugural award. "Out of the blue," Wayne recalled, "in front of five hundred people, Tom calls me up and gives me this award. I couldn't even talk afterwards I was so emotional."

People crave recognition, not only for results but also for their ideas. Applaud their efforts (literally) every chance you get—in team meetings, informal settings, group e-mails, and newsletters. After Scott McPhee, our retail operations chief, suggested we create a "head of automotive services," I never let him forget it. Years later, I was bragging about Scott's RBI (Really Big Idea) to anybody who worked with him. "You're the man, Scott!" I'd say, turning to the others. "Do you know how much money this guy made for us?" Sure, people may turn red when you pour on the praise, but don't be fooled for a second. They can't get enough of it.

CHAPTER 18

HONOR THY EMPLOYEE

Putting People First Produces Higher Profits

This is not your father's workplace. The once impenetrable barrier between work and home has crumbled in the wake of the baby-boomer-fueled personal-growth movement. In the span of a generation, a hunger for meaning that grew even more ravenous after 9/11 has spurred an unprecedented demand for integration (within an employee's own life) and interconnectedness (with the lives of others).

High-tech wizardry also contributes to blurred boundaries. It's now commonplace to e-mail extra work home—or remotely tap into the office network—for relaxed, after-dinner analysis. We sit in our offices and monitor our stock portfolios, place bids on eBay, and e-mail our kids instructions for dinner. We take partial "tele-vacations" to sandy beaches in the tropics, and we placate customers on a cell phone in our pajamas (I can hear Groucho: *How a cell phone got in your pajamas, I'll never know*).

Cultural aftershocks ripple from these psychological and technological tremors. Employees are clamoring for fulfillment *and* flexibility, and wondering if they'll ever have an undivided moment that's protected from cell phones and BlackBerrys and IMs. To sooth the anxiety, enlightened entre-preneurs:

Honor employees. During a routine visit to a Minneapolis Tires Plus store, I asked a young salesman named Gabe Lopez how things were going. "To be honest with you," he said, "not too well." Gabe said he had recently clocked a seventy-hour week only to be told after the fact that he had been "promoted" from an hourly to a salaried position. He felt chumped, that he was owed the overtime money. He had me-thodically climbed his grievance up the corporate ladder, but felt his protest had fallen on deaf ears.

On the spot, I called our head of HR for an explanation. Gabe's situ-ation was a "gray area," I was told, and we had a good case for not pay-ing him the overtime cash. If there's a gray area, I told her, the employee should be given the benefit of the doubt; after all, that's what we do for our customers when there's a dispute. I hung up and apologized to Gabe. He got his check the next day. "I was just a nineteen-year-old kid out of high school working in an entry-level position," recalled Gabe, now a Tires Plus assistant district manager. "The fact that Tom took the time to listen to me and resolve the situation without hesitation re-ally wowed me. It's something that will always stay with me."

Gabe's story illustrates why you can't leapfrog your employees—your internal customers—and focus solely on pleasing your external customers. It's a simple matter of connecting the dots. Honor your people and care about their well-being and they'll reward you with loyalty and set a new standard for customer service.

Expect greatness. Don't worry about setting expectations just be-yond the moon. It will pull the best out of them. Jim Pascale, our vice president of franchise operations, saw this a lot. "Working for Tom was like playing for a coach who says, 'We expect to win champion-ships here,'" Jim said. "You find out what you're made of. You rise up to that level, you practice harder, and you have higher expectations."

But watch out. Setting high standards can actually undermine pro-ductivity and morale unless individual expectations are clearly defined *in relation to team goals* and the players appreciate how the two are related. That's why the strategic-planning process (chapter 23) is critical. It establishes a clear, measurable relationship between organizational objectives and individual goals.

Accommodate family priorities. Contrary to business mythology, putting family first in a disciplined, achievement-oriented culture will actually *enhance* productivity, not diminish it. Countless times I've seen grateful employees tackle their work with renewed vigor after returning from a family-related absence. Maybe parents don't need to take in every single soccer game, dance line performance, or spelling bee, but a high attendance rate is important to them and to their child. Keep their bodies at work during these events and you'll lose their hearts and minds.

One afternoon each week, for seven summers, Larry Brandt left work early to cheer at his son Andrew's baseball game. A key Tires Plus exec and our third-largest shareholder, Larry also ducked out occasionally to root for his other son, Barett, as he worked his way up to a black belt in karate. To compensate for his absences during the workday, Larry worked at night and on weekends.

Remember, output equals quantity of hours worked multiplied by the quality of those hours. Allowing your people, whether single or married, to play hooky for important family events—where their absence would overshadow the event—is a goodwill gesture sure to boost morale. It's also a competitive advantage that may prevent otherwise resentful employees from seeking more family-friendly pastures.

Seat-of-the-pantsers typically don't connect the dots between how they treat employees' families and employee loyalty and performance. I'll never forget the time my wife and I were visiting my buddy and Shell Oil colleague, Art Davis, in Dayton, Ohio, over thirty years ago. The phone rang and Art's wife went into the kitchen to answer it. Seconds later she was back. It was Art's boss. After Art left the room, she said, "That jerk, he doesn't even bother to say hello. Just, 'Is Art there?'" Now really, how hard is it to say, "Hi, Judy, this is Bill, how are you?" Think about it. A spouse has more influence over your employee than anyone else. I wasn't surprised when, less than a year later, Art told me he had found another job.

Trust employees to deliver. We had a caring, family-oriented culture, but also a hardworking culture. The two naturally go hand in hand. Of course, we also had systems in place, like weekly reports and one-on-one coaching, to ensure that employees stayed on track. If people didn't live up to their end of the bargain, their privilege parameters were tightened a bit. Honoring and valuing your people and going out of your way to accommodate their personal needs—not to advance your own agenda, but because it's the right thing to do—produces dedicated employees.

Remember, quality employees want to be trusted, and they want balanced lives. That's why Best Buy designed ROWE (results-oriented work environment)—to attract top-notch candidates. The program goes light-years beyond typical flexibility benefits like condensed work weeks and telecommuting. People are free to work when and where they want. All that matters is results—did the job get done? Granted, this approach isn't a cure-all and it's probably not doable at many organizations, but evidence suggests that appreciative Best Buy employees are living up to their end of the bargain.

In stark contrast, a seat-of-the-pants office is like a prison. It drains and frustrates its denizens. The only thing they look forward to is giving their two-week notice. Moving from that kind of fear-based, spirit-deadening atmosphere to our company gave Doug, one of our top execs, a severe case of culture shock. Doug had spent nineteen years at a well-known national firm. "The executive vice president of operations was confrontational with his staff and pitted his managers against each other," Doug said. "Because he was unwilling to make a decision he could be held accountable for, we were left to figure out for ourselves what direction our divisions should go." The inevitable turf wars that followed caused some capable managers to bolt. Even though these were smart, sought-after pros, Doug's boss spun every loss as a victory. "He would boast to the board that he had weeded out another malcontent," Doug recalled. "That created a culture of managers who were afraid to make decisions, take risks, or offer creative suggestions. It just became a very stressful place to work."

CHAPTER 19

HR SOLUTIONS

Shifting Focus from Paperwork to Partnership

HR is like Ellis Island. Everyone—your newly hired huddled masses, yearning for a paycheck—passes through the human resources department to enter a new world of opportunity. To some seat-of-the-pantsers, HR is nothing more than a profit-suction that should only distribute paychecks, manuals, and benefits answers. To those guys I say, wake up and smell the new century.

Progressive companies regard HR as a strategic partner that pumps up the people side of the business with policies and programs that jibe with their mission, vision, and values. HR delivers a consistent brand message to employees. It also works with management to shape cultural values, to develop quality and safety programs, and to recruit, train, and retain stars. Many small businesses outsource basic HR functions while maintaining an in-house HR presence that coordinates programs and maintains standards. Consultants and outside agencies also help with everything from benefits, payroll, and workers comp to recruiting, hiring, even "employee leasing." Based on your circumstances, mix and match these tips to enrich your people.

HR is your culture keeper. The best HR reps advocate for both employees and management. They're a people-friendly bridge between the two. Your cultural tone is set by the way HR relates to workers through one-on-ones, group sessions, and communications. Ideally, employees walk away from HR encounters feeling heard, respected, valued—by both HR and management. It's also imperative that HR reps speak candidly with company leaders if they feel that decisions, even at the highest level, could damage employee relations. One amazing statistic that points to this importance: On average, only 50 percent of new hires stick around longer than six months. HR's capacity to elevate the culture and provide outstanding internal "customer service" can keep turnover low and training costs lower.

Pull HR into the inner circle. At executive-committee meetings and strategic-planning sessions, make a place at the table for your HR chief. He'll prod you to see every issue through the eyes of employees and in the context of your company's capabilities and goals. Really, what issue isn't an employee issue? HR's guidance on various protocols and legalities that pop up is also valuable. Consider HR the go-to leader for big-picture thinking that balances human, financial, technological, and market factors.

Print your policies. A comprehensive employee manual proves that everyone receives fair and consistent treatment, and that your company respects the balance between work and life. The manual covers a variety of issues, including company benefits, compensation guidelines, work rules, employment conditions, and leaves of absence. Committing policies to print improves the odds that supervisors will correctly administer them. The manual might also protect you from spurious legal claims (chapter 6).

Offer competitive compensation. The healthiest of companies pay competitive wages but are also fiscally responsible. That second part isn't easy. Too many owners dig a financial hole for themselves by over-committing resources to attract and retain talent. Our base salaries were fair but unexceptional, although go-getters fattened their paychecks through individual and team performance bonuses. What put us at the top of the "Best Places to Work" list was the caring culture. Don't scoff. Study after study reveals that employees value culture more than compensation (chapter 37). You're on track when the office is full of joking and laughing on Monday morning.

Provide healthy health benefits. Offering competitive health benefits (medical, dental, disability, vision, chiropractic coverage) helps recruit and retain topflight employees. That boosts morale, productivity, and commitment to the company and its goals. Roughly 60 percent of employees value health insurance more than any other benefit. (Hint: Set clear cost-sharing expectations.)

Remarkably, small employers tend to think they can withhold health benefits without suffering blowback. According to a recent Employee Benefit Research Institute Small Employer Health Benefits Survey, companies that provide health benefits have overwhelmingly stronger cultures than those that don't. Moreover, businesses without benefits tend to pay considerably lower salaries and have a smaller proportion of full-time employees. Those same firms report that most of their employees quit after a few months. Shocker.

Offer an Employee Assistance Program (EAP). EAP providers offer phone banks staffed by trained counselors. Your people can call for help with nearly any issue—including emotional health, family crisis, financial stress, and chemical dependency. Any one of these issues can inflict enormous emotional suffering, torpedo job performance, and damage your culture. Many EAPs, typically offered in conjunction with a health insurance plan, can also guide you through legal land mines, and most are surprisingly affordable on a per-employee basis.

CHAPTER 20

FUN, FRIENDLY, AND FLEXIBLE

Loosening Up Keeps Grumbling Down

Your employees are on board with the mission, they're stoked about the vision and they feel honored and valued. With a little more effort, you can crank up the culture and make the place so enjoyable that people wouldn't dream of working anywhere else. As Herb Kelleher, the pioneering former CEO of Southwest Airlines, says:

> *If people come to a place that they regard*
> *as fun, entertaining, and stimulating, their*
> *minds are turned on. They're looking for*
> *solutions and they'll find them.*

Start with yourself. Fair or not, your relationships with people under your watch set the tone for the entire staff. My dad and his World War II army buddies told me they saw the same thing. "There were some leaders we'd gladly follow out of a foxhole into battle," they said. "But there were others we wanted to shoot in the back." It's no different in the corporate foxholes. As commander in chief you can make every day feel like a slice of heaven or a glimpse of hell.

Let your guard down. Be accessible. Listen. Every so often, start a meeting by asking everyone to share something interesting going on in his or her personal life. Or, start with a humorous, self-deprecating story. Ever spill food on yourself at an important business dinner? Make a bonehead play in a basketball game? Lock yourself out of the house in your bathrobe?

Your gentle humor and humility encourage others to follow suit. Build on that. Every so often, organize a potluck lunch or have take-out food delivered. If weather permits, make it a picnic lunch. Breaking bread is a wonderful way to bring people together and strengthen bonds. Filling people's stomachs is also a good way to show you appreciate great work. Every year, our executive team donned aprons and served lunch to the employees. During huge snowstorms, we tried to keep our crews fueled with pizza while they worked sixteen-hour days to serve panicked drivers.

Don't stop there. Sponsor a softball, golf, or bowling team. Maybe a volleyball or archery league. Gardening or chess club, anyone? Welcome the spouses of employees and former employees—whoever wants in on the fun. Some of these things might spill into company time, but that's okay. It's not wasted time. People who sit anonymously in rows of cubicles can get to know their neighbors better in one afternoon at a bowling alley than three years' worth of hallway hellos.

That camaraderie is priceless, especially when leaders participate. I was a force to be reckoned with on the company basketball team, played in our annual golf outing, and took on countless Ping-Pong challengers determined to beat the boss. By keeping "rank-and-file" diversions like this at arm's length, management promotes an us-versus-them mentality. If nothing else, show up on the sidelines once in a while. I had a blast cheering on our softball team.

Enlightened entrepreneurs also recognize that most employees have busy, complicated lives. Do what you can to reduce their stress. If circumstances allow (and often they don't), provide flexible start and finish times. Let people run errands during the workday. As long as the work gets done, and gets done well and on time, loosen the rules and give people the freedom to be responsible adults.

Want to be a hero to your employees and help them consistently hit their targets? Convert an underused room into a nap space. It's a common-sense solution—an exhausted employee is an unproductive employee. *The Art of Napping at Work,* by William Anthony, director of the Center for Psychiatric

Rehabilitation at Boston University, and his wife, Camille, argues that losing just one hour of sleep a night for a week slashes work productivity. When American workers feel sleep deprived, 51 percent say they do less work and 40 percent admit the quality of their work suffers, according to the International Labour Organization (ILO). I know many executives will think on-the-job napping is goofy, but the concept is catching on; 16 percent of workers surveyed by ILO were allowed to take naps at work. I expect that number to grow. Employees who take catnaps make fewer mistakes, are more productive, and—here's the best part—are eternally grateful they work at such an employee-friendly company.

Creating a can't-wait-to-get-to-work-on-Monday culture not only helps retain people, it can even lure them back once they've left. Before a departing employee slipped out the exit door, I made sure he saw the WELCOME BACK sign taped to the other side. Many employers dub them persona non grata. Big mistake. We thought of former employees as "lifetime alumni," and invited them back for special events as though it were high school homecoming week. We also checked in with them to see how they were getting along (we knew once people had a taste of our culture, it was hard to settle for less). If a former employee was happy at his new company, I was happy. But if he felt like a fish out of water, I'd jump at the chance to reel him back into our pond.

Once, a larger company offered our director of loss prevention, Eric Randa, a major boost in salary and responsibility. After reviewing the facts, I shook his hand. "I hate to lose you, Eric," I said, "but you're obviously making the right decision." Almost five years later, we had grown from 40 stores to 150. I got a wild hair, called Eric, and asked if he'd like to come back, as a vice president, with stock options. "I was fairly content where I was," Eric recalled, "but the new job hadn't been nearly as enjoyable. At Tires Plus, I had put in long hours, but I learned a lot and it had been a lot of fun. It didn't take long to accept Tom's offer. It was a breath of fresh air to come back."

Maintaining cordial relations with ex-employees was an important part of our culture. It wasn't just because we hoped they'd return; it was also one of our values. If I heard an employee bad-mouth a former teammate, I slammed on the brakes. "You're glad he's gone?" I'd say. "Yes, he made some mistakes. But don't we all? Overall, he's a good person, he contributed, and I hope he's happy at his new company." Speaking well of former colleagues shows your people your concern is authentic, and that you won't treat them like stale toast should they leave. That authenticity is the glue that binds a healthy culture together. You can't fake it any more than you can put a price on it.

Okay, reality check: No matter how much effort you put into making your office a fun, stimulating place, a small pocket of employees are still going to grouse. It's always left me scratching my head about some folks—the happier other people are, the unhappier they seem to get. It's the if-you're-okay-I-must-not-be-okay syndrome. But that's okay.

Changing your culture is hard, but rewarding, work. There are no quick fixes. But take heart. Once you begin engaging hearts and minds with the idea that work can be exciting and enjoyable, the process crosses a tipping point. As Stanford University professor Everett M. Rogers noted, "When approximately five percent of a population adopts a new idea, it becomes 'embedded.' When it's accepted by twenty percent of the people, it is unstoppable."

CHAPTER 21

WORKPLACE WELLNESS

Nurturing Healthy and Productive Employees

A healthy culture requires healthy employees. My executive committee objected when I proposed building a fitness center, massage area, and meditation room in our new suburban Minneapolis headquarters. "Why waste valuable square footage on luxuries?" some argued. "They're not luxuries, they're necessities," I said. "When we take care of our people, we take care of ourselves." They weren't the only skeptics. Dave Wilhelmi, our vice president of marketing, was dumbfounded. "Our home office was going to include a meditation room, an exercise room, a basketball court, and afternoon classes on dieting and yoga?" Dave said. "My first thought was, *You've gotta be kidding me. We're in the tire business, aren't we?*"

It didn't take long to win Dave over. "When I think back," he said, "I remember the swelling pride I felt in showing off all those features to a group of out-of-town guests and watching their eyes pop as I toured them around." Dave explained why we offered those amenities, along with an in-house university with mock showroom and service bays, and a hundred-seat break room furnished with a state-of-the-art kitchen and a woodsy view. Visitors were especially impressed with the grand staircase that cascaded down to the two-story glass windows overlooking a pond.

Pride and productivity aren't easy to sustain when you feel ill, physically or emotionally. Common sense tells you productivity suffers if employees don't exercise; if they eat too much junk food; if they're stressed out and sleep-deprived; if they don't feel good about themselves. Now, I'm not suggesting that you pry into personal lives. Even casually telling people what they *should* be doing crosses the line. With that caveat in mind, I came up with a three-step process that, over the years, inspired hundreds of employees to make healthier lifestyle choices.

1. **Model Healthy Behavior and Habits.** An overweight, cantankerous boss who chain-smokes and guzzles sugar-water all day long broadcasts a very different message than a fit, energetic, and emotionally grounded leader with a ready smile and encouraging word. But don't wait till you're a paragon of healthy habits before you send out the positive self-care vibe. In fact, employees may relate better to someone who's struggling with, and taking responsibility for, his own unhealthy ways.

2. **Encourage Others (Gently) to Take Better Care of Themselves.** When an employee was noticeably sleep-deprived or lethargic, I'd say, "Gosh, Ken, are you doing okay? You don't seem to be your usual energetic self." Judging from his response, I'd urge him to get caught up on sleep or to take time to exercise regularly, even if it meant working a little less. Of course, if he wasn't receptive, I'd wish him well and move on. Too many seat-of-the-pantsers send an unspoken message: "What's this nonsense about going to the gym and eating 'better' food? What do you think this is, a resort? We pay you good money to work your butt off." Enlightened entrepreneurs understand that when employees devote a few hours a week to self-care, *the hours they do spend at work will be more productive.*

Seat-of-the-pants cultures are notorious for discouraging people from taking sick days. Hello? Coming to work sick often extends the illness and may put other employees at risk. If someone is sniffling, shivering, and sneezing, thank her for her dedication and tell her to go home, get some rest, and get healthy.

3. **Create Opportunities for Employees to Make Healthier Choices.** Our corporate wellness program, led by an in-house wellness coach, wasn't limited to nutrition and exercise. It covered everything from stress reduction, weight management, and smoking cessation to back care, emotional health, and substance abuse. Info and programming were accessible through on-site workshops, brown-bag classes, newsletters, e-mail alerts, our intranet, an in-house library, and an EAP (employee assistance program). Once a week, everyone from computer jockeys in the home office to in-store mechanics could sign up for a fifteen-minute shiatsu massage for a company-subsidized five bucks.

Sure, not everyone took advantage. But the benefits were dramatic for many who did. People dragging by lunchtime returned from a workout invigorated. Employees struggling with emotional challenges had a better shot at beating them thanks to internal support and professional help. A lot of people simply didn't know how to make the first step toward a healthier lifestyle. It was a joy to watch them take the ball and run with it.

This is one of the most misunderstood benefits a business owner can provide, maybe because results of wellness initiatives are hard to measure. But conservative data I've seen estimates a three-to-one return on investment. It makes sense. The benefits are obvious—health-care costs and absenteeism go down; creativity, efficiency, and performance go up. They're programs people enjoy and appreciate, which translates into better employee relations. Bottom line: It's a no-brainer.

CHAPTER 22

GET PERSONAL

The Rules of Engagement

Joe was half human, half cyborg. The guy was a rock, a street-smart, twenty-year veteran with a friendly smile. He ran his Tires Plus store in Iowa by the book, and sales were always near the top of the charts. So I was more than a little puzzled when I saw his numbers plummet over the course of three months. When complaints from customers and employees began rolling in, I knew we had a mystery on our hands that needed solving, fast. I scheduled a quick trip south and set aside a little extra time for his district manager and me to take Joe to dinner. Joe was wary. By the time the appetizers arrived, however, he had let his guard down and confessed he was in the midst of a messy divorce. No wonder he could barely function; he was distracted, disoriented, depressed.

No stranger to a painful divorce, I asked him what he was doing to take care of himself. Nothing, he said, he was just trying to tough it out. Joe was a man's man, a real blue-collar guy who thought asking for help was a sign of weakness. I asked if he cared to hear how I got through a similar rough patch. He nodded, so I told him how counseling had helped. I recommended he consider it. He was skeptical, but recognized what was at stake. Joe's next two monthly store reports showed him moving in the right direction. The month after that looked even better. Later, he called and told me about the "shrink" he was seeing. "Wow," he said, "that's powerful stuff." He went on and on about how much he appreciated my feedback, and promised he wouldn't cause me any more fitful trips to Iowa. He kept his word.

Why is a chapter that's basically about psychological health in a business book? Because the most troubling and potentially dangerous challenges in the workplace aren't caused by knowledge gaps. They're caused by behavior gaps.

Dysfunctional behavior is a deadly serious business issue, yet business owners rarely deal with it. The consequences are staggering, both in terms of the emotional toll on brittle employees and in cold, hard cash. Mind-body research performed in the past decade has proven conclusively that, without intervention, emotional or psychological turmoil can weaken the body's immune system and lead to physical illness. The upshot? More absenteeism, a productivity plunge, rising health insurance costs, and high turnover. One employee's personal problems can set in motion a chain of events that could threaten the health of an entire organization. As the old proverb goes, "For want of a nail, the kingdom was lost."

Joe's struggle illustrates that whether it's a marital crisis, illness in the family, or demons dragged around since childhood, everyone's personal baggage spills out in the office. Does that mean you have to be an amateur psychologist? Maybe. Let's revisit the definition of enlightened entrepreneur: *A tough-minded, warm-hearted, systems-disciplined leader who inspires people to actively embody the organization's mission, vision, and values.*

By my lights, it's impossible to be a master motivator without understanding what makes people tick. All leaders would do well to learn the basic tools psychologists use to help clients work through problems. I wasn't blessed from birth with the skills to recognize warning signs in the next guy, or to follow up with open-ended questions, or to coach him toward a healthier attitude and lifestyle. What I know I gained through a lot of couch time.

There isn't an honest person alive who hasn't unconsciously indulged in mind games at one time or another—control freaking, defensiveness, intimidation, workaholism, sabotaging, perfectionism, procrastination, displaced anger, victimology. Study that list for a second. They're games your employees are playing *right now,* and many feel perfectly justified to play hardball.

Suggestion: Consider asking key employees to take a standardized psychological test (first consult with a corporate attorney). Tests like the Myers-Briggs Type Indicator or Riso-Hudson Enneagram Type Indicator can help you better understand various personality types. As your grasp of interpersonal dynamics grows, these tests become less important.

Leaders must compassionately confront workers who are underperforming or over-annoying. You'll find that employees are often relieved to tell you why they've been acting up. More often than not, as in Joe's case, it doesn't demand heavy lifting—just a question or two here, a suggestion or insight there. When you finally penetrate a dysfunction barricade and make contact with the human being on the other side, you help her find confidence and courage. You also strengthen your professional relationship.

Occasionally you get lucky, and a few minutes of probing sweeps away years of secrecy and shame. After a few frustrating encounters with Mike, one of my mid-level managers, I suspected he was playing dumb about a key issue I knew he was aware of. During our next one-on-one, when he feigned ignorance about an important detail, I quizzed him, gently but persistently, until he boxed himself into a corner. With tears running down his cheeks, he confessed he had been lying. "I'm sorry to break down," he said. "Mike," I said, "this isn't a breakdown, it's a breakthrough. Congratulations."

After composing himself, Mike explained that he was raised by a cold-hearted father. Whenever Mike did something wrong, his father relentlessly interrogated him until he extracted every last humiliating detail. Then Mike was punished mercilessly. His survival instinct quickly taught him that aloofness or, when necessary lying, was a good form of protection. I assured Mike that this was a safe place, and he could feel free to talk about anything without fear of reprisal. The look of relief and gratitude on his face was a joy to behold.

In extreme cases, I've used something called the "Two-Chair Technique." I don't know anything better for clearing the clouds on pressing personal or professional storms. One afternoon, one of my VPs was depressed and questioning his value as an employee and human being. "Mark," I said, "you're such a hard worker and you do so many things right. This may sound strange, but if you're willing to have a conversation with yourself and also look at things from a positive perspective, we can try something I learned from my therapist. It helped me bounce back when I was in the frame of mind you're in."

With a flash of alarm and amusement, Mark shrugged. "Sure," he said, "what the heck." I arranged two chairs facing each other—a "negative" chair and a "positive" chair. He chose the negative chair, naturally. Now I said, imagine you're also seated in the positive chair. I told him to make the case to his other, positive self, that he was a failure. Given his mood, that wasn't difficult. He said, "You're bad news, Mark. You keep on screwing up. What's the point of even trying anymore?" Then I asked him to change chairs and respond to what Mark in the negative chair had just said. Addressing the negative chair, Mark defended himself with his positive qualities and all the great things he'd done. It wasn't exactly trial-lawyer stuff, but it was a convincing argument. Fifteen minutes later, Mark felt energized after realizing he was a good guy after all. Over the following months, Mark confided that the Two-Chair Technique had also helped him resolve some personal problems.

Some people simply won't budge the door on their inner lives. That's okay. Don't force it. A lot more people *will* tell you what's on their mind if you follow these tips.

Earn trust. People open up if they sense they can trust you. They need to know you care, and that the personal information they're sharing won't come back to them from another source. Establishing that trust begins today—right now—through respectful interaction. That way, when an issue does bubble up, an employee will trust that his secret will be safe with you. As former Secretary of State Colin Powell observed:

> *The day people stop bringing you their problems*
> *is the day you stopped leading them.*

Stop, drop, and listen. When an employee needs to talk, stop thinking about business, drop what you're doing, and give him your full attention. The words of Brad Burley, one of our regional managers, demonstrate why. Brad's three-year-old daughter had been having earaches and developmental problems that stumped her doctors. Touring the stores one day, I asked Brad how she was doing. "Normally, Tom was very focused on business while we were driving around," Brad recalled. "But I bet he spent an hour and a half with me sitting in a store parking lot talking about alternative medicine options and giving me the names of doctors who may be able to help. He even told me that if I couldn't get in to see them, to call him and he'd help me get an appointment." Brad and his wife tried a few dietary changes I suggested and noticed some progress. Eventually, their daughter's ears healed and her health improved. "That was pretty powerful," Brad said. "You know, for a leader to spend that much time talking about one of my kids, well, it was an impression that will last the rest of my life."

Be humble. Joe's struggle with his divorce showed that employees respond better to an empathetic leader than to an imperious autocrat looking down his nose at them. Sharing my vulnerabilities with Joe, telling him how therapy helped me deal with divorce, bridged the boss-employee gap and enabled us to forge a deeper connection. Imagine if I had allowed my ego to maintain the distance between us and had simply told him to go see a therapist. I doubt Joe would be lighting up the charts in Iowa today.

Eliminate barriers. Step out from behind your big, imposing, all-hail-the-chief desk and sit toe-to-toe with employees as equals. If you have two extra chairs in your office, that'll do. Or stake out neutral territory—perhaps an empty conference room or cafeteria table.

Get permission. The introduction of personal issues into a workplace discussion requires—unequivocally—the employee's consent. How to get it? Recap the underlying performance issue, then empathize: "Are there any roadblocks preventing you from doing the great work we both know you're capable of?" "Are you comfortable sharing whatever's affecting your performance?" "I'm sensing there's a deeper issue at work here. How do you feel about discussing it?" My batting average was about .800. Better than .000, which is what you'll be swinging if you don't ask how you can help.

Stay objective. If you've struggled with a similar issue, don't assume your fix is universal or that your recovery timetable is relevant. Sure, your experiences are good points of reference. But recognize that the circumstances and rhythms of your employee's life created a very different scenario. Proceed with caution. Be patient, and open yourself to her point of view.

Walk the talk. It's one thing to assure people they can tell you anything; to tell them you'll respond with understanding; to say you'll help them work things out and regain their footing. But you cripple your credibility if you respond in a way that puts the lie to your assurances. You can't be judgmental, you can't condescend, you can't trivialize. Breach that trust *even once* and the gossip gourmets and gourmands in the office will serve it up in the cafeteria for weeks to come.

Do right by your teammate. Your goal as coach is to maximize each employee's value. To do that, never lose sight of the fact that her well-being takes precedence over her work responsibilities. Heresy? Only to a boss running the shop by the seat of his pants. Putting the health and happiness of employees first unquestionably benefits an organization in ways both measurable and intangible.

Be ready with outside resources. Sometimes you have to call in the professional—chemical dependency, anger management, clinical depression, marital strife, physical abuse. The first step is to subscribe to an EAP (employee assistance program), a phone bank staffed by trained counselors. Don't stop there. Compile a list of programs, support groups, and organizations whose mission is to help people who are severely stressed out or consumed by a full-blown crisis. Post the list in the office (on your intranet or bulletin board) and remind people it's there. Encouraging your staff to consider outside help adds credibility to those options and may blunt their shame. Remember, troubled employees don't always know which way to turn. Pointing them in the right direction might be a lifesaver.

KEY POINTS

GROWING THE CULTURE

> **Culture requires constant nurturing.** Sustaining an energized, team-oriented atmosphere is an ongoing process. It begins with ethical leaders who authentically model the organization's mission, vision, and values. Attention must be paid to people's social, physical, emotional, and motivational needs.

> **Mold individual egos into a team ego.** There's nothing so heady as being on a winning team. Use formal and informal channels to communicate that long-term success depends on harmony with coworkers. More important, lead by example.

> **Apply the laws of cultural leadership.** Great leaders are born— and made. Seat-of-the-pants bosses can begin improving their leadership skills today by putting these essential laws—huddle up, respond rapidly, invite dissent—into practice.

> **Honor your people and accommodate their priorities.** Great employees seek fulfillment and flexibility. They expect to be held accountable. They welcome challenging and meaningful work. They put family first. They hate micromanagement.

> **Leverage your HR assets.** Consider HR a strategic partner that pumps up the people side of your business with policies and programs that jibe with your mission, vision, and values. Work with HR to shape cultural values, provide fiscally responsible compensation packages, develop quality and safety programs, and recruit, train, and retain stars.

> **Give employees opportunities to be healthier and happier.** Establish a wellness program and encourage camaraderie through humility, humor, and occasional diversions. The better you take care of your people, the better they'll take care of business.

> **Realize that personal issues spill into the workplace.** People are human beings first and employees second. That means nobody

sails through life without some behavioral issues or the occasional crisis. Both impair performance. Recognize warning signs so that you can either help them deal with it or direct people to appropriate resources.

➤ **Don't hesitate to ask if everything is all right.** Keep in mind that people who act dysfunctionally believe they're justified in doing so. Consequently, many are receptive to probing. Others, however, force a smile and deny that anything's amiss. You're not a miracle worker. All you can do is coach people who are open to it and keep a compassionate eye on those who aren't.

BUILDING A SYSTEMS-DISCIPLINED ORGANIZATION

Crafting Pitch-Perfect Processes

Imagine you're at the Kentucky Derby, the Run for the Roses, the Super Bowl of horse racing. Betting is brisk. The horses are champing at the bit for the electronic gates to fling open. The jockeys position their steeds. The flag goes up, the bell sounds, and the gates—stay closed. The jockeys curse, the horses bray, track officials scramble. Propriety unravels as minutes tick by. The crowd's grumble swells into a roar. It's an unbridled nightmare.

You can be a walking billboard for your company's mission, vision, and values. You can have a stable stocked with talented, motivated thoroughbreds. You can take pride in your enlightened, healthy culture. But if you don't have the right systems in place, nobody's going anywhere.

Quality guru W. Edwards Deming declared that 80 percent of all errors are systems errors. While Deming was referring chiefly to manufacturing, the essence of his observation applies to any of your systems and procedures. Even if that percentage were halved, it's clear that developing sophisticated, user-friendly procedures—for everything from strategic planning to conducting meetings to phone etiquette—can help you blow past the competition. Structural integrity makes it easier to

- define roles, responsibilities, and relationships
- coordinate, communicate, and make decisions
- allocate and deploy resources
- convert strategy into reality
- respond to change
- develop employees
- provide stability

The structural linchpin is the "org chart." Keep it current and visible so everyone knows who does what and who reports to whom. Even if everybody in a small firm wears three hats, the org chart still lets everyone know how they fit into the big picture. The flatter the org chart—meaning more people reporting directly to you—the better. The more levels between you and department heads—and between you and your customers—the more communication snafus you can expect in both directions. For instance, CEOs often have IT (information technology) and human resources, functions critical to overall success, report to the CFO. Without direct contact, it's more difficult to keep your fingers on front-page issues. Don't worry, having more people report to you won't drain your time—if you're hiring the right people, empowering them, and regularly meeting one-on-one. The org chart is the official power grid, but it's just as important to know who wields the unofficial clout. A CEO's executive assistant, for instance, often has more influence than some high-level execs.

Without a framework, any organization—corporation, government, nonprofit—is doomed to mediocrity and chaos. A taut system is like a trampoline—it keeps you bounding higher. Slip and it bounces you right back up. Yet relying heavily on structure is a tough leap of faith for creative, right-brained leaders who view well-defined systems as blood-sucking bureaucracies. The challenge is to find the sweet spot between too much and too little bureaucracy. Large corporations tend to be top-heavy with regulations, while small businesses too often ad-lib it. It's easy to see why. Most entrepreneurs run their own show because they feel suffocated by bulky bureaucracies. But they tend to overcompensate by going from too many rules to too few. That's why inefficiency and waste are common causes of death for small businesses.

Make sure employees focus on all the options and freedom within your structure rather than on its limitations. A long list of don't dos—accompanied by incessant harping—stifles creativity. Worse, fixing attention on what not to do can bring about the very result you're trying to avoid. Karl Wallenda, founder of the Great Wallendas, a daredevil circus troupe famous for performing death-defying feats without a safety net, tragically illustrated this in 1978. At the age of seventy-three, he attempted to "walk the wire" between two hotels in San Juan, Puerto Rico. His widow said afterward that, for the first time in his life, her husband had "put all his energies into not falling rather than walking the tightrope."

CHAPTER 23

STRATEGIC PLANNING

Drawing Up Tomorrow's Road Map

We went from contender to champ the day we implemented a strategic planning process. The strategic plan is the sun in your solar system. It illuminates the purpose of every proposal, every process, every project. Everything revolves around it. Everything radiates from it. It flows from team objectives into operating plans into individual goals into action plans and, finally, into bottom-line results. "Our strategic plan put us all on the same page," said Jim Bemis, our CFO. "It made everyone accountable and helped us work more cohesively together. Without it, the level of success we achieved would have been unthinkable." It's not too much to say that every choice, every decision, every single action traces back to (drum roll) the strategic plan.

Seat-of-the-pantsers, particularly in smaller organizations, pooh-pooh strategic planning as a waste of time. Markets change too rapidly, they say. It's true, long-term plans are subject to the whim of unexpected events. Strategic planning is totally conceptual, looking out five to seven years. But short-term and mid-range planning is absolutely necessary. Certainly you can't prepare for every possibility, but failing to methodically look out a year or two can be fatal.

PLANNING CHANGE, CHANGING PLANS

Show me a leader who avoids planning and I'll show you a leader afraid of change. It's human nature. Grooves are safe and comfortable. Too much comfort, however, dulls the senses. You may think you're at the top of your game when you're actually skating on thin ice. A hockey player who rushes to the puck instead of to where it's going to be next doesn't score many goals.

The best leaders expect change, embrace it, and inspire others with its promise of new opportunities. They do it without losing sight of day-to-day operations and challenging their people to raise their game through developmental education. Managers who stubbornly cling to the status quo—out of fear, denial—only hasten a change in their own status. I'm reminded of a woman who attended a Change Management seminar only to walk away disappointed that the subject was managing change, not changing managers.

Managing change doesn't work on the run. Nor can you grapple with it in a vacuum. Every action causes a series of reactions in every corner of the company. Plumbing the depths of change requires focused, structured, and strategic input from throughout the company. That's why it's woven tightly into your strategic-planning process. Also, twice a month, at executive-committee meetings, your people should report on what's new in the field. (Fast-breaking seismic shifts warrant special war-room sessions.) Which disruptive technology is at the front door of the marketplace? What new products and services is the competition launching? What do customers want now that they didn't want a year ago? How about a month ago? Continuously challenging assumptions keeps you on our toes, and out of the red.

Don't get caught flat-footed like New World Pasta. The nation's largest maker of dry pasta filed for Chapter 11 bankruptcy protection in May 2004, two weeks before Krispy Kreme Doughnuts reported its first quarterly net loss

($24.4 million) since going public four years prior. The culprit? The low-carb diet craze—the very phenomenon a New World Pasta veep had called "a fad" that would soon fade. Fade it did, but not before permanently embedding itself in our cultural consciousness and leaving a trail of corporate carcasses in its wake. Misjudge cultural cues and it's your company that will fade.

Janet Dolan knows how to stay sharply in focus. In March 2000, the CEO of Tennant Company, the U.S. leader in power-cleaning equipment, summoned her top fifty people to a two-day strategy marathon. The objective, she told them, was nothing less than total transformation. The response was a collective "Huh?" Business had never been better. Tennant was on schedule to close the year with $28 million in earnings on sales of $454 million. The publicly traded company's earnings-per-share were hitting historic highs. Cash flow was healthy, debt inconsequential.

But Janet looked beyond the numbers. It was a month before the dot-com bubble burst, and she felt the winds of change kicking up. She and her executive team believed that an imminent recession and industry trends were about to permanently alter the power-cleaning landscape. More agile competitors were siphoning away Tennant's customers. Others were moving their manufacturing operations overseas. Technology was on the verge of rendering many cleaning solutions obsolete.

Convinced that innovation paves the road to salvation, Janet's team tore up and rebuilt every premise and process. Surveys revealed that customers cared more about health and safety than clean factory floors. They were also demanding highly specialized cleaning teams. Invigorated, Team Tennant brainstormed how to build and leverage the company's brand. It worked. While the 2001 recession chomped 86 percent out of earnings, the damage might have been fatal had Tennant stayed the course on its profitable-yet-aging business model. Tennant's numbers continue their smooth ascent. Most important, the company is positioned for explosive future growth.

Whether you're running with the bulls or laying low with the bears, strategic planning is straightforward. Frame it with a searching question: *How can we take advantage of our strengths and opportunities and neutralize our weaknesses and threats?* Fix your eye on your SWOTs (strengths, weaknesses, opportunities, threats), and the right plan unfolds.

Strategic planning's eight steps are:

1. Identify SWOTs. Get clarity on every issue you're facing. In July (or six months prior to the next fiscal year), schedule a series of two-hour brainstorming sessions with reps from every group of stakeholders, from department heads and customers to vendors and the rank and file. Each group has its own point of view. Collect plenty of observations—macro, micro, and everything in between—about internal strengths and weaknesses and external opportunities and threats. Keep it simple—ask everyone to fill out a single sheet listing the four SWOT categories. Then merge the results into one report.

2. Set Priorities. Come September, gather the executive committee and other key people for a daylong priority-setting meeting. (The "executive committee" in smaller shops may simply be the owner and her three top people.) First, establish context by summarizing industry trends, competitor activity, last year's performance, and this year's financial forecasts. Next, vigorously debate which issues (gleaned from your SWOT list in step one) deserve priority in the coming year, and which make the list for the next two to four years. Best use a pencil for anything more than eighteen months out. Simplify both lists by grouping similar issues under the same macro heading (approve no more than eight macro issues per time period). Now that priorities are set and ranked, assign them to the appropriate leader.

3. Task-force It, and Plan, Plan, Plan. Each priority earns its own task force, composed of the company's subject-matter experts. For the next two months, they research the priority and design an action plan that assigns responsibilities and accountabilities, sets deadlines, allocates resources, and establishes controls.

4. Present Action Plans. Schedule a review meeting (a day or two) in early November that includes the same folks from the early-September gathering. Here, taskforce leaders present their action plans. Each presentation is like a Ph.D. dissertation—it must be defended. That means respectful disagreement is essential. It pushes the task force to thoroughly prepare benchmarking protocols, ROI (return on investment) projections, and other necessities.

With the task-force plans presented, start green-lighting. Some plans will be good to go; others will need modifying based on available resources. (Plans requiring revision should be redistributed within two weeks.) Of course, each strategic objective is generally multidepartmental—hence the team approach. If the goal, for instance, is to open a dozen new stores, the exec in charge of real estate secures locations and oversees construction. Meanwhile, the CFO arranges financing; the retail operations people groom new store managers; marketing folks study the markets, develop a plan, and negotiate ad rates; IT analyzes and preps data systems.

Now that action plans are established, incorporate them into the annual grand (ours ran ten pages) strategic plan. This plan has two major sections. It kicks off, of course, with your mission, vision, and operating values. Fundamental business-plan issues follow—product and service offerings, the marketplace and how you'll target it (much of this is carried over year to year with minor tweaks). The second section explores the company's SWOTs and details its action plans. It may sound counterintuitive, but your strategic plan is not a top-secret document. Portions are ideal calling cards for bankers, vendors, and potential partners.

5. Present Departmental Operating Plans. Now break each action plan into pieces and parcel them out to the right people. Those employees who have others reporting to them create individual operating plans to execute the pieces assigned to them. Department heads collect these operating plans, approve them, and roll them into departmental operating plans. In December (or the final month of your fiscal year), round up the same group as in November to review and approve these departmental plans. Example: *The accounting plan looks good except we need the financials two days earlier.* Then update departmental and individual operating plans.

6. Budget It. Start the budgeting process in early November. All four parts of the corporate budget—projected P&L statement, projected monthly cash flows, projected balance sheet, capital expenditure plan—should be built off last year's performance and this year's SWOT-powered operating plan.

7. Follow-up. A poorly executed plan isn't worth the paper it's printed on. Follow-up is critical. Enthusiasm can wane. Attention gets diverted. Here are three ways to avoid that and monitor results:

- Six months after approval (and again six months later), convene the executive committee for an operating-plan review. Each department head introduces her key reps (from the accounting department, it may be the controller, treasurer, and accounts payable manager) to present progress reports comparing accomplishments to operating-plan goals. The presenters, and the department chief, grade their own performance. The group's accomplishments and grades (later factored into employee annual bonus calculations) are open to compliments and challenges. The department head wraps things up with a summary of successes and shortfalls over the last six months as well as expectations for the next six months. Once complete, all but the department head who sits on the executive committee are excused, and another department files in.
- Each manager keeps the operating plan humming by meeting one-on-one two to four times a month with everyone who reports to her (chapter 32).
- Regular, one-to-three-hour executive-committee meetings throughout the year also keep the strategic plan on track. Aim for weekly or monthly, depending on team experience and the pace of change (we met every two weeks). The agenda includes
  - mid-month review of the P&L, including department-by-department response
  - monthly review of key departmental metrics
  - brainstorming on inter- and intra-departmental challenges

- round-robin sharing of new ideas or recent successes
- competitive updates
- introduction of new enterprise-wide policies and programs

8. Team Update. Gather the entire company for a few hours each month or quarter to motivate, inform, celebrate, and educate. Have department heads update people on wins and losses, what needs to be done over the next period, and how everyone can make it happen. Solicit ideas and questions. It's also a good time to salute birthdays, births, and employment anniversaries.

COMPRESS FOR SUCCESS

Of course, six days of strategic planning can choke a small company. Rather than abandon it, compress it into a two-day in-house meeting. Get a lot done ahead of time by e-mailing attendees a request for their views on the company's SWOTs. The CFO or operations chief merges and purges the responses. This consolidated list, which displays the SWOT items in order of the frequency (in parentheses) with which they're mentioned, replaces an entire day of roundtable debate and chatter.

Now you're ready for the meeting. After an introduction where you outline the meeting protocols (chapter 26), establish some context (part of step two, above) with a ninety-minute summary about industry trends, competitor moves, last year's performance, and this year's financial forecasts. Allocate the remainder of the two days to brainstorming and coming up with action plans for the top seven to eight issues on the SWOT survey.

Give more time to issues higher on the list. Chances are these issues burn hot and brief during board meetings, executive-committee meetings, and one-on-ones. Now they can get a full airing among the company's key people. (You should average about two hours per subject.) The days are certainly long, with working lunches. But it's worth the direction and cohesion that you produce. The action plans you come up with divvy up responsibilities and accountabilities, set deadlines, allocate resources, and establish controls.

A note taker records the action plans by issue and sends them to all the players after the meeting.

On first blush, the creation and execution of a strategic plan may seem like learning a foreign language. It may also seem like death by a thousand meetings. But these eight steps can lead you to the Promised Land. After upgrading our strategic planning, our profits increased tenfold and revenue soared from $40 million to $200 million in just eight years. Coincidence?

CHAPTER 24

EXECUTION IS EVERYTHING

Ensuring It's Done Right

The best operating plans aren't worth a plugged quarter (even clichés need to keep pace with inflation) without thorough execution. My four-step execution solution helps employees hurdle obstacles *and* pick themselves up when they stumble: Define expectations, inspire, teach, follow up.

The simplicity is deceptive. Let's say an employee poorly executes a piece of her operating plan and blames it on colleagues who failed to fill out a form correctly and on time.

- First, did she **define the expectation**? Ask if she spelled out what needed to be done and by when. Did she write a clear memo (bullet-point format with key points bolded)? Did the subject line or first sentence clearly convey her key message?
- Second, did she **inspire**? Ask if she explained why it was important to completely and accurately fill out the form, and why speed was essential.
- Next, did she **teach**? Ask if she demonstrated how to fill out the

form. For more complex issues, did she resort to the Confucius Checklist (chapter 41)?

- Last, did she **follow up**? Ask if a system was in place to ensure accuracy and timeliness. If so, does it call for instant feedback for noncompliance?

Did she answer yes to each question? If not, tell her you're happy to listen to what somebody else needs to do *after* she's done what she needs to do—execute all four steps. Until then, the ball stays in her court.

CHAPTER 25

RESOLVE ROADBLOCKS

Helping Individuals and Groups Solve Problems

Blame, shame, panic, pander—enlightened entrepreneurs don't do any of these to employees that miss their marks. Sure, these execs may feel frustrated. But they're cooperative and exploratory, not combative and accusatory. They know that a disciplined attitude, tight procedures, and plenty of intellectual elbow grease can make problem solving more like piecing together a puzzle than pulling teeth.

Say your department's sales report reveals that Bill's in free fall. When you ask Bill what's up, he points to a deskful of factors beyond his control. "I'm doing everything I can," he insists. "But the deck's been stacked against me for weeks. Business is down all over, man. Those new guys are really underpricing us. And the weather!"

The stage is set for the one-two knockout punch—*external comparison* followed by *internal analysis*. Be direct and upbeat. Express curiosity, not condescension, or you may plant seeds of anger and resentment. "Really?" you might reply. "According to this report, Debbie and Max hit their numbers in the same environment. Let's take a look at how well you're following the system. The plan calls for you to make twelve to fifteen cold calls daily, and I see only a handful of calls on your cold-call sheet. Why is that? By the way, have you notified your customers about the specials we posted? I see checks by only half the names on your log. Sorry, not to belabor the point, but your new-account follow-up matrix has only a few chicken scratches on it. Sure you're doing everything you can?" What can he say? He's cornered, and he knows that you know that he knows. Hopefully, this jolts him out of denial. After he takes responsibility, nudge him with some kind words: "I know you've got what it takes to do a lot better than this, Bill. If you plug back into the program, you'll be back on track."

I should say in passing, a streamlined system works for *procedure problem solving,* but it's useless for *people problem solving* (chapter 22). Emotions and feelings need more than precision-guided procedures.

Not all problems can be solved one-on-one. That's why it's important to learn my group problem-solving technique. When I hit the road for store visits, it was fun to identify and resolve roadblocks as a group. The process can yield a big harvest wherever you go.

The seven steps for group problem solving are:

1. Build Rapport. Learn or confirm everybody's name: "Nice to meet you, Mary; glad you're on the team." "Great to see you again, George; you're looking good." Ask about spouses and kids, and whether anyone's had recent accomplishments or adventures. Genuinely making the effort to connect, one human being to another, builds the bonds of an effective working relationship. The goal here is to get everyone to chill and loosen up. A lighthearted clubhouse atmosphere teases out the creativity essential for solving problems.

2. Offer Assistance. Confirm that everyone's getting all the support they need. Somebody's almost always thinking, *How can we take on something new when we can't even get support for what we're doing now?* Maybe one employee isn't receiving an important report on time. Perhaps marketing isn't providing someone else with enough lead time on promotions. Promise you'll check into things and get some answers. Some people hesitate to mention irritants because they don't want to be branded a kvetcher. But they'll open up if you demonstrate a willingness to unplug blocked channels. Later, when you do discuss concerns with the appropriate managers, *do not* name names. Prefacing your comments with "Jill said this about you" plants seeds of resentment and leads to unhealthy triangulation and a corrosive culture. If you absolutely must reveal a source, positively frame her suggestion: "Jill had a terrific idea for how we can make this process even better. But I need your help."

3. Review the Numbers. Ask for stats—revenue, customer satisfaction surveys, ad-response rates—that reflect the group's performance. For instance, I'd ask the store manager for last month's profit-and-loss statement and up-to-the-second leading indicators. That info provided valuable context. It's also a reality check to the *Everything is great!* syndrome (phony optimism is a huge red flag).

4. Compliment and Congratulate. Recognize and praise individual and team successes. Get the applause meter jumping. In exceptional cases, promise to pick up the tab for a team outing. Praising people in front of their peers pumps up the team and sends the message that excellence is expected, appreciated, and rewarded.

5. Identify Roadblocks. Ask everyone where improvement is most needed and where they see obstacles. In an atmosphere of trust and security, it's amazing how a simple question like "What's going on?" produces all sorts of valuable info. At the first hint of a problem, drill down with Columbo-like questions until you hit a gusher. If revenues are lackluster, find out if basic protocols were followed. In our stores that meant pulling work orders and asking questions: "Were the brakes inspected?" "Was it noted on the inspection sheet?" "Was the customer told?" "Was her response recorded properly?" Remember, the answer to every problem is in that room.

6. Cast the Net Again. To ensure real candor, hand out blank sheets of paper and ask everyone to anonymously describe the best things about the unit and its biggest challenges. This always produces eye-openers. If it's a small group, collect the responses and mix them up to preserve anonymity. Then address them one by one, cheering the positive ones and digging into the challenges. For large groups, schedule a follow-up meeting so an assistant can merge-and-purge the comments and distribute the results. No matter how supportive you are, however, some employees may still hold back, especially if the issue involves singling out a colleague. So wrap up with a reminder that you're always available to discuss sensitive issues one-on-one.

7. Get Commitments. It's natural for somebody to be embarrassed when they're identified as a roadblock in front of their teammates. Disarm the situation by warmly pointing out what the person is doing right and framing the matter as a teachable moment: "I'm really glad this came up, because it's a great reminder that every single step in our process impacts customer service, store earnings, and, ultimately, your bonuses." Gently ask the employee how he can make things right. If you're satisfied with his answer, agree on a course of action. Then—and this is pivotal—ask for a commitment to make it happen and set a date for a progress report. Finish with a dollop of genuine praise: "Great, John. You're a sharp guy and I know you can do it. We're all cheering for you." You'll get great results, as long as the room doesn't feel like someone's just been offered up as a sacrificial goat.

The magic of candid group sessions can illuminate every angle of a problem. That leads to better decision making and deeper support for the decisions—and for procedures already in place. It was a rare brainstorming session that failed to produce effective solutions. It's like Voltaire said:

No problem can withstand the assault of
sustained thinking.

CHAPTER 26

ADD MUSCLE TO MEETINGS

How to Run Tight, Productive Meetings

I t's been said that a meeting is an event where minutes are kept and hours are lost. So why have meetings at all? Simple: the huge payoff. They leverage your time—you can impart vital information to many key people at once, so the choir sings from the same song sheet. They tap into the power of brainstorming—one plus one can equal three when viewpoints converge. Meetings tamp down turf wars—when a group solves each other's problems, people magically become less turf-conscious. Yet you'll waste a year of your life in meetings—unless you announce agendas and expectations with a bullhorn. Get tough. Set tight parameters. Otherwise, you'll be listening to disorganized people ramble on deep into the weeds about God knows what. Here are my battle-tested protocols to get you in, out, and back to your desk before all the muffins are gone.

Ready

- Cancel it. Or, at least, ask yourself whether the meeting truly needs to happen. So many issues can be handled via memo, e-mail, or a quick one-on-one.
- Still gotta do it? Okay, but invite only the A-listers, and make sure you have a quorum.
- Confirm the meeting room's availability, and be darn sure the necessary audiovisual gear will be assembled and working.
- If it's a teleconference or videoconference, confirm timing with the vendor. Do not screw around with cheap speakerphones; state-of-the-art phones won't waste the time of long-distance participants. E-mail the agenda, handouts, and step-by-step access instructions to all participants (noting start time in both your time zone and theirs). Add a note to remind teleconference participants to identify themselves before speaking.

Set

- Prep an agenda that includes time limits for presentations and discussions. Circulate it via e-mail, clearly laying out the meeting's date, time, and place.
- Remind presenters to come armed with handouts that minimize questions and note taking.
- Appoint a time sheriff to signal you whenever people run long.
- Designate a note taker to record the action steps produced by agenda items.

Go

- Start on time, to the minute. It enforces promptness. George W. Bush was known to lock the door when he began his meetings.

Starting ten minutes late sends people a bad message—that it's okay to mosey on in whenever they feel like it.

- We'd sometimes start with sixty seconds of quiet time to just breathe and relax (some people needed to catch their breath after running to get there on time). It's amazing how this simple exercise can get people grounded and ready to go.
- If it feels natural, go around the table for (very) brief updates on everyone's personal lives. It lifts spirits and bonds the group.
- Devote thirty seconds to the meeting's objective and importance. Don't assume that everyone takes their seat ready to hand over their full attention (even after a breathing exercise). You need to capture the attention of the woman who just finished arguing with her husband. That guy frantically dousing a departmental fire? You need him, too. A quick pep talk energizes and focuses everyone.
- Quickly review the agenda, then ask for late-breaking additions or deletions.

Pick Up the Pace

- Firmly, but tactfully, bat away remarks that stray from the meeting's target. Positive comments get the point across without embarrassing anyone: "Sue, that sounds important. Why don't we get that on the agenda for next time?"
- Urge ramblers, even when they're on message, to keep it moving: "Hey, Tony, FYI, we've got five more minutes for this segment. Better finish up so we have time for questions." If time is running out: "Hey, Tony, great point. Can you bottom-line it?"
- Beware "piling on," the tendency we have to toss in our two cents. Rather than allow everyone to say the same thing in slightly different ways, ask people to call out ditto to signal agreement.
- Deep-six side conversations by looking directly at the talker and injecting his name into what you're saying: "So this solution, Jim, should solve that problem."
- Drawn-out discussions make it hard to wrap up an issue. Bring it to a head by saying, "We've got two minutes. What are the action

steps?" If that's not practical, either defer the topic to the next meeting or appoint a committee to explore it. I know, committees get a bad rap. As former House of Commons clerk Sir Barnett Cocks delicately put it, "A committee is a cul-de-sac down which ideas are lured and then quietly strangled." But when they're quarterbacked with discipline, committees save time and produce results.

Stretch Run

- Think high-stakes poker. Hold your cards close and betray nothing with your facial expressions. Why? Play your cards too soon and the pot won't have time to grow. In other words, a leader's opinion influences others' opinions, the mental equivalent of a pile of chips. Keep a poker face and you're more likely to draw out the quiet types and make it hard for the sycophants to parrot your ideas. (Ask a trusted team member to cue you if you're too quick to seize the reins.)
- Get everyone to ante up. Don't let the Silent Sams get through a meeting without contributing. Call on individuals if you sense they're stifling their ideas. Resort to the round-robin technique if too many people are holding back.
- Use secret balloting when serious issues require a vote. When I staked out a position, I found others were sometimes reluctant to openly vote against me. Still, you may occasionally have to trump an outcome by playing the executive-privilege veto card. In the end, you're the chief protector of the company's mission, vision, and values.
- Ask open-ended questions. You'll hear thoughtful and often revealing answers.
- Indulge wisecracks. You're keeper of the tone, and laughing and kibitzing with everyone else keeps it light and fosters strong relationships.
- Stand and stretch every hour or so to keep people invigorated and focused. Let people stand if they begin to feel uncomfortable or fatigued.

Finish Line

- Close out every issue by defining action steps: "Okay, exactly what are we going to do, who's going to do it, and when are they going to do it?" Skip this critical step and you waste everyone's time. Plus, the next meeting will have a bloated, déjà vu agenda.
- Try putting the meeting "on the couch" every so often for post-game analysis. Ask the group what they liked about the meeting, and if they have any ideas for making the process better.
- Finally, schedule the next meeting.

Cooling Down

- As people leave, strike up a conversation with anyone who was straying during the meeting: "Hey, Jim, good distribution idea. But I couldn't help noticing you strayed off the mark a few times. That's not like you. Everything all right?"
- Ask the designated note taker to e-mail attendees a bulleted action-step summary within twenty-four hours. Succinct bullet points get read more thoroughly than long paragraphs.
- The note taker also updates the Meeting Follow-up Log, a list of items whose progress you want to assess during subsequent meetings.

Tight team meetings generate two powerful side effects. First, you teach participants by example how to efficiently conduct their own staff meetings. Second, you broadcast a message that reverberates through the entire culture: *We value efficiency and teamwork, and we need your help to solve our problems.*

CHAPTER 27

THE BEST NEVER REST

Continuous Systems Improvement

Success has many fathers, as the saying goes. One sire to my company's exponential growth was our obsession with improving the way we did things. We were fanatical about identifying roadblocks, unearthing errors, and fine-tuning our system. Part of our campaign included benchmarking the highfliers; one way we did that was an occasional intel-gathering field trip. Once, we chartered a twin-prop plane for our regional managers, Wayne Shimer, and me to investigate a top national chain's Omaha locations. The company had a great reputation and did a lot of things right—and they were about to invade the twin cities, our most lucrative market.

We split into three teams, rented cars, and went shopping. We got oil changes at every store and watched their MO. "While we waited," Wayne recalled, "I'd say to the manager, 'That looks like a great computer system. How does it work?' And he'd explain the whole thing in detail." We flew home fat with improvements that we immediately clicked into place, like installing windows between the bays and the lobby so customers could watch the progress on their cars. "Looking back," Wayne said, "the cost and the time to load us all onto a charter and fly us back and forth to Omaha, I mean, that's crazy. Or is it? It takes a lot of passion and drive to be the best."

The big boys tend to pursue structural precision through a process called Lean Enterprise, a hybrid of TQM (Total Quality Management) and JIT (Just In Time). Essentially, Lean Enterprise integrates quality commitment, waste elimination, and employee involvement within a structured management system. Its primary purpose is to perform all functions—from product development and production to sales and customer service—so that steps that don't create value for the end user are eliminated. This allows steps that do create value to flow unimpeded in the value stream. Clearly, Lean Enterprise demands a thorough understanding of customer needs, as does Six Sigma, a rigorous, empirical method of eliminating defects in all systems. Six Sigma, conceived by the late Bill Smith, a reliability engineer at Motorola, defines a defect as anything outside of customer specifications. General Electric claims that Six Sigma produced $10 billion in benefits in just five years.

There aren't many companies *saving* $2 billion annually. And small businesses often don't have budgets for TQM, JIT, or Lean Enterprise. But you can save plenty on systems issues by troubleshooting the disease rather than the symptom. Seat-of-the-pantsers do the exact opposite—they focus on the errors (symptoms) caused by the system (disease). Don't have a formal strategy for improvement? Get in the game by taking these steps.

- Seek **employee input.** They're in the thick of the action, so every month ask each person, "What's working and what isn't?"
- Implore employees to **report all errors** as soon as they happen. Welcome mistakes with open arms. Finding and fixing errors prevents major headaches down the road.
- **Abandon any part of the system** as soon as a better way emerges.
- Set up a **hotline number.** Some employees aren't comfortable making even the smallest wave. Partner with a loss-prevention company to provide a hotline for employees to confidentially offer suggestions and point out problems.
- Establish **system-improvement committees** to hunt bottlenecks in your systems, from machines and materials to communication and training. Do whatever it takes to repair broken links.

- **Partner with a consultant** specializing in Lean Enterprise, Six Sigma, or some other highly regarded system-improvement specialist, if the expected benefits exceed the cost in time and money.

KEY POINTS

BUILDING A SYSTEMS-DISCIPLINED ORGANIZATION

➤ **Focus on strategic planning.** It's the cornerstone of a proactive, healthy organization. Don't let the process intimidate you. Strategic planning exploits your strengths and opportunities and diminishes your weaknesses and threats.

➤ **Execute in four steps.** Define expectations, then inspire, teach, and follow up. The execution solution helps employees avoid obstacles, or get back on track when they do trip up.

➤ **Methodically solve problems.** When an individual or department underperforms, don't blame, shame, panic, or pander. Cooperate and explore, don't fight and accuse. The right attitude and the right systems turn problem solving into no problem at all.

➤ **Manage your meetings.** Disorganized meetings waste time and drain energy. Productive meetings run on tight premeeting preparation and strict protocol.

➤ **Troubleshooting is a year-round sport.** Beyond high-concept theories like Total Quality Management, tell your people that their company is a work in progress. Dedicate yourself to continuous process improvement. Constantly scout the competition, abandon bad systems, establish internal hotlines, and consider partnering with consultants.

COMMUNICATING CLEARLY

Sending Static-Free Signals

Back in 1968, I graduated from Indiana University into the HR department of Shell Oil Company's Midwest regional headquarters in Chicago. At twenty-one years old, it was my job to ensure that proposed salary increases were commensurate with corporate policy. I threw myself into the fray with all the youthful, bullheaded passion of an idealistic college grad. I kicked up a storm, to put it mildly. After I had butted heads with department leaders for a week, my manager, Neal Pettit, was deluged with complaints about me.

Thank God Neal saw the uproar as a teachable moment. He asked me to tag along as he visited a few poodles I had turned into South Side pit bulls. Neal put on a diplomacy clinic. He started with a smile and some small talk, then eased into inquiring about the logic of the raises I had rejected. He listened intently and praised each supervisor's approach. But he didn't hesitate to scratch his head over a few things that didn't track for him. It was a humble, help-me-out-here approach (think Peter Falk in the old detective show *Columbo*). Neal patiently worked with each manager to explore options and find solutions. I was amazed at how effortlessly he patched up the relationships.

Neal taught me two simple but important lessons. First, it takes great communication skills to build and manage relationships. Second, every single thing you do requires building and managing relationships. It's the quality of your bonds that ultimately determine how well you communicate, and vice versa. Remember this four-word mantra: *Less ego, more empathy.*

Egotism and empathy are opposites. They repel each other like poles of magnets. The more you pour ego into your consciousness, the less room there is for empathy. But our culture rewards big egos a lot more than big empathy. If you could see the thought-bubbles floating through America's cartoonish executive suites, many would contain variations on, *The world revolves around me; my needs first.*

Neal taught me that people care not only about *what* is said but about *how* it's said. Years later, Scott McPhee, one of our top execs, learned the same lesson. One afternoon, Scott's colleague teared up as she confided to me that Scott's body language proved his disdain for her. She feared for her job. I called Scott in for a briefing. "When Tom explained it to me," Scott said, "I thought, *Wow, I've heard the same thing from my wife.*" That insight helped Scott understand the impression he left on people. He apologized to his colleague and repaired the damage.

If you're quarreling with colleagues, step back. Think of yourself as a complex communications network that processes the messages you receive and assembles the messages you send out. Are your lines open and clear, or is the signal distorted by static generated by, say, a giant ego? If it's the latter, get used to endless loops of miscommunication and misunderstanding.

CHAPTER 28

LISTEN UP

Practicing Active Listening

Hi, my name is Tom and I'm a talkaholic." That's right, if there were a support group for dialogue hogs, I would've been a charter member. I used to see every conversation as a race—first one to get their point across wins. But cutting off a conversation without considering what the other person can offer is like tearing up a lottery ticket before the winning number is announced.

It never occurred to me that I was a lousy listener. Heck, listening was like breathing—I never thought about it, I just did it. My Aha! moment came at C. J. Hegarty's "Active Listening" seminar in the mid-eighties. His theme: *Hearing is involuntary, but listening is an acquired skill.* When it dawned on me that listening involved more than noticing noise emitting from a mouth, my transition to enlightened entrepreneur picked up steam.

Lousy listening wastes precious resources and damages relationships. How can we discipline an employee if we don't listen—really listen—to her side of the story? How can we expect employees to nail deadlines if we don't listen to their questions and concerns?

In small businesses—where people wear multiple hats, chase deadlines, and move fast and talk even faster—listening better be a core competency. Imagine what can be lost or misinterpreted in a simple exchange between two people of different genders, ages, and socioeconomic and cultural backgrounds.

Five listening lessons:

1. Seek First to Understand Before Seeking to be Understood. These nine simple words, from the timeless prayer of St. Francis of Assisi, are powerful. Challenging myself to view things through another person's eyes expanded my powers of perception and deepened my connection to—and appreciation of—others. It was further proof that empathy trumps ego. Another benefit: The more you listen, the better informed you are when it's your turn to talk.

2. Be a Human Mirror. We expect colleagues to hang on our every word. Yet if we don't first listen to *them*—so we can lock onto their communication style and mirror it back to them—we might as well be speaking different languages. For instance, if you're brainstorming with a coworker who thoughtfully chooses every word, your brilliant idea might zip by her if you spew sentences at the speed of light. The same goes for decibel level; your pithy points may not register if you overwhelm her soft-spoken sensibilities with bluster.

3. Value the Speaker as Well as the Speech. It's easy for people to tell when their boss is listening *against* them instead of *to* them. A dead giveaway is the wall he throws up—leaning back in a chair and folding his arms across his chest. No matter what comes out of his mouth, all they're going to hear is, *I have nothing but contempt for you and your ideas. Stop wasting my time.* If this sounds like you, you won't be crowned Mr. Motivation anytime soon—people are certainly not going to share all their great ideas just to see them shot down. Conversely, a caring approach—a smile, leaning into the conversation, eye contact—lets employees know they're taken seriously.

The mind-set is *What's right with what she's saying and how can I learn from it?* rather than *What's wrong and how can I object to it?* A leader who actively listens sets the tone for the entire department or company; people he listens to will listen to their people more carefully, and so on down the line.

4. Hear the Unspoken. Subtle messages flow through facial expressions, body language, and tone of voice. That awareness came in handy during store visits when I queried customers about our service. I recall one typically over-polite Minnesotan who called the service "fine." But her steady foot-tapping and the restless way she flipped through her magazine told a different story. I pressed her. "Are you sure?" I asked. "Anything I can help you with?" She paused, then confessed her car was twenty minutes overdue. Information in hand, we addressed the problem.

5. Repeat What You Hear. Try not to ape the speaker, of course, but play back your interpretation of what you heard. Paraphrasing her message shows you listened carefully and gives you both a chance to clear up miscommunication. (Remember that one of our deepest desires is to be heard.) Skipping this step can set off a chain reaction of misunderstanding that culminates in dented feelings and awkward apologies.

Active listening is grounded in courtesy, empathy, and a desire for clarity at all costs. You don't have to agree with what you hear. But your attentiveness and attitude speak the unspoken: *I want to understand where you're coming from. Tell me how you see this.* Practiced conscientiously, active listening engenders trust, reduces errors, and encourages people to speak their mind.

The same dynamics apply to groups. Eric Randa left the company and returned four years later only to notice a distinct change around the conference table. "There had been a tendency for some executive-committee members, including Tom, to go for the jugular," recalled Eric. "It made people feel lousy and drove wedges between team members." Eric's right. Thankfully,

I wised up. I told the team that corrosive, vindictive behavior was no longer acceptable. I reminded them that our mission statement and operating values called for caring, respectful interactions. "Once Tom put a stop to that kind of behavior, things really turned around," Eric said. "Nobody dreaded meetings anymore. We all realized that challenging each other in a professional way would help us all grow."

CHAPTER 29

EXPRESS YOURSELF

Writing and Speaking Effectively

One day, Eric, our vice president of loss prevention, dropped off a three-page memo. I scanned it and called him back into my office. "Eric," I said, "this is a great memo, but I need you to condense it and make it simpler." In fact, I said, write every memo like it's for the president of a company, someone who has to read a hundred memos a day and doesn't have time to read two pages, let alone three. Eric did exactly that. At the next executive-committee meeting, I handed Eric's memo out and said I wanted all memos done in that format—short paragraphs, subheads, crisp writing, *and lots of bullet points.* "Tom called it the 'President Randa format' and everyone had a good laugh," Eric recalled.

For all the effort to keep it plain and simple, the near universal use of e-mail, instant messaging, and phone-texting tempts us to backslide into vagueness. Digital communication lends itself to shorthand and slang, with new abbreviations invented daily. To avoid confusion, write full sentences that err on the side of polite formality. Also, treat e-mail the way a driver approaches her car—don't use it if you're tired or tipsy, or you may steer your business into a ditch.

I have a low tolerance for sloppy verbal communication, too. The breaking point for me was a high-level team meeting where a key exec stated a "fact" that threatened to reverse an important decision we were about to make. I asked if she was 100 percent certain. "Absolutely," she replied. That wasn't the way I recalled the matter, so I asked her for supporting documentation. Sure enough, she had erred. Bad information creates chaos and sabotages team goals. Recognizing, however, that this exec was already embarrassed by her mistake, I reined in my frustration and stressed to the team that success hinged on airtight info. Effective immediately, I said, we need to be precise with our language and extraordinarily careful not to confuse "probably" or "pretty sure" with "absolutely." My executive's red face and my own exasperation were a small price to pay for purifying the process.

Stepping up a level of communication, the bully pulpit can spread the word fast. Seize every opportunity to address your troops. One well-crafted speech saves time and magnifies impact. For that matter, don't pass up outside engagements—speaking to community groups extends your company's goodwill (and brand). How to perform like a pro?

SETTING THE STAGE

Know your audience. Chat up the organizer (or, for in-house talks, the employee closest to the action). First, nail the facts: number of attendees, average age, gender breakdown. Next, ask three questions to gauge the attendees' state of mind: *Do they know who I am? Is attendance voluntary? How much do they know about the topic?* Finally, ask what's dominating watercooler chatter so you can slide into their rhythm.

Assemble the bones. Ask yourself three questions: *What's the goal of this talk? How can I take the audience from here to there? What could block their understanding or acceptance?* The answers will provide the perfect bulleted outline and a talk title that conveys your core message.

Personify your talk. Put your fingerprints on the content, especially if you're covering familiar territory. Spring off audience concerns to explain the connection between your words and their immediate future. Remember, the audience is consumed with one thing: What's in it for me?

Keep it conversational. Jot down key words on recipe cards to keep your train of thought on track. If you must write out the whole thing, say it out loud as you write, like you're telling a friend what's on your mind.

Polish the apple. Put away your notes for a day or two, then review them with fresh eyes. Look for ways to clarify points and trim fat. Does your opening clearly state your message? Does your kicker summarize your big points and link them to action steps?

Practice, practice, practice. Do a run-through with a colleague. Or, speak in front of an empty chair, a stand-in for the audience. Speak conversationally. Slow. When you're finished, do it again—and again and again and again, until it's second nature. (Cures for stage fright: Dale Carnegie courses and Toastmasters.)

Proof your intro. Find out who's introducing you and ask if you can see her remarks in advance. Check that the title of your talk is correct. Fix any errors and offer updated info.

Create a checklist. Detail everything you need: laptop, note cards, charts, handouts, Prozac. Using audiovisual equipment? Do a dry run to avoid game-day fumbles.

WAITING IN THE WINGS

Walk the room. Before anyone arrives, get a feel for the place. Practice your entrance and exit. Test the microphone. Ask someone to stand at the back of the room to confirm that your voice will carry. Locate the lights and power sockets. Make sure all systems are *go* (for PowerPoint presentations, position a laptop screen in front of you as you face the audience).

Think drink. Keep a bottle of water nearby. Periodic sips keep your voice strong. But don't overdo it—unless the talk is long enough for you to take a bathroom break.

Relax. Before stepping into the spotlight, breathe slowly and deeply for thirty seconds, preferably with your eyes closed. Slow, deliberate breathing calms your nerves and opens your mind.

Lift your gaze. Silently ask for guidance to find the best words to benefit your audience.

REAL-TIME REMINDERS

Don't hide behind the podium. It's a home base, not a planting pot. A wireless lavalier mic lets you roam among the audience.

Slow down. Novices can jabber at warp speed, making it hard for audiences to digest the message. Don't underestimate the value of a pause; few things grab an audience's attention quicker.

Be yourself. Talk with the audience, not at them. It may help to pretend you're chatting with close friends. Keep your head up. Establish eye contact. If you know your material well, believe that the words will come. Better to stumble occasionally—and come off as genuine—than robotically recite every point from a canned script. Key words on note cards or a PowerPoint presentation can help avoid losing a lot of eye contact.

SHOW TIME

Blast out of the gate. For some reason, audiences aren't always breathlessly anticipating your pearls of wisdom. Stomachs will growl. Dozers will daydream. Somebody will come fresh from a fight with her boss (or husband). Grab the room's attention, or its funny bone.

That first minute sets the tone. Do not slam that window of opportunity by droning on about how happy you are to be there, in Kansas City—I mean, Cleveland. And for the love of God, do not try to lower expectations by claiming to be a poor speaker, or that you're unprepared, or not feeling well. If you do, that splashing sound you'll hear will be your presentation falling into the toilet.

Give it your heart and soul. Infect your audience with your passion and enthusiasm. Only your very best will get the room buzzing.

Interact. Pepper your talk with questions to the group as a whole and to individual audience members by name: *What would you do if that happened, Sharon?* When appropriate, role-play with a volunteer—"showing" always trumps "telling."

Spin a yarn. Facts and figures get their attention. But a good story gets them thinking, feeling, and caring. Your audience will lap up every word when you tell them how getting booted from your first job saved your career. Or, how your top sales guy hurdled a roadblock to close the deal of the century. Messages delivered with inspirational stories are like mixing cod liver oil into a milkshake—it goes down easily and gets absorbed.

Call to action. Firing them up is pointless unless you demonstrate how to stoke the coals. Show how to translate your lessons into everyday actions that yield results.

Finish strong and on time. Save your best for last and leave 'em wanting more. I like to close with a favorite story that never fails to get a big laugh.

CHAPTER 30

COMMUNICATE EXPECTATIONS

Achieving Airtight Accountability

After you get the hang of it, straight talk opens a lot of opportunity. The law of diminishing dedication (chapter 15) holds that malaise develops when employees aren't challenged, inspired partners in their own fate. For most, purpose and enthusiasm have the shelf life of sushi. So I developed the four-step Ask/Tell Technique to get them to open up. It keeps managers' and employees' expectations in line so there are no surprises.

This is how it works:

Ask: "What are your expectations?" Know your team members' needs, desires, and expectations—for their job and their career. Do you know what your people value most? Is it making more money? A promotion? Meaningful work? Time off for family?

Relationships, personal and professional, break down if they're taken for granted, if we focus exclusively on our own needs. In business, this is called "turnover." Don't kid yourself, turnover is always about employees' unmet needs. Ask them what they need from you and from the organization, and then do what you can to give it to them.

Tell: "Here are my expectations." Do your people know exactly what's expected of them? If there's a chance you're not on the same page, don't wait till the end of the book. Get clear by committing your expectations (whether operating-plan-related or task-oriented) to paper and defining how you'll measure them. Then ask employees to sign off, literally or figuratively. This kind of detail prevents crossed wires and builds benchmarks by which to tally momentum.

Think that formally defining expectations is overkill? Just the opposite is true—it's liberating for people to know what's expected of them. Done with care, clarifying mutual expectations stokes initiative and leads to professional growth. It also sets the stage for a continual exchange of constructive feedback.

Ask: "How am I doing?" We're imperfect creatures. Daily brush fires can divert our attention and scorch our commitments. Checking in with colleagues who report to you brings us back. But be realistic. Don't expect employees to rattle off opinions when you ask how you've been doing as a leader. Some may respond without reservation. Others will hesitate even if they have a laundry list of gripes—unless they've noticed you're open to hearing honest feedback. Even then, you may have to resort to the Rule of Three Technique (ask three times, digging deeper each time, before you get honest answers). Or, try ASU—*Ask and Shut Up.* Just smile and look him in the eye until he expresses himself. People get an energy boost when they empty the buffer between what's on their mind and what's on their lips. It frees up psychic energy so they can focus on their work in a more positive, constructive way. Here is a typical exchange:

REQUEST ONE: Is there anything I could do differently to improve how things work around here?
RESPONSE: Uh, no, not really.
REQUEST TWO: I really value your opinion, Scott. You're telling me there's *nothing* I need to change?
RESPONSE: (*Pause*) No, everything's fine.
REQUEST THREE: (*Now get specific.*) C'mon, I bet you can name three things I'm doing right and three things I could do better.

RESPONSE: Well, yeah, I guess I could think of something. It's no big deal, but you always seem to have broccoli stuck in your teeth.

Tell: "Here's how you're doing." Use the cardinal rules of coaching:

- Mold, don't scold.
- A spoonful of sugar helps the criticism go down.
- Leave people feeling empowered, not embittered.

People are more likely to take corrective feedback to heart if it's imparted with care and—this is critical—accompanied by kudos. That's to say, shy away from striding up to an employee, brusquely pointing out an error, and warning it had better not happen again. Any short-term productivity gain will be offset by a steady decline into hostility. And please, never, ever reprimand anybody in front of her colleagues. Not only is it demeaning, it leaves employees seething. I don't care how busy or moody you are, it's inexcusable to disrespect people. Call it entrepreneurial karma, but if the day comes when you find yourself flailing away in the unforgiving grip of company quicksand, it's the dead weight of all your damaged relationships that will drag you, and your company, down.

The Ask/Tell Technique also helped me monitor how the people who reported to me were dealing with the people who reported to them. Every so often I asked my executive committee to list the names of everyone on their team. Then I asked them to grade each relationship based on four Ask/Tell questions.

1. How well do you understand her needs, desires, and expectations?
2. Do you think she perfectly understands what you expect of her?
3. Is she comfortable letting you know her likes and dislikes?
4. Are you giving her regular feedback?

For grades lower than A, I didn't even bother to ask why. My execs knew the drill. They busted out their planners and scheduled meetings with the people they needed to get to know better. Nobody knew his people better than Wayne Shimer. He was master of what I called the "inner-view," chatting up employees in the hall, during lunch, or before getting down to business around the conference table. It's nothing more complex than a series of simple inquiries: "What's up with your kids?" "How's your dad feeling?" After that, the four questions above go down a lot easier.

Wayne read his people like sports fans read box scores. "Full-time or part-time, sales or mechanic," Wayne said, "I want to know your name, whether you're married, got kids, pets, and anything else I could learn about you. I knew if somebody was ready to quit, and why, long before their manager did." Good inner-viewers don't just go through the motions. People knew I genuinely cared about them. "Tom always looked you straight in the eye and you could tell he was listening," said Brad Burley, a regional manager, "that he really did want to know. That was the key to Tom's success: caring." Point the Ask/Tell Technique at your subordinates or at external business partners. It's a key to motivating and keeping everyone's expectations clear and aboveboard.

CHAPTER 31

ASK FOR ADVICE

Soliciting Employee Ideas

Hoping to grab a preflight bite one night, I scanned the slim choices at an airport concession stand—chili-cheese dogs, chocolate muffins, ice cream sandwiches. Nothing remotely qualified as healthy. I suggested to the kid behind the counter that he urge the owner to add veggie burgers to the menu. His blank look morphed into a laugh. "Are you kidding?" he said. "The boss would never listen to me." That's a portrait of a boss taking a pass on success. Employees in constant contact with customers are like the waitstaff at a small-town diner. They know the inside scoop on just about everything.

Fresh ideas are the lifeblood of any organization, and it's often the non-managerial players on the front lines that come up with the biggest corkers. But woe to the employee who tells a seat-of-the-pants entrepreneur how to do things better. Those firms all have legends of The Transfer to Siberia. So problem-talk is just passed among peers rather than handed up to the boss (that's you). The cure? Keep the ideas flowing and the heart of your operations pumping with clear, convenient channels of employee communication. It reminds me of a line from poet Mark Van Doren:

Bring ideas in and entertain them royally,
for one of them may be the king.

Don't get so caught up in popping champagne corks that you overlook the occasional squashed grape. Every culture, no matter how enlightened, has its share of saboteurs lurking in the shadows—the incompetent employee, inappropriate Internet surfing, a weak link in the production chain. The longer you wait to root out the problem the more entrenched—and costlier—it becomes. The challenge is breaking the code of silence among employees, without wreaking havoc on morale and solidarity.

To excavate the gold of employee intelligence:

Forecast brainstorms for staff meetings. At meetings, I'd say, "Give me your RBIs" (Really Big Ideas). One by one, around the table we'd go. One person might propose a new policy or procedure. Another passed along an idea from a customer or vendor. Somebody else described a team member's innovation. The brainstorms were torrential, and livened up the place. If you try it, vary the format and occasionally provide incentives to keep the creative juices flowing. For the best RBI of the day, we often awarded a dinner certificate or small cash bonus.

Poll the people. Our annual culture/climate survey asked employees what they liked about our operation, what they thought we could do better, and what they would do if they ran the place. HR sorted the feedback by topic and presented summaries to the executive team. Some suggestions were good and others comically bad. Some were real *Eureka!* moments. The e-mail we sent to employees broke it all down: "Based on your recommendations, here are some things we'll be changing . . ." and "We won't be able to implement the following suggestions because . . ." We also surveyed the troops during our annual strategic planning process (chapter 23).

Query new recruits. New hires have the fresh eyes of a consultant, minus the enormous price tag. But get them before they've slid too deeply into the status quo. Tapping newbies for advice also makes them feel valued, which engages and motivates them. Even if their suggestion is a stinker, react positively so the feedback channel stays open.

One morning a new salesman in one of our suburban Minneapolis stores mentioned that he sensed a rift between the mechanics and sales staff. "The tire-mounters come across as pretty resentful," he said innocently, "like they think we've got a cushy job." Ten minutes later, when I met with the store manager, I asked how things were between the mechanics and the sales team. Reluctantly, he acknowledged some brewing tension. "Oh, really," I said. "How do you think we can fix that?" He and I brainstormed a few minutes and decided to call a huddle to find out what people were thinking. It was like a group therapy session. Grievances were aired and addressed and, what do you know, cooperation improved.

Quiz departing employees. Here's an overlooked resource. Denial and rationalization tell us we aren't losing much so we don't need to listen to deserters. These people have the dirt you want. Simply ask, "What do you think we need to change around here?" Take notes. A person packing up his office has little to lose and, typically, is only too happy to tell you what he thinks. Sometimes the grapes are sour but diplomatic follow-up questions can separate the sweet from the sour. For best results, have the soon-to-be-ex-employee talk to his boss *and,* separately, to his boss's boss.

Be prepared to hear things you don't want to hear, but need to. Employees who had given their notice occasionally said their manager had paid little attention to them, that they hadn't been given enough responsibility. I'd immediately remind my executive team that staying connected to our people was priority one. "Tom often said a little bit of attention, a little bit of love, goes a long way," said Wayne Shimer, a key VP. "But Tom wasn't realistic. When you have sixteen hundred employees scattered throughout ten states, all with different personalities and supervisors, some are going to slip through the cracks." Wayne may be right, but that didn't stop me from trying to caulk every last crack. Good employees are hard to find and costly to train.

When you reel in suggestions, criticisms, and company secrets, be sure to:

- Show appreciation no matter how surprised or upset you may be.
- Ask how the person would resolve the situation. People are more likely to back a solution they helped create.
- Keep it confidential. If it's impossible to conceal your source, make it clear to everyone that you sought out—and will continue to seek out—information to improve the organization and everyone in it.

Break these rules even once—by going ballistic, imposing unilateral solutions, or identifying your source of information—and your intel pipeline will run dry. Worse, resentful employees may retaliate against the whistle-blower or idea person.

CHAPTER 32

FACE-TO-FACE FEEDBACK

Delivering One-on-One Critiques

A good boss helps his people correct course and work through roadblocks. This is obvious, perhaps. But tricky in practice. Be careful to avoid coming off like Judge Judy, CEO. In other words, give feedback that's welcomed rather than dreaded. Take the time Brad Burley and I drove north a few hours to Duluth, Minnesota, to inspect a store. It took all of ten minutes to understand that the store manager was just skating by. I was more than a little disappointed, in both Brad and the manager.

Brad and I walked to a gas station across the street, grabbed something to drink, and planned the next move. "First," Brad said, "Tom looked me in the eye and said, 'You're too good to allow this to happen.' Then, before we covered what I needed to do, he talked through everything I was doing right." Before leaving, I made sure Brad was in the right frame of mind. "Hey," I said, "you *can* do better and you *will* do better, because you've shown me you can. Don't let this guy get away with it."

Hammering away at how Brad had screwed up would have left him wallowing in negativity, unable to think clearly and creatively. Today, Brad uses the same MO with his managers—and his family. "When I'm upset with my kids," Brad said, "the first thing I tell them is how great they are and how much I love them. Then I single out the specific behavior that isn't acceptable. I look them straight in the eye when I'm doing it. I learned that from Tom."

Delivering timely feedback to everyone who reports to you may sound overwhelming. That's why I broke it down into four manageable pieces. They help transform the process from grating and stressful to gratifying and successful.

Level One: Weekly meetings to review status of projects (chapter 32).
Level Two: Quarterly twenty-minute reviews (chapter 32).
Level Three: Biannual operating-plan reviews (chapter 23).
Level Four: Annual performance review (chapter 36).

Each level reminds people what's expected of them and redirects them when they stray off course. Mind you, this sort of structured feedback doesn't replace your obligation to give quick, floor-coaching critiques whenever opportunity knocks—both on what an employee is doing well and on what I call NTIs (need-to-improve areas). Don't worry about overkill. Artfully delivered repetition is the backbone of effective coaching. It can take months to change habits, so be that broken record. Human nature demands it.

THE SANDWICH TECHNIQUE

A lot of leaders are wildly inconsistent with reprimands. They manage to restrain themselves when someone makes a huge mistake, only to erupt later over a penny-ante infraction. That's when you see employees shaking their heads (or muttering, "What a psycho"). Well, that was me back in the old days. I didn't hesitate to light into employees who had messed up and hurt the company. But I'm embarrassed to say, I blew my fuse over lesser offenses just as often. It was the classic "React in haste, regret in leisure." Why the outbursts? Growing a company made me feel as if I were saddled in on a bucking bronco, holding on for dear life. Patience was a luxury I thought I could ill afford.

How do people feel after you've reprimanded or corrected them? Ready to take on the world? Or are they cursing you on a coffee break? In time, thankfully, I got a grip. Instead of breaking people's spirits, I learned to make them soar. How? By serving up the Sandwich Technique, which slides the meat of the matter between two slices of organic praise. Here's what it looks like:

A positive slice. Ask if she's open to hearing a concern. Look her in the eye; establish trust. Smile, pay her a bona fide compliment: "Sally, I can't tell you how much I appreciate the care you put into your work."

The meat of the matter. Ask a question or two about the issue at hand to get her take on it. Then, focus on *your* feelings and what *you* see rather than *her* behavior. Telling her she screwed up backs her into a corner, whereas telling her how you *feel* about what she did will produce a more cooperative response. People can't help but relate to how you feel; they *can't* relate to getting smacked upside the head. Remember, our egos are fragile. The second you sense a defense mechanism kicking in, clarify that you're talking about something she *did,* and that you're not evaluating her net human worth: "This has nothing to do with who you are, Sally. You know we value you and care about you very much. This is strictly a performance issue." If you can't resolve the issue on the spot, agree on when she'll get back to you with recommendations.

A positive slice. Sprinkle in a compliment: "Overall, Sally, you're doing a super job. Thanks for your efforts." This final step can mean the difference between leaving someone elated, deflated, or just plain mad.

Taste tip: Take a bite out of the Sandwich from time to time. If you habitually follow up praise with a helping of corrective criticism, people will develop a Pavlovian response, and wince whenever a compliment escapes your lips. (*Uh-oh, here comes the high heat!*) That's counterproductive any way you slice it. I can vouch that the praise-criticism-praise habit is hard to break; it was on my NTI list for years. Avoid that syndrome by throwing out plenty of stand-alone high fives and *way-to-go*'s.

TÊTE-À-TÊTE

"No excuses," I told Ron, a client who owns a midwestern manufacturing firm. "Meet one-on-one every single week with every employee who reports to you." His eyes bulged and he sputtered, "Where am I going to find that kind of time? I've got a business to run. Besides, I already talk to people dozens of times a day." One of the most common blunders leaders make, I told him, is believing that office drop-ins and hallway encounters are the same as regular one-on-ones. To cement my point, I rattled off some benefits of meeting face-to-face:

- Clears fog from mission-critical projects and speeds problem solving
- Straightens the paths of misguided workers
- Deepens loyalty by opening up your schedule
- Prevents brush fires and saves time and money by nipping mistakes in the bud
- Produces prepared employees geared toward weekly project check-ins
- Speeds the idea-to-implementation cycle
- Reduces interruptions by delaying minor questions until the next meeting
- Unearths deeper issues through open-ended questions and big-picture thinking

Hold the meetings weekly or every other week, and anywhere from thirty minutes to two hours, depending on the employee's responsibilities and performance. The agenda is simple and direct.

Check in. Kick things off by asking how things are in general. Every month, also ask how he *feels* about his job. Keeping tabs on an employee's state of mind yields clues about whether he's ready for a new challenge. Tapping into feelings also provides a window into wellness issues that could affect performance.

Review tasks. Look over his Goals Activity Report (opposite page). It tracks projects related to the operating plan, plus other tasks added throughout the year. Each goal is listed along with its status and three due dates—rough draft, final draft, implementation. Career and behavioral goals are also listed (often without due dates) to heighten their awareness. The Goals Activity Report is a reminder of the expectations you created together in the first two steps of the Ask/Tell Technique (chapter 30). This document—either as a hard copy or a spreadsheet attachment to an e-mail—should be available at your request.

The Goals Activity Report tracks all the moving pieces that propel your business. Wayne Shimer, who headed up a few divisions for us, swore by it. He also at times swore at it. "Everybody was plowing full speed ahead," Wayne said. "We all had 135 things on our plate. Then Tom would go on what we called 'a ride'—visiting some stores. I don't care what region he rode in, we had to have a meeting when he came back. He'd have a couple hundred more need-to-dos, all broken out by category. One by one, they'd hit somebody's Goals Activity Report for follow-up, and suddenly we'd all have 175 things to do."

After I sold Tires Plus, Wayne brought the report to his new company. "It absolutely works," Wayne said. "It shows me very quickly what each person needs from me and how they respond to priorities and timelines. Bottom line, it will make them better.

Keep hot projects moving. For each high-priority project, ask six questions (vary the phrasing to keep it fresh):

1. How do you see yourself proceeding?
2. What roadblocks do you anticipate?
3. How do you plan to skirt the roadblocks?
4. What do you need from others to be successful?
5. What do you need from me?
6. When do you expect to complete this? (Verify—and, if necessary, adjust—the three due dates listed.)

Tackle any project-specific NTIs (need-to-improve areas). Another deadline has come and gone? Zero in: "We've talked about the

GOALS ACTIVITY REPORT
Adam Lehrke

GOAL	STATUS/NEXT STEP	DUE DATE ROUGH DRAFT	DUE DATE FINAL	DUE DATE IMPLEMENTATION
Projects				
Annual rebid of vendors (Target = 5% savings)	*Ask Bob for specs*	JUL 12	JUL 24	AUG 8
Review Yellow Page ad, reposition ad prototype	*Ask rep about costs*	JUL 5	JUL 12	AUG 1
Develop and implement Frequent Customer program	*Meet with Chuck*	JUL 7	JUL 12	JUL 21
Do market labor rate assessment, revise rates accordingly	*Strategize with team*	AUG 3	AUG 28	SEP 15
Negotiate with credit card companies for TP credit card	*Start calling for bids*	JUL 5	JUL 10	JUL 24
Develop and execute annual advertising plan	*Call account rep*	JUL 6	JUL 17	AUG 14
Plan and implement Tent Sale or 72-hour sale promotion	*Meet with Joanie*	JUL 8	JUL 17	JUL 20
Ongoing Tasks	**Frequency**			
Role-playing selling (show tread depth, ask about ride quality)	*Tuesday and Friday p.m.*			
Place weekly newspaper ads (*Star Tribune, Pioneer Press*)	*Monday a.m.*			
Monitor and report on Guest Enthusiasm Index	*Thursday a.m.*			
Weekly night-school course at U of M	*Wednesdays*			

importance of meeting deadlines on urgent projects, and you've missed the last three. What's happening, Joe? You're generally on time." The gravity of your reaction depends on

- the project's importance
- the project's time frame
- how close the project is to completion
- the number of warnings you've given
- the employee's record for hitting deadlines
- the employee's level of denial

For each project, generously compliment any progress. If he's enthusiastic about a particular assignment, encourage his passion. Wrap up this section with a scoop of praise: "It's nice to have someone on the team who's so diligent, Joe. I'm impressed with how you collected and summarized everyone's input on the new campaign."

Throughout the process, avoid yes-no questions. Open-ended questions like "What do you suggest?" give his mind room to roam and nudge him along until he arrives at his own solutions. Answer any monosyllabic responses by digging deeper. If your question "How do you feel about this project?" is met with, "Good," ask, "Good in what way?"

Feedback. Ask for concerns. If he says nothing comes to mind, prompt him: "What would you do differently if you were in charge?" You may have to resort to prying him open with the Rule of Three Technique (chapter 30): "C'mon, I *know* you can give me three things you'd like to see different around here." It's the rare employee who wouldn't enjoy tweaking the status quo.

QUARTERLY REVIEWS

Most people are dying to know what the boss thinks of them. I certainly was when I worked for Shell Oil Company. So I started doing my people a favor. Every few months, as a weekly one-on-one wound down, I'd ask, "Are you open to a quick review of what I think is going well, and hearing a few ideas on how you can do even better?" Granted, not many people will say, "No, thanks," to the boss. But I rarely sensed resistance. In fact, eyes lit up virtually every time I offered a twenty-minute miniperformance review. The boss's critique generated some anxiety, sure, but they were eager to hear what I had to say.

I started by writing bullet points on everything the employee was doing well, and salted in some detailed anecdotes: "The way you reformatted the sales report is a big help, Charlene, and it's on my desk first thing Monday morning just like I asked. I can't tell you how much I appreciate you making that happen." I relied on memory, but also scanned my recent notes.

Next, I addressed NTIs in quick-hit summaries only, since they were ongoing coaching issues. Remember, putting NTIs squarely on the table won't be seen as going negative as long as they're presented fairly and offset by things the employee is doing right. But again, choose your words carefully. If she feels under attack, the tips you're trying to embed in her consciousness won't pierce her barriers of shame, guilt, and fear. There's a world of difference between "Boy, if you nail that, you'll be in superstar territory" and "Damn, you really screwed up. What the heck were you thinking?"

Tie a bow on the meeting by briefly putting it all into perspective: "Everyone's really happy you're on the team, Charlene. You always seem to find a way to do what needs to get done, and that's a rare quality. I'm confident you'll resolve those NTIs and continue to grow with us."

CHAPTER 33

FACE YOUR FLAWS

Soliciting Frank Feedback About Your Performance

t was 1994, but I can still see the shell-shocked faces of the other CEOs. In Quebec City for an American Management Association conference, I had just shared the results of my annual Roundtable Review (chapter 36), in which the six vice presidents (departmental head coaches) who reported to me anonymously listed their view of my strengths and NTIs. The NTIs were things like:

- You're very careful of your own time, but not always with others' time. You get too involved in microissues and often cause meetings to run late.
- In quizzing deeply for problems, you come up with small, insignificant things that waste people's time on follow-up.
- You try to come across as caring, but you're not always genuine. Example: You asked an employee in the presence of his spouse the name of another employee's spouse. The first spouse then heard you go up and say, "How's it going, Mary?" The two spouses got together and joked about it afterward.

The CEOs were aghast. "I can't believe you let your people talk to you like that," one said. "Hey," I said, "if they're thinking it, I wanna know. At least then I can deal with it." Was it painful to read the negative stuff? Absolutely. You always like to think that your employees admire you. Don't kid yourself. If you're committed to being the best leader you can be, you've gotta let Toto pull back the curtain and expose the flaws of the great and powerful Oz (that would be you).

Yes, the "Tell me how I'm doing" step in the Ask/Tell Technique (chapter 30) extracts some useful information, but there are some things employees just won't say to your face. Digging up the really good dirt requires three conditions:

Confidentiality. For my annual Roundtable Review, the people who reported directly to me wrote their critiques and submitted them to HR, who merged and purged the comments and presented them to me anonymously.

Receptivity. Solicited brutally frank feedback must be accepted with grace. Early on, I often heard comments like, "You say you're open to us giving you feedback, but you should see your facial contortions when we do; it's a kill-the-messenger look." They were right. My spoken gratitude was belied by body language that said I'd rather be walking barefoot over hot coals. I had to train myself to listen reflectively, rather than defensively. Your organization will be unhealthy unless your people can speak their minds (respectfully) without fear of reprisal.

Action. Confidential feedback has to be acted upon—quickly—lest your people quit bothering to drop comments into the pipeline. I basically had three responses: "That's valid and I'll try to do better," "I hear what you're saying, but this is why I do it like that," and "I totally disagree and here's why."

For the record, here's how I responded to the three NTIs listed at the beginning of this chapter:

- *You're very careful of your own time, but not always with others' time.* Valid. I am recommitting myself to be timelier and to better respect your time and schedules.
- *In quizzing deeply for problems, you come up with small, insignificant things that waste people's time on follow-up.* Some nitpicking probably occurs. I'll try to be better at backing off if there really isn't a problem. But I know that real problems tend to stay hidden from leaders and surface only after deep probing. It's a lesser of two evils thing, and the way I'm going about it is better than not finding the bigger problems. Therefore, I will continue to actively seek out challenges facing our team.
- *You try to come across as caring, but you're not always genuine.* With the number of employees and spouses we have, I'm not able to remember every name. I have asked, and will continue to ask, somebody's name when I don't know it. I will, however, make sure no one else hears me doing so. I would hope, though, that if someone does overhear me they would think, "What's wrong with asking someone's name?" It's better than avoiding somebody or not caring that I don't know their name. (In hindsight, I think I was a bit too prickly here. I see how people might find it insincere to ask someone's name from a third party and then approach that person like an old friend. I'm a bit more straightforward today and willing to tell someone that I'm embarrassed to say I can't remember his or her name.)

Occasionally I was hurt and frequently humbled by the criticisms. But I tried hard to take them to heart and change what needed changing in order to become a better person *and* a better businessman. Burying my head in the sand was not an option. As Winston Churchill said:

> *Criticism may not be agreeable, but it is*
> *necessary. It fulfills the same function as*
> *pain in the human body. It calls attention*
> *to an unhealthy state of things.*

KEY POINTS

COMMUNICATING CLEARLY

➤ **Less egotism, more empathy.** These four words enhance work relationships because they scrub the vagueness out of communication. Ultimately, success depends on how well you communicate your ideas and how well you receive feedback.

➤ **Acquire listening skills.** Conversations aren't competitions. They're successful only when both parties win. People feel free to express themselves when they feel appreciated, and nothing shows appreciation in the business world like the scarce resource of undivided attention.

➤ **Be concise.** Keep memos short, sweet, and readable. Use subheads, quick paragraphs, crisp writing, and lots of bullets. Be clear and precise in verbal communications, especially when the stakes are high.

➤ **Sharpen your public-speaking skills.** Speaking to groups internally and externally leverages the power of your words and spreads your company's goodwill. For best results, prepare a killer outline, maintain eye contact, use stories, and interact with your audience.

➤ **Ask and tell.** Superior communication is the secret to keeping your people engaged, informed, involved, and connected.

➤ **Cast a wide idea net.** Fresh ideas fuel organizations. Tap your people, especially if they have direct contact with customers. Make sure they communicate their rich intel through meetings, surveys, and informal chats.

➤ **Structure feedback.** Breaking operational reviews into varying formats and frequency (weekly, quarterly, biannual, annual) makes them manageable. Capitalize on opportunities to offer spontaneous praise and corrective critiques.

➤ **Schedule regular one-on-ones with employees.** Private meetings strengthen relationships, sharpen analytical skills, encourage attention to detail, prevent the brush fires that flare up in a seat-of-the-pants culture, and allow deeper issues to emerge. Occasionally add to regular one-on-ones a twenty-minute review to share your thoughts on what an employee's doing well and how she can do even better.

➤ **Request brutally honest feedback.** Painful as it may be, you're best off knowing what employees think of you. Keep it anonymous, accept it graciously, and offer a detailed response to show you take their input seriously.

COACHING OTHERS

Cheering and Steering, Not Domineering

*P*eople make decisions emotionally and justify them intellectually. That's the first thing I share with business owners who tell me they're baffled by their employees. "Man," they say, "I just don't know how to deal with these attitude problems." It's difficult for seat-of-the-pantsers to realize that it takes more than raw wits or charisma to inspire employees. People will not run through walls for you unless you forge some sort of emotional connection.

My dad preached the virtues of humility and empathy for as long as I can recall. Louis Schmidt, my dad's platoon officer in World War II, poignantly recalled his example. "When Bill came in as first lieutenant, he was a breath of fresh air because we got somebody who really cared about the guys," Louis said, pausing to compose himself, "more than he cared about himself." Never forget: People don't care how much you know until they know how much you care.

The late A. Bartlett Giamatti, former president of Yale University, called leadership "the assertion of a vision, not simply the exercise of a style." Allow me to build on that. Enlightened leadership demands the *vision* that inspires followers, the *values* that earn their trust, and the *vitality* to march them to the Promised Land. With all three in place, a leader is like a lantern that lights the road, beckoning, *Come, follow me.*

Burn four words into your consciousness: *Manage things, coach people.* Manage people impersonally and they'll resent being treated like cogs in a machine. Coach them individually and they'll flourish. It's your choice—your people will either get bitter or better. Is the shift from managing to coaching easy? Depends. If you're a hard-nosed boss—the kind of guy who's convinced that, dammit, a regular paycheck is all the motivation employees need—then the shift will be a grind. You'll only make things worse if you apply these principles without buying into them. People can smell insincerity.

Seat-of-the-pantsers typically come in two types: Type A, dictator, hard-driving, self-centered, gets results but leaves a trail of human debris; or Type B, doormat, passive, people pleaser, tolerates less productivity. Enlightened leaders—let's call them Type E—produce uncommon, sustainable results through firm, but caring, leadership coupled with "best practices." Type E leaders are ever alert and nurturing. They leverage intellectual, physical, emotional, and spiritual well-being to deepen connections and inspire achievement.

The good news is, Type E leadership is contagious. The more you act like an enlightened entrepreneur, the more likely you are to infect employees with the Type E bug. Symptoms include decisive movements, a sparkle in the eye, and a spring in the step. Enlightened entrepreneurs realize they're at the service of their employees. That means that personnel development ranks up there with locking up the store at night. When people sense you've got their best interests at heart, they'll rise to the occasion, if only to justify your confidence in them. Novelist Hermann Hesse illustrated the service-leadership connection in *Journey to the East,* in which a humble servant in a mystical organization is revealed to be the group's wise and exalted leader.

What kind of coaching are we talking about? A Lamaze childbirth coach comes to mind. Or a golf or tennis coach. Someone who stays close to the action, offers tips, and patiently corrects technique. Good coaches are incurable optimists. They view people as unique human beings, each capable of greatness. They ask insightful questions and nudge people to craft their own solutions.

With the right attitude, anyone can become a good coach. Soon after Scott McPhee joined us as regional manager, we relocated him to Iowa, our first market outside Minnesota. We had big expansion plans, and a lot was riding on our twelve stores down there. Trouble was, a lot of Iowans kept riding on tires they purchased somewhere else. Scott struggled. He had been a hard-driving regional manager elsewhere, but his my-way-or-the-highway style wasn't in sync with our culture.

Scott was a systematic guy, but a poor listener. "I didn't pay much attention to what others thought," he admitted. "I always got results by ordering employees around, but that starts to wear on people." He started noticing that the Iowa store managers were working against him. Moribund sales and high turnover signaled that it was time to pay a call on Scott. A stand-up guy, he admitted he was in over his head. Again, I urged him to coach rather than manage, to get to know his team and learn what made them tick. Ask more questions, I said. Partner with people instead of laying down the law. "I finally got it," Scott said. "I realized I had to transition from preaching to teaching. Instead of *telling* people what to do I had to *inspire* them to do it."

After our meeting, Scott scheduled weekly team meetings for his dozen managers, some of whom had to drive halfway across the state to attend. He kicked them off with news and small talk, then coached his managers on coaching each other. "Immediately, everything changed," Scott said, "beginning with the camaraderie. They started helping each other, sharing best practices, and putting their heads together on recruiting and staffing." In a few months, Scott was back on course. Sales shot up. Turnover dropped. Three years later, we promoted Scott to vice president of retail operations.

Good coaches also know that leading is more important than doing. Devote more of your time to inspiring and educating the people who report to you. Otherwise, they'll feel you're oblivious of their hard work. They'll think, *Why should I knock myself out? I'll just do enough to get by. Nobody will notice anyway.* That leads to—you guessed it—lots more work for you. I learned this lesson firsthand from observing one of my Shell Oil dealers in Chicago. Roger was one of the smartest guys I knew. He was also the most frenzied.

Every time I stopped by, he was working his tail off while his employees pretty much stood around and watched. I remember thinking, *There's a management lesson if ever I saw one.* I wasn't surprised a few years later when I heard Roger had gone out of business.

Sometime in the early 1990s, I started feeling uneasy about the titles we were using—"CEO," "vice president," "supervisor." Traditional titles just seemed to separate and isolate people. There had to be a better way to promote the ideals of employee development and teamwork. As I watched an Indiana University basketball game, it came to me: We're all coaches, when it comes down to it. After a lifetime in athletics, it seemed natural to transfer the coaching mentality from the court to the office.

Convinced I had discovered the Holy Grail of workplace harmony, I pitched a title overhaul to my executive committee. Instead of CEO, I would be Head Coach. Our CFO would become Chief Financial Coach. Store managers would be converted to Store Coaches. Employees would transform into teammates and customers into guests ("fans" seemed a bit presumptuous). I explained to the committee that the effects would be electrifying—our people would stride with purpose, relationships would blossom, morale would soar.

The executive-committee vote was unanimous. They hated it. Down to my last option, I turned benevolent dictator and overruled them (a rare move). The grumbling didn't last long. Within months, the new titles started to feel like cozy old sweaters. A year later, nearly everyone was on board and extolling the new names to visitors and recruits. (It was just more validation that most new ideas go through four stages: rejection, ridicule, acceptance, and "I knew it all along.")

As far as I know, we were the first company to adopt coaching titles; I'm still waiting to hear about the second. I'm not surprised no one has followed suit. It is a radical change. For the sake of clarity, some teammates carried two sets of business cards—one displaying their "coaching" title, chiefly for internal circulation, and the other displaying their traditional title, for select external contacts.

Coaching titles haven't caught on, but the coach approach has swept through Corporate America. Twelve years ago, when I met Lee Iacocca at Executive Focus International's annual forum in Orlando, Florida, I asked him if he'd consider consulting for Tires Plus. Sure, he said, and asked for my business card. He looked at it and saw "Head Coach" under my name. "What's wrong with you, boy," Lee said, "don't you want to be a CEO?" I said no, I liked being a Head Coach. He looked at me like I was crazy. I told the Iacocca story to Nike CEO Phil Knight when I ran into him in Indianapolis at a NCAA Final Four game. "You're right on and Lee was dead wrong," Phil said. "It's all about coaching." Titles can be powerful instruments of change. But what's more important is switching from a managerial mind-set to a coaching philosophy.

CHAPTER 34

DARE TO CARE

Kindness and Empathy Wins Hearts and Minds

Dee Hock, chairman emeritus of Visa International, penned some of the wisest words ever written about coaching. Essentially, he supersized the Golden Rule:

> *Make a careful list of all things done to you that*
> *you abhorred. Don't do them to others, ever.*
> *Make another list of things done for you that*
> *you loved. Do them for others, always.*

Reading between the lines, two of the qualities a good coach must have are kindness and empathy. I'm not talking namby-pamby pushover—an empathetic coach also wears steel-toe boots and holds people accountable. He's equal parts teacher and taskmaster, dreamer and disciplinarian. He's mastered the "hard" skills of leadership—from strategic planning to managing meetings. But it's unquestionably the "soft" people skills that help him win hearts and minds. To coach you have to lead with your heart, not your head. You need to treat people as human beings first, employees second.

Still not buying the kindness quotient? An undercurrent of mean-spiritedness, or even benign neglect, produces a culture of fear and loathing. Things gradually get worse because an ill-tempered boss is usually oblivious of his impact; for every snide comment he tosses off, a seething employee raids the supply cabinet to exact revenge.

All my life, till I was forty-two, I had scoffed at the notion that kindness and empathy were the bedrock on which leadership was built. My faith was in ruthless efficiency and the cold numbers of a balance sheet. Truth be told, I was so tough on people because I lived in constant fear that my business was on the brink of collapse. It never occurred to me that caring about my employees would lead to greater stability and higher profits.

When I started my own company, I vowed to take only the best elements of Shell Oil with me. But some of the bad ones tagged along, too. I was like the product of a dysfunctional home who rebels against his family's unhealthy behavior only to unwittingly perpetuate it in his own family. I soon found myself tilting at some of the same windmills that had exasperated me at Shell. I was a typical seat-of-the-pantser: an ego the size of Texas and more concerned about proving how great I was than about being a good leader. I didn't understand that I was managing too much with my head and not enough with my heart.

It wasn't until I shook off the trauma of personal and professional calamities that I realized that learning how to be a better leader begins with learning how to be a better human being. Turns out it's never too late to become an enlightened entrepreneur. The first step is a commitment to continual improvement. As French critic Charles DuBois wrote:

> *The important thing is this: to be able*
> *at any moment to sacrifice what we*
> *are for what we could become.*

Don't pay attention just when people are screwing up. Add some drive-by praising into the mix. When you notice what they're doing well, they'll listen to your constructive criticism in the right spirit. They'll think, *My boss is a good guy and he's always fair, so if he's got something to say, I wanna hear it.*

There simply wasn't anyone better than Dorie Thrall, my executive assistant at Tires Plus. She was smart, quick, and dogged. She knew when I needed help before I even knew I needed help. One morning I called her into my office. "Dorie," I said, "I just wanted to tell you I think you're doing a super job." For ten minutes I rambled on about her skills, dedication, and cheerfulness. Her efforts meant a great deal to me personally and professionally, and I told her so. The odd thing was that Dorie, a perfectly stoic Minnesotan, just sat there stone-faced, occasionally nodding her head. All in all she looked rather blasé, like I was giving a dish-by-dish of every meal I'd eaten for a week. *That's okay,* I remember thinking, *I just want to make sure she knows how much I appreciate her contributions.* Later, Dorie's teammates told a different story. One stopped me in the hallway. "What did you say to Dorie?" he said. "She's beaming from ear to ear and telling everyone about all the compliments you paid her."

Praise sticks when it's personal. Extend the life of your compliment by naming who the smooth moves helped, and why you appreciate it so much. Everyone likes to hear "Hey, nice work." But to leave a tattoolike impression, try, "Wow, heck of a job. That really helped the team and our customers. Thanks for caring enough to make it happen."

If nothing revs an employee's motivational motor like positive strokes, why are bosses so miserly about handing them out? A recent Gallup Poll showed that 65 percent of workers received zero recognition for good work *in the preceding year.* I've rounded up seven of the usual suspects:

1. Not Enough Time. Baloney. It takes ten seconds to light someone's afterburners. All you have to do is pay attention to what, and who, is right in front of you.

2. They're Just Meeting Expectations. Seat-of-the-pantsers think, *What, I'm supposed to congratulate people for doing what I pay them to do?* Yes, if you want those results to be repeated, if not eclipsed, and you don't want employees jumping ship. Don't wait till they climb over the rail. If someone goes from 70 percent of goal to 78 percent of goal, hey, that's reason to celebrate. One of my mottos is, *Even if you're not performing, you get kudos for trending!*

3. Too Touchy-Feely. The sad truth is that relating to an employee on anything resembling a personal level is foreign to a lot of leaders.

To give someone a genuine compliment, you've got to connect, one human being to another. No disrespect, but if something's preventing you from doing that, deal with it.

4. I Get No Reaction. As I discovered with Dorie, raving about an employee to her face can produce deadpan looks. But the praise still makes a huge impact. Tell a child how wonderful he is and he beams. That joy doesn't fade as we get older; many of us are just too reserved to express it in front of an authority figure.

5. Don't Wanna Overdo It. Ever hear of somebody overdosing on genuine compliments? Have *you* ever been fed up with too many? Our appetite for praise is bottomless. The operative word here is "genuine." Don't bother setting a weekly compliment quota; employees will see through it.

6. Gotta Hold On to Power. It takes a strong ego to lift up somebody else's. Too many seat-of-the-pantsers play one-upmanship with rules that assume *If I acknowledge how good you are, I mustn't be as good; but if I'm putting you down, I feel better about myself.* Zero-sum thinking like that is destructive.

7. I'll Pay for It. Let's get this straight. You think keeping your mouth shut will dissuade people from thinking better of themselves, and therefore less likely to ask for a raise? C'mon. Motivated people perform better. That leads to a healthier culture, higher morale, and higher profits. The real cost you pay is for *not* dishing out praise.

CHAPTER 35

SET CHALLENGING GOALS

Helping Employees to Grow Through Goal Setting

Without a little stretching, goal setting can be an exercise in futility. If a goal is too easy, productivity drops off as soon as you clear that first hurdle. Good coaches know just how far to push. Their people stay excited about scoring bull's-eyes because each target is freshly painted and placed just beyond their previous best effort. To turn employees into goal-getters:

Make it mutual. Wise and all-knowing leader that I was, I used to unilaterally assign goals to people. When no one was as excited as I was about reaching them, as was often the case, I was mystified. It finally dawned on me that employees get more fired up about their goals if they have a hand in shaping them. So, we sat down together, negotiated a bit, and arrived at something we both liked. But they walked away with *their* goals, not *my* goals. And that, to paraphrase Robert Frost, has made all the difference.

Don't overstretch. For too long, my philosophy toward employees was, "Shoot for the moon! Even if you come up short, you're still up there among the stars." What I was oblivious of was that this actually created a locomotive streaking toward a head-on collision with human nature. I assumed that people would just barrel along until they ran out of steam. But people don't work that way. A goal that's too far out of reach is a *demotivator*. Discouraged employees think, *What's the point of even trying? I could work 24/7 and still come up light-years short.* That hopelessness is contagious, and team morale inevitably nose-dives.

The solution? Either scale back the goal or help your employee put it into perspective. Stretch goals don't necessarily need to be hit to serve a purpose. Instead of focusing solely on the numerical target (doubling sales or slicing three months off time-to-market), shift some attention to the *process* you're trying to stimulate. When people came up short, I told them not to worry—*if* they were following our system and working hard. Whatever the outcome, stretch goals help people realize they are infinitely capable of improvement.

When it comes to motivating employees, it's not always your job to do the heavy lifting. Ask team members to name three ways they could improve their performance. (Vary the question to avoid stale responses.) As you get to know everyone's strengths, capabilities, and mentality, it's easier to inspire them. Remember, people do things for their reasons, not yours. Learn what they want, then help them get it.

CHAPTER 36

THE ANNUAL REVIEW

Turning the Review into a Coaching Session

One day two decades ago, I was sitting at my desk, flipping through an employee's annual review and growing more frustrated by the minute. I remember thinking, *Man, what a waste of time. There's gotta be a better way to do this.* My compliance-conscious HR people had insisted I use the same tired performance review form that had been around since the Industrial Revolution: Ask generic questions, circle "meets expectations" or "exceeds expectations," drop in the employee's file.

I recalled the words of W. Edwards Deming, the father of Total Quality Management. He said the standard review "nourishes short-term performance, annihilates long-term planning, builds fear, demolishes teamwork, nourishes rivalry, and leaves people bitter." No wonder so many entrepreneurs feel like going on vacation come review time. Sitting at my desk, I thought, *These multiple-choice questions are pointless. What should I really discover about employees at review time?* I jotted down four questions:

1. What's he done in the past year versus what he said he would do?
2. What's he doing well that I can reinforce?

3. What could he do better, and how can we help him?
4. Where does he want his career to go, and how can we help?

The best snapshot of this, I figured, would require observations from four angles: the employee's, his subordinates' (if applicable), his peers', and mine. So I sketched out a Teammate Review Form. The employee under review fills out a form himself, and asks five or six subordinates and five or six peers (all of my choosing) to do the same. The employee's form also asks him to list his career goals. The anonymous forms get submitted to HR, which merges and purges the responses and compiles separate results for peers and subordinates. Raw feedback like this packs a powerful punch. Sure, people respect the boss's comments, but nothing sinks in like a written self-appraisal and the straight scoop from subordinates and peers.

Armed with this no-holds-barred critique, I'd sit down with the employee and go over his Goals Activity Report and his individual operating plan (annual goals derived from the company's strategic plan). The meeting shaped up like this:

Review results. We'd briefly check the status of his operating-plan goals and other high-priority objectives that he was assigned during the year. This was largely an overview, since I'd been monitoring his progress during our weekly one-on-ones (chapter 32).

Assess strengths and developmental needs. First, I'd ask the employee to read me the positive attributes he listed in his self-appraisal. I'd endorse his assessment, then share his subordinates' laudatory observations: "Okay, Joe, here's what your team members had to say. Four of them said you're really caring; three say you're running tighter meetings . . ." Next came favorable feedback from his peers: "Wow, a couple of your peers also noticed you've been more empathetic. You must be putting extra effort into that. Way to go." Then it was my turn. I'd affirm everyone else's positive remarks and compliment him on anything else I noticed over the past year. (Although I have a pretty good memory, I'd also rely on the reminder notes I dropped into his file throughout the year.)

Next, it was time to move on to NTIs (need-to-improve areas). I'd

TEAMMATE COMMENTS
2005 Roundtable Review

Feedback for _____

I would appreciate feedback on what you perceive I'm doing well. I'd also like suggestions for how I can improve my performance and further my development.

Strengths:

_____
_____
_____
_____
_____
_____

NTIs ("Needs To Improve" areas):

_____
_____
_____
_____
_____
_____

Teammate Review Form

say, "Now, let's review everyone's tips, including your own, for how you can perform even better." As he read aloud his own suggestions, I'd acknowledge each one with a nod or comment. After reviewing what his subordinates and peers had written, I'd share my critique. Then we'd develop action plans to fix what we agreed was broken. If he had a temper, he might enroll in an anger-management class. If he was exceeding payroll projections, I'd get the CFO to mentor him. For broader NTIs—"Always running late," for instance—we'd add to his Goals Activity Report his desire to arrive to appointments five minutes early; that way I could monitor his progress via our weekly one-on-ones. One more check-and-balance move: I'd note the goal in the section of the performance review called "Bring Up at Next Annual Review." (I always prepped by studying the employee's previous annual reviews.)

The best employees were realistic about the review and used it to their advantage. "All that honest feedback taught me a lot about myself," said Hank, a key exec. "But if I had ten or twelve things that needed improving, I was never crazy enough to think I could fix all of them. I'd pick out the top five and work on those for the year." Hank paid particular attention to the multiple complaints and ignored the one-offs. "Maybe you ticked somebody off and it was payback time," he said. "Welcome to the world of management."

After wrapping up the NTIs, I'd recap and affirm what was going well: "Overall, Joe, you're doing a super job. You've got a great outlook, a superior work ethic, and you interact well with your people. I'm impressed with your determination to get on top of the challenges we discussed, like keeping your temper in check, clamping down on payroll expenses, and getting more disciplined."

Look to the future. I'd ask him to read me his self-appraisal's career goals, both two and five years out. If his abilities matched his ambitions, I'd help him determine the action steps that would take him from daydreaming to day-doing. If he wanted to nab a promotion, I'd suggest a seminar or mentor, which he'd duly record in his Goals Activity Report. Finally, I'd congratulate him and thank him for his efforts.

Brad Burley credits the Roundtable Review for his promotions. "I was very comfortable expressing my career goals to my supervisor," Brad said. "Out of those discussions, I went from being a store manager to being a wholesale sales manager to being a regional manager. That kind of upward mobility was built into our system."

The Roundtable Review is a potent developmental tool. So I got upset when a sales associate at our Milwaukee store told me he hadn't had a review in two years. I apologized and told the store manager and regional manager who were there with me to do his review before the week was out. At the next executive-committee meeting, I brought up the incident and said lapses like that were intolerable. I asked for a monthly listing of every employee whose Roundtable Review was thirty days or more past due. The company-wide memo issued the next day said managers violating our review policy could expect to answer not only to their boss, but also in person to the executive committee. End of problem.

CHAPTER 37

REWARD RESULTS

Matching Incentives to Outcomes

Like all entrepreneurs who pour every last dime into their company, my cofounder, Don, and I got nervous whenever business hit the skids. What made me really nervous early on, though, was when nobody else was nervous. *No wonder there's no urgency,* I remember thinking. *Everybody else is on straight salary. They don't have an incentive to make us more profitable. Yet if revenues dry up, Don and I don't get paid.*

What was wrong with this picture? Seeing the flaw changed everything. A couple months later, we installed an incentive-based compensation plan. It took awhile to coach everybody through it, but we tied a portion of most every employee's salary to individual, team, and organizational performance. Suddenly, a gust of wind hit our sails. Slackers were exposed and cut loose. Stars netted big bonuses. Productivity soared.

Yet it wasn't all about money. "Fat paycheck" barely cracks the top ten in employee motivation surveys. Consistently topping the list are intangibles like "challenging and interesting work," "involvement in decision making," "feeling respected and valued," "the ability to make a contribution." Salary and vacation time are closer to the bottom, believe it or not. Wanna know what seat-of-the-pantsers call motivators? Turn that list upside down.

By my lights, compensation lures employees more than surveys suggest and less than employers would like to think. Sacks full of cash might make people stick around, but they aren't necessarily going to make happy campers. Likewise, stimulating work at below-market wages might produce quality for a while, but top performers eventually follow the money. The best results come from providing opportunities to flourish in an enlightened environment where extra effort equals extra pay.

Bonuses are a good way to tie it all together. I'd set a bonus target of around 30 percent above a nonadministrative employee's base salary. That meant she'd get paid below market value if she failed to reach any goals, above market value if she achieved half, and significantly more if she hit all of them.

The X-factor here is human nature. Motivational motors sputter and stall, so you've gotta get inside people's heads if you hope to match incentives to outcomes. Business writer Steven Kerr explored this dynamic in his classic essay, "On the Folly of Rewarding A While Hoping for B," which appeared in the esoteric *Academy of Management Journal.* "Managers who complain about lack of motivation in their workers," Kerr wrote, "might do well to consider the possibility that the reward systems they have installed are paying off for behavior other than what they are seeking." A few institutional follies:

- We hope for teamwork and collaboration, yet reward only individual effort.
- We hope for innovation and risk taking, yet reward the errorless status quo.
- We hope for long-term strategic thinking, yet reward quarterly earnings.

They sound like obvious and curable maladies until you realize how deeply they're ingrained in the business world. After reading Kerr, whenever I saw something that just didn't seem right, I asked myself, *What behavior are we really rewarding?* This led me to create the "farm system" to reward store managers for developing assistant managers (chapter 16). Without the farm system, many of our efforts to trumpet teamwork rang hollow. Rhetoric must be backed up by reward. It's folly to tie a store manager's bonus to his team's performance, and then expect him to tell us when his assistant manager was ready for promotion. The first time he sees one of his protégés whisked off to manage someplace else will be the last. He'll keep the next little secret weapon to himself.

Human nature is a powerful force that must be reckoned with. Before launching a new initiative, shut your office door and take a few minutes to consider its real-world consequences. Close your eyes. Slip on the shoes of an employee. Step by empathetic step, walk through—and work through—your own gut reaction to the new incentives. Ask yourself, *If I were on the receiving end of this policy, how would it change the way I do things?* Remember, employees see through slick packaging to what management truly values. It's pretty simple, really. They watch what raises the boss's eyebrows. If you don't notice promptness, they're going to be late. If you focus on promptness and ignore quality, you'll have an office full of punctual mediocrity.

One last thought on incentive. Ask yourself, *Would I work as hard if I didn't have a piece of the action?* Where appropriate, we let key execs invest in the company. The payback was phenomenal. "My commitment and loyalty were heightened when I became a shareholder," said Jim Pascale, who headed up our franchise operations. Jim's equity spurred a no-limits attitude. "It made me care about every aspect, not just the division I was running," Jim said. "I was willing to help everybody and work more cooperatively to do whatever had to be done."

CHAPTER 38

GOOD-BYE AND GOOD LUCK

Freeing Up the Future of Underachievers

In the early days, I was so doggedly loyal that I terminated people only for serious underperformance or egregious offenses. It was a major shift to realize that welfare management—failing to hold people accountable and allowing the wrong people to stay in key positions—hurts everyone. It took years to learn to be both compassionate and tough. Once I balanced my personal resolutions with my professional duty, the termination process took on a life of its own. In fact, it often culminated with an underachieving employee offering to terminate himself, and there was almost always a sense of relief.

Take one of my former top execs. A nice guy, he had been with us for years but repeatedly failed to provide accurate, timely reporting on critical issues. After one too many broken promises, I called him into my office. I asked how important he thought it was to consistently produce these reports. He agreed it was essential. He also acknowledged that we had established mutually defined objectives and that he had consistently fallen short of the mark. I then asked, "What do you think should happen here?" Crestfallen but with honor intact, he replied, "I think I should probably leave." I hesitated for a moment,

225

to acknowledge how difficult this was for him. "Yes," I said, "I think you're right. Congratulations for that awareness. I really appreciate everything you've done for this company, and we'll do everything we can to make this a smooth transition." Visibly relieved, he left to type his resignation letter. We supported him until he found another job.

Deciding whether to free up someone's future demands a detached viewpoint. Detachment does not imply callousness. It simply means caring deeply, but from an objective place. Ask yourself, *Does this person have what it takes to get the job done?* Hopefully, you're now better equipped to answer that question. Personnel pioneer Robert Half had a nice way of putting it:

> *There's something more scarce than ability;*
> *it's the ability to recognize ability.*

KEY POINTS

COACHING OTHERS

➤ **Aspire to Type E (Enlightened) leadership.** People make decisions emotionally and justify them intellectually. People will run through walls for you once you've forged bonds. Type E leaders achieve sustainable results through firm, but caring, leadership.

➤ **Manage things, coach people.** See each person as a unique human being capable of greatness. Become a steady stream of constructive feedback. Ask insightful questions and nudge people to craft their own solutions. Coaching is the best way to maximize the potential of everyone in your organization.

➤ **Care about your people.** Yes, business leaders need to master "hard" skills like strategic planning and meeting management. But don't forget that kindness and empathy are bedrock values of enlightened leadership. Caring for the well-being of your employees has a big impact on profits.

➤ **Pour on the praise.** Sincere words of praise are necessities, not luxuries. They inspire confidence, shore up self-esteem, and reinforce good habits. People will go the extra mile when you start tossing out drive-by praising.

➤ **Cocreate challenging (not impossible) goals.** Goal setting is part art and part science. On one hand, it's hard to squeeze motivation out of an easy goal. On the other, a goal that's out of reach can demotivate. Avoid either extreme by involving people in the process.

➤ **Exploit performance reviews.** Transform this annual rite into a real-world educational tool. Toss the generic forms in favor of an interactive process that reinforces success, corrects stumbles, and advances career and personal goals.

➤ **Match incentives to outcomes.** Examine your reward system when you find yourself wondering why you have listless employees. Ask yourself, *What behaviors are we really encouraging?* You may be unwittingly rewarding the wrong kind of conduct.

➤ **Avoid welfare management.** The drawbacks to loyalty reveal themselves when you hold on to underperformers who're pulling everyone else down. Be compassionate and tough, ask good questions, and people will often terminate themselves. Unless fired for cause, support departing employees and help them in their transition.

EDUCATING EMPLOYEES

Riding Employee Development to the Top

Some years ago, a junior IBM executive lost the company $10 million when a deal blew up. Shortly afterward, CEO Tom Watson Sr. called the young man into his office. When the contrite exec said, "I guess you want my resignation," Watson replied, "You can't be serious, son. We've just spent $10 million educating you." Elementary, my dear Watson. Whether it's Big Blue or a business of two, PR&D (people research and development) should be a big-ticket item on any budget.

Hard-line fiscal hawks may squawk, but the yields on human-capital upgrades are better than on most other capital expenses. It's cause and effect. Educated employees are more likely to visualize a bright future, and to create and execute a plan to get there.

Our competition always lagged a few steps behind. Scrambling to catch up, our seat-of-the-pants rivals imitated everything we did, from store design to our commercials. They even swiped our phone greeting. What they couldn't copy was our people and culture, a proprietary blend of personalities and values. Whether you're teaching an employee to manage payroll or coaching him to get organized, you're doing more than shoveling information into his brain. You're equipping him with the wisdom and skills to meet your team's needs. That adds up to profitable days and restful nights.

IDENTIFYING ROOKIES, PROS, AND FALLEN STARS

Enlightened entrepreneurs take into account the natural four-stage process of learning and unlearning that governs most people's career arc. As Alvin Toffler wrote, "The illiterate of the 21st century will not be those who cannot read and write, but those who cannot learn, unlearn, and relearn." Here's my spin:

Conscious incompetent. Out of the gate, your newbie is perfectly aware he doesn't know what he needs to know to do the job well. Nevertheless, he's determined to succeed. The excitement of a new challenge propels him to study systems, ask questions, listen hard, and follow even the tiniest rule.

Unconscious competent. This is learning's sweet spot. He's sharpened his skills and is starting to shine. Yet he's still humble, and eager to master every challenge that comes along. He sees with "the beginner's mind," as Japanese Zen priest Shunryu Suzuki-roshi calls it, a mind fertile for limitless learning and growth.

Conscious competent. He's darn good and he knows it. Coaches dream of a team full of players at this stage—confident and capable, passionate and productive, a skilled professional. But beware. Once he scales the hill of success, it's painfully easy to tumble down the other side, like Sisyphus and his rock. Confidence can rot into arrogance. Now, corners are tempting to cut. *Sure, I'll try that* morphs into *Been there, done that.* A good coach recognizes the signs and issues a wake-up call. Some of your employees will respond; the others will hit the snooze button and drift into the next stage.

Unconscious incompetent. It's the twilight of his career, if he's not careful. He no longer knows what he needs to know in order to keep pace. The golden boy's glitter has faded, but he's too busy taking long lunches and admiring old press clips to notice. He's flying by the seat of his pants straight into turbulence—shifting trends, technological advances, competitive pressures—but he's on autopilot. A good coach knows that it takes some jolting to get him back to stage one, pressing *restart*. If he's too proud to take a few steps back, well, I hope he's packed a parachute.

Sometimes an involuntary plunge is precisely what a former star performer needs to break his sense of entitlement. After years as one of our top store managers, Warren was neglecting the basics. His store's revenue and morale were tanking. Motivation didn't work. Probation didn't work. After eighteen months, concerned about the message we were sending to other employees, we were forced to let him go. A few years later, Warren called and offered a heartfelt mea culpa. He said he had matured and asked for another shot. After two months of retraining, he roared back and reclaimed his star status.

Warren's comeback illustrates the value of customized coaching. A seat-of-the-pants leader acts impulsively without seeing employees as individuals. He sometimes reaches for motivation when he should grab education. Sure, an inspired employee will try to leap over a moat of alligators—but it's safer for everyone if you teach him how to lower the drawbridge. The following rules may have a whiff of Management 101, but seat-of-the-pantsers violate them like speed limits.

- If you want something done, and know somebody who wants to do it and knows how to do it—Delegate.

- If somebody knows how to do it but doesn't want to do it—Motivate.

- If somebody wants to do it but doesn't know how to do it—Educate.

- If somebody doesn't want to do it, doesn't know how to do it, and motivation and education haven't worked—Terminate.

	KNOWS HOW	DOESN'T KNOW HOW
WANTS TO	Delegate (who to)	Educate (how to)
DOESN'T WANT TO	Motivate (why to)	Terminate (show the door to)

CHAPTER 39

ON-THE-JOB LEARNING

Building Your Educational Infrastructure

The employee-education equation is Zen simple: *more input = more output*. Input education and your people will output more productivity. You're the conduit: Share what you know about building a business. If you keep it to yourself, you're the one who's a roadblock, perpetually frustrated that nobody else "gets it." The same goes for sharing best practices. If one department or store builds a better mousetrap, see that it's replicated throughout your company.

Employee education stretches beyond work-related subjects. The best education is multidisciplinary, reaching across all of life's artificial boundaries. Well-rounded employees with mature, sophisticated viewpoints are more likely to become happy masters of their craft. "Focus on education had a lot to do with our low turnover," noted Jim Pascale, our franchise operations veep. "The more educated you are, the more productive and fulfilled you are.

The building blocks of employee education are:

Training. Consuming eight thousand square feet in our suburban Minneapolis headquarters, Tires Plus University included classrooms, an auditorium, and a virtual store complete with showroom and service bays. (In-house universities are expensive, but ours paid for itself in no time.) We enrolled new employees in weeklong courses with three primary objectives. First, TPU, as we called it, taught standardization—indispensable to an explosive outfit with employees from Milwaukee to Denver. Second, TPU made store responsibilities second nature for new hires, so they hit the ground running at their first store. Third, TPU taught product knowledge. Nobody in the tire industry knew their "black gold" like our staff. With reassurance and a smile, they provided customers with manufacturer specs—as well as value and safety metrics—for every brand.

TPU's Accelerated Management program put select employees on the fast track, a must for a growing company. "Eventually," said Chris Koepsell, TPU's dean, "we reduced the training timeline from six to twelve months down to three months." The approach was simple— identify the skills necessary for the position, identify an employee's skills, train to the gap.

The formula also applies to bosses, especially the entrepreneurial variety. Most people start a business because it allows them to make a living doing something they love. Unlike me, some of my car-loving competitors paid more attention to brakes and oil pans than budgets and operating plans. Every minute under the hood was another minute they weren't sharpening their leadership skills. (By all means, tinker away if staying comfortably small is your game plan.) The sad truth is, if a restaurateur is more passionate about her dishes than improving her business skills, she'll gradually become overwhelmed by the daily demands of a growing business. The inevitable frustration that follows may crush the food passion that led her into business in the first place.

Motivational speakers. Familiarity breeds boredom. A new face in the office complements your in-house experts. Mike Norman, a franchisee for Dale Carnegie Training, lit a fire under a hundred of our regional and store managers during a half-day leadership workshop. "At the time, we needed to reinvent ourselves and quit relying so much on internal leaders to educate and motivate employees," said Chris Koepsell. I always looked to the horizon for fascinating specialists who could speak on anything from business trends to psychology. Our roster of memorable speakers ran the gamut from basketball firebrand Bobby Knight to mind-body author Deepak Chopra. Chalk it up to human nature, but when an outside speaker says something, chances are it's going to be heard and valued more. But don't just hand over the agenda. Before Mike Norman took the stage, we made sure his message jibed with our mission, vision, and values.

Seminars. Send employees to workshops that fit their positions—and don't neglect yourself. I took notes and collected handouts at numerous classes, conventions, and seminars so I could re-present the content to our management team.

Books. I periodically asked my executive team to read a business or personal-growth book. I'd assign everyone a chapter or two to summarize at an upcoming meeting. The reaction was predictable—nobody liked homework, but everybody liked having done it. "I have a belated appreciation for Tom's emphasis on downloading information about successful people and companies," said Dave Wilhelmi, vice president of marketing. "I found myself reading more books at Tires Plus than I ever did in school. It was like getting an additional education while going to work every day."

Mentors. Mentoring is a terrific way a business owner can leverage one employee's strengths to educate another. Mentors and mentees typically trade phone calls and regularly get together for lunch. If the right internal match doesn't exist, go outside the company. Eric Randa, our vice president of loss prevention, trained under Gary Kasper more than twenty years ago at Montgomery Ward. Later, when we hired Eric to start up our loss-prevention program, he often called Gary to ask him how he'd handle a particular challenge. "It's always good to talk to somebody who's been there," Eric said, "rather than try to reinvent the wheel."

Tuition assistance. In the early days, Steve Varner was a wholesale rep eager for a fresh challenge. We obliged with an assignment to the collections department, followed by a bump up to credit manager that required him to squeeze people for money. Figuring there was more to the job, Steve signed up for a credit-and-financial-management course at the University of Minnesota. We were thrilled, and paid half of Steve's tuition for every class in which he earned a B or better. "If I hadn't gone back to school," Steve said, "they would've eventually replaced me with somebody from the outside." He's right. Our rapid growth demanded that Steve know everything from calculating a customer's credit risk to interpreting antitrust and collection laws. It was a classic win-win. Steve's bad-debt ratio was well below industry benchmarks, and his stewardship played a key role in the growth of our wholesale division.

Encourage your people to advance their education however it fits into their busy lives. It's dangerous to assume they already have what it takes to play in the big leagues. Night and weekend courses make an immediate impact. Web-based distance learning makes formal education more convenient than ever.

CHAPTER 40

DELEGATE OR DIE

Deputizing Your Staff Multiplies Your Impact

O ver-delegation is in the eye of the delegator. One of my key execs listed "delegates too much" as a weakness on his annual review. His staff disagreed—70 percent said he didn't delegate enough. My advice on delegating can be summed up in three words: Let 'er rip! It develops employees like nothing else can. Hand over anything your people can do

- better than you
- quicker than you
- at less cost than you
- that will add to their development
- that will free you for more important pursuits

Under-delegation is rampant. Micromanagers, take note. Many seat-of-the-pantsers wear their resistance to parceling out tasks like a badge of honor. Others conceal it behind a wall of bravado. There are myriad excuses for under-delegating. There's the *I-can-do-it-better-myself syndrome,* which, even if it's true, doesn't change the fact that your time would be better spent elsewhere. There's the classic *I-can-save-time-doing-it-myself syndrome*. Sure, it might take awhile to train someone to do a repetitive task, but once it's learned you're home free. Do the math—delegating just one additional assignment each week to seven people who report to you crosses thirty assignments off your to-do list every month. Another malady is the *Somebody-else-might-make-a-mistake syndrome*. Mistakes *will* be made, but that's exactly how people develop the experience needed to free you up for more meaningful activities.

Other conditions that cause under-delegation include the *Fear-of-giving-the-wrong-impression syndrome,* marked by concern that you'll appear to be carrying less than your own weight. In fact, respect deepens when you place your trust in others and focus on the big picture. There's also the *I-feel-threatened syndrome*—fear of being shown up by a subordinate. That leads to a mediocrity mind-set and an idle, cynical staff whose poor performance reflects poorly on you. Last, there's the *I-might-lose-control syndrome*. Hey, no problem, people love working for a control freak in an office gulag.

Good leaders occasionally use overt nondelegation to emphasize a point. Take the Monday morning Eric Randa, our loss-prevention czar, and Wayne Shimer, head of recruiting and retention, our retail operation's V.P. at the time, stopped by a Wisconsin Tires Plus store. They walked past soda cans and other weekend detritus spotting the lawn on their way inside only to discover the store manager and two associates standing around. Now, understand that we viewed cleanliness as next to godliness, which set us apart in an industry synonymous with "grease monkey" and "industrial waste." Wayne walked back outside and, for all to see, picked up the trash. "You never saw Wayne have to pick up trash at that store again," Eric recalled.

Nobody ever accused me of under-delegating. "Tom was a dedicated delegator," Wayne recalled. "He forced me to be better by getting me to do things I didn't think I could do. The downside was that Tom was so strong at it he would sometimes over-delegate. His logic was that he never knew how far he could challenge you to find your end point, and Tom wanted to find that end point. If your optimum capacity was 98, he wanted you at 97.9."

I do tend to overload people. But that's so they learn to unload lesser priorities. But there's a fine line. You have to trust that people will yell "Uncle!" Back in chapter 32, Wayne mentioned the time he had 135 items on his Goals Activity Report. "I just became adept at figuring out what Tom really wanted done," Wayne said. "What were the $10 items, what were the $5 items, what were the $1 items? I took the $10 items and worked the heck out of 'em. If he hit me on an uncompleted $5 item, he'd grill me some, but he never brought up the $1 items. His motto is, 'Be tough, not rough.' I'm convinced he walked out of the building at night smiling and thinking, *Let's see how he handles this one.*"

Experience has taught me that tough-not-rough delegation benefits everyone. Still, I'm not surprised that many seat-of-the-pantsers refuse to hand off enough work: willy-nilly delegation creates more problems than it solves. Before plopping assignments on desks, do your delegation due diligence.

Here are ten delegation directives:

1. Transfer Ownership. Be clear: "Here you go, this baby's all yours now."

2. Tell Why. An employee who understands why she's being asked to handle a task is more likely to execute it thoroughly.

3. Get the Wheels Turning. For complex projects, help the delegatee develop an action plan by asking open-ended questions like "How do you see this unfolding?" and "What roadblocks do you anticipate, and how will you overcome them?"

4. Set Deadlines. Mutually agree on a completion date and time. Otherwise, the task may sink to the bottom of the delegatee's priority list.

5. Ask for a Recap. Don't assume the delegatee perfectly understands the assignment. Always double-check: "To make sure I communicated clearly, please explain what you're planning to do and why." The answer may surprise you.

6. Monitor (but don't smother). The point is liberation, so don't micromanage unless the delegatee is untested or timing is critical. If she starts down the wrong path, say something like, "That might work, but have you considered going in this direction? What do you think that could yield?" Remember, the weekly one-on-one employee meeting (chapter 32) is your forum for pinpoint advising.

7. No Take-Backs. Don't retract an assignment at the first sign of trouble. That hurts confidence. Setbacks are learning opportunities, so coach the delegatee back on track.

8. Play to a Delegatee's Strong Suit. Tailor assignments to people's strengths. Don't saddle a big-picture thinker with a pointillism project.

9. Don't Duplicate. Assign specific duties to specific people, with zero overlap. If there are two people involved, make it clear who's in charge.

10. Distribute Evenly. Up-and-comers need challenges, too. Avoid the temptation to overload your stars.

CHAPTER 41

TEACH, DON'T PREACH

Making Lessons Stick

I told him what to do and how to do it—and he still screwed it up!" Whenever I hear this complaint, I agree that someone indeed screwed up. The culprit, however, was usually the guy doing the venting. You can't just throw information at people and expect them to process it the same way you do. Nobody shares your precise experiences and frame of reference, so a few links in their chain of understanding may be missing. How do you get them to understand? Stated gastronomically: Digesting and assimilating raw information requires a committed chef to chop it into bite-size chunks and sauté it in encouragement.

Teaching is as simple as the Confucius Checklist. But seat-of-the-pantsers usually abandon it after the first step, oblivious that barking orders on the run wastes more time than it saves. Each step takes them a quarter of the way toward learning what you know.

1. Tell him.
2. Show him.

3. Watch him do it and offer feedback.
4. Watch him do it again.

Say you're coaching an employee to field calls. Start by reviewing the protocols point by point. Next, take a call yourself and handle it with your usual aplomb. After hanging up, smile and ask him to take a stab. Watch closely. When he finishes his call, critique his performance: "Nice job, Larry. You were polite and friendly, the qualities we look for. A couple minor things. Remember to offer your name before, 'How can I help you?' Try not to hem and haw so much. Project confidence. All right, let's try it again." Watch and listen once more. If he nails it, give him the thumbs-up and move on to the next student.

The Confucius Checklist is grounded in a basic truth—information turns into knowledge when we understand how it applies to us, and knowledge turns into wisdom when we absorb it and act on it. This process has inspired leaders for twenty-five hundred years, ever since Confucius (one of the earliest enlightened entrepreneurs) said:

Tell me and I will forget.
Show me and I might remember.
Involve me and I will understand.

CHAPTER 42

SUCCESSION STRATEGIES

Putting the "Success" in Succession

Business abhors a vacuum. I tossed and turned many a night worrying whether we could fill fresh and soon-to-be created vacancies. It's a tricky balancing act, but focusing on your employees' current performance *and* future potential turns your staff into a major-league team while also producing a resource-rich farm club. You'll sleep better when you're confident about facing the next surprise departure or summoning the courage to act when an employee's poor performance forces your hand.

Here are ten succession strategies:

1. Don't Procrastinate. Begin today planning developmental experiences for tomorrow's leaders. People need a chance to test their wings before you push them out of the nest. Focusing solely on the here and now carries a high cost—frequent turnover, operational interruptions, squandered human capital. To paraphrase Professor Harold Hill from Broadway's *The Music Man*, "Planning Purely for the Present" starts with *P*, which rhymes with *T*, and that stands for "Trouble."

2. Develop a Deep Bench. Routinely prepping people to take on more responsibility minimizes the chaos created by a surprise resignation. "I never knew when I was going to need a new store manager," said regional manager Brad Burley, "so I always had two or three candidates lined up. It was great for morale because people knew there was a plan to help them advance." Employees can sense when their departure will hurt you, and sometimes they subtly exploit it.

3. Ask, Don't Assume. It's easy to think, *Jake's a sales guy; I can't see him as a customer service rep.* Well, maybe Jake can. Don't wait for an annual review to discuss career goals. It's a natural thing to chat about in the parking lot. Ask about employees' interests and where they see themselves two years and five years down the road.

4. Cross-Train. Challenge people to learn new skills, especially in unfamiliar areas of the company. Start by asking them to back up colleagues during vacations, illnesses, and so-busy-I-can't-think periods. If they resist, nudge them out of their comfort zone and encourage them to stretch. You won't produce any butterflies if you allow people to stay tucked in the seductive safety of their cubicle cocoons.

5. Prevent Paranoia. It's a safe bet people will feel threatened if they're asked to train somebody else to do their job. Assure them their job isn't at risk. Explain that it's critical for the company to build in redundancy in order to run seamlessly when people get ill or if, God forbid, the proverbial bus takes somebody out. Toss in this fringe benefit: Their desk won't be piled high with projects when they return from vacation.

6. Move People Around. Don't nail people's feet to the floor. Some companies transfer managers to other departments every few years to keep them fresh and flexible. (Newspapers routinely move reporters from one beat to the next so they don't get stale.) It creates a petri dish for innovation, and gives people a better sense of how all the disparate parts of the company fit together. Although it might not be an option for smaller firms, orchestrating an occasional round of managerial musical chairs sharpens skills.

7. Use 'em or Lose 'em. There's a tendency to keep a potential all-star right where he is because you don't want to risk replacing him with someone less capable. Who knows how many Chris Speakes there are out there. In the course of eight years, Chris climbed from part-time tire tech to full-time sales to service manager to store manager to, finally, franchise store owner. If you don't allow people to explore and express the full range of their God-given abilities, they'll find somebody who will.

8. Promote from Within. When a job opens, the first impulse should be to pass the baton to one of your own. Choking off advancement by regularly hiring outsiders for key positions dashes employees' hopes and creates a culture of complacency. On the other hand, investing in your people's professional development, and then rewarding them with plum promotions, delivers a powerful message: If you apply yourself, anything is possible. It took years—and plenty of kvetching employees—before I wised up to this one.

9. Avoid Ruffled Feathers. Sure, sometimes it's necessary to recruit a heavy hitter with years of specialized training. In that case, let insiders know that you took them and their feelings into account. Like the time our less-than-effective CFO resigned. Daily cash crises were poking holes in our suddenly porous financial foundation. Somebody had to step up—fast—and plug the leaks. Luckily, we countered the wolf at our door with a Wolf of our own—Jim Wolf, our treasurer. Jim had briefly served as the CFO of a start-up, but a company our size was a different ball game. "I basically operated in survival mode," Jim recalled, "and managed the cash on a daily basis to help us limp through the first half of the year. It was a stressful time, but it was also a great opportunity to learn and perform under fire." Six months later we hired Jim Bemis as permanent CFO, but Jim Wolf was strongly considered. "Tom was sensitive about my feelings, but I actually felt good about the decision," Jim said. "Jim Bemis came in with better credentials and proved to be a successful CFO." Moral of the story? Even though Jim Wolf didn't get the job, in the end he felt valued and appreciated. He continued to play a key role, with treasury and planning.

10. Collect Names. Keep a short list of all-star outsiders in case a high-level position opens up that no staffer is qualified for (or interested in). When I ran across, say, an impressive CFO, I jotted down his contact info. Ditto for quality referrals and great candidates we didn't hire.

KEY POINTS

EDUCATING EMPLOYEES

➤ **Invest in education.** Make a healthy PR&D (people research and development) budget a priority. Skills-obsessed employees run laps around rivals. They visualize a brighter future and know how to turn that vision into reality.

➤ **Learn how people learn and unlearn.** There are four stages of learning and unlearning—conscious incompetent, unconscious competent, conscious competent, unconscious incompetent. Good leaders recognize the signs of the stages and guide each person accordingly.

➤ **More input=more output.** Capitalize on the link between increased employee education and increased productivity. Improve their skills through every means, from books and seminars to mentors and tuition assistance.

➤ **Develop via delegation.** Tough-not-rough delegation benefits everyone. Increasing employees' responsibilities develops their confidence and expertise. That frees you up for more important pursuits.

➤ **Follow the Confucius Checklist.** Tell an employee how to do something and she'll forget. Show her how to do it and she might remember. Involve her and she'll understand.

➤ **Plan for succession.** Development programs put the "success" in succession. Strike a balance between improving candidates' productivity in their current job and grooming them for their next move.

COACHING YOURSELF

Guiding Yourself to Peak Personal Performance

By this section, you've learned a strong management methodology. But setting it in motion, day after day, requires discipline, and that requires self-coaching. Huh? "Self-coaching?" What does that have to do with meeting management or marketing? Good question. It's a little bit like business psychology. Let's start with a definition—self-coaching is a systematic way to inspire, educate, and lead yourself so you can be an effective, enlightened leader. Are you thinking, *There's nothing wrong with me that doubling my profits won't cure*? I used to think that, too. But I can assure you that self-coaching—coupled with enlightened business methods—will double your profits. Self-coaching strengthens your organizational skills as well as your intellect, body, psyche, and spirit. That expands your capacity to lead.

Simply holding *The Big Book* means you're ahead of where I was at forty-one, a year before life went all Humpty-Dumpty on me, before I was interested in self-coaching. Had you met me back in 1988, you would've seen the facade of the Classic American Dream. I had the handsome family, the beautiful home. Every week I had time for church and shooting hoops with pals. I had the growing company and prominence in the community. I would've told you with an ear-to-ear grin and a firm handshake that life was good. Real good.

Next thing I knew, divorce, cancer, and a business crisis laid me flat. My twitchy nerves forced people to tread lightly around me as I tried to glue things back together. I lashed out at the suggestion that I look in the mirror. I snapped at a friend not long after my divorce: "Show me anywhere in writing where it says it's healthy to feel my feelings." A wicked internal storm started splintering my defenses. I pummeled myself for six months: *You really screwed up. You hurt your family. You ruined your business. There's no way out of this one.*

If I could just get my old self back, I thought, the pieces of my life would snap back together. I clung to the belief that brainpower and force of will would pull me through. I ignored airy-fairy talk from friends about "emotional breakthroughs" and "spiritual connections." *Maybe a shrink can tell me what's wrong with everyone else,* I remember thinking. *This mess sure can't be my fault.*

Enter psychologist Brenda Schaeffer—contacting her was one of the smartest calls I ever made. She helped me see that my choices and behavior were the shovels that had dug the cesspool I was floating in. It dawned on me that maybe there was a higher purpose for the sledgehammer that had walloped me. The words of philosopher Soren Kierkegaard started speaking to me:

> *A man may perform astonishing feats and*
> *comprehend a vast amount of knowledge,*
> *and yet have no understanding of himself.*
> *But suffering directs a man to look within.*
> *If it succeeds, then there, within him, is*
> *the beginning of his learning.*

Humbled, I began exploring healthier lifestyles. I read books and attended seminars on psychological and spiritual wellness. I overhauled my diet. Meditation, massages, tai chi (a Chinese discipline of meditative movements), and individual and group therapy sessions filled my calendar. I solicited blunt, objective feedback from friends and colleagues. Without naming it, or knowing where it would lead, I had begun the process of self-coaching.

Sure enough, the pieces of my life started snapping back together. Deeper clarity and self-awareness enhanced my efficiency and management skills. My strategic and operational thinking grew sharper. To my delight, I was connecting deeply with teammates. Better still, my healthier frame of mind inspired healthier behavior in employees, who in turn produced a healthier bottom line. Now I'm actually grateful for that humbling trauma. It shook up my priorities and steered me down the road toward enlightenment. Maybe you can turn my screwups into signposts that keep you out of the ditch.

Self-coaching will help you:

Fulfill your promise. There isn't much wiggle room in professional sports contracts. Athletes must take care of themselves so that they play at the top of their game. Likewise, you're agreeing to give your best to your employees and customers when you start your own business. If you don't take care of yourself physically, emotionally, intellectually, and spiritually, you won't find the stamina or know-how to lead your team.

Coach your team. Leadership demands a passionate sense of purpose, clarity of mind, and stratospheric levels of integrity, energy, and interpersonal skills. You can't get there without self-coaching. As Dee Hock, founder of Visa International, said, "If you look to lead, invest at least 40 percent of your time managing yourself." If you can't manage to manage yourself, you're doomed to inspire your troops about as well as Dilbert's pointy-haired boss.

Improve relationships. It's an aphorism that bears repeating: *People don't care how much you know until they know how much you care.* If you have more "issues" than *National Geographic,* you're too mired in your own muck to care for the people under your watch. You'll also remain mystified why people don't pay you the respect you think you deserve.

Save time. Time management improves because you're focused, organized, and alert. Better interpersonal and decision-making skills also help dispatch more issues as they arise, preventing future course-correction headaches. Sure, it's tough to find time to do everything that coaching yourself entails, but avoiding it altogether will make life harder than it should be.

Keep your antennae up. Get in touch with your emotions, motivations, and feelings. You'll have a better sense of what makes people tick, and you'll know what to ask and when and how to ask it. Approaching and comforting a struggling employee is an underrated skill—and difficult to pull off without going to school on it.

Positively influence others. Think like a parent, even at work. Whether or not you realize it, your attitude and behavior seep through your entire company or department. If you're cheerful and optimistic, your teammates are more likely to be upbeat and positive. If you're moody and negative, you'll have an office full of grouches.

Make work more enjoyable. Office life gets easier the harder you work at self-improvement. You start going with the flow instead of fighting the current. As you get to know yourself better, you'll engage people more authentically throughout life. You'll think more clearly. You'll laugh more. You'll feel more caring and energized. You might just get that Zen feeling that life is unfolding exactly like it's supposed to.

Enhance your people skills. Among the more valuable currencies in a team environment are superior organizational, management, and people skills. Master them, and you'll respond to crises with the calmness and clarity of Sherlock Holmes.

All coaches need a playbook that spells out their championship strategy, even for coaching yourself. Yours is the next seven chapters. It starts by clarifying the life you were born to lead, then shows you how to realize that vision by setting and reaching goals and treating yourself right. Remember, the healthier you are, the healthier your business will be.

CHAPTER 43

GOT MISSION?

Crafting Your Personal Mission Statement

One way to sharpen your focus is to put pen to paper—or fingers to keyboard—and craft a personal mission statement. It helps zero in on why you're here (surely there's more to life than worrying your mother). Which gets us thinking big thoughts about what we want to give and get out of life. Think of your mission as a beacon in the darkness that helps you navigate indecision. It prevents dreams from drifting off course and getting dashed on the rocks of inertia. Whether a single paragraph or a page, your mission can mean the difference between living a life of choice or a life of chance.

The act of writing out a vision crystallizes conviction and trues up your internal compass. It also unpacks the wisdom of the adage, "The purpose of life is a life of purpose." When I act in concert with my mission, opportunities are more obvious, big decisions come easier.

You'll avoid bolting up in bed some night with the horrible realization that your dreams have gone unfulfilled, scattered to the wind like wisps of smoke. Do the work you need to do, right now. Don't wait until you find yourself on your knees, awash in regrets. Been there, hated that. Writing my mission statement reconnected my head to my soul. Yet I don't expect it to shield me from life's vicissitudes. Chaos and calamity may pay me another visit, especially when I lose focus and drift. The difference now is that it's easier to regain my footing. Thanks to the stability and perspective of my mission statement.

FIRST THINGS FIRST

In the time it takes to see a movie, you can finish the first draft of your mission statement. It's a small price to pay—skipping the latest action flick—for supercharging your own life story. To set the stage:

Isolate yourself. Find a quiet place and turn off the phones. You may even want to tape a DO NOT DISTURB sign on the door.

Get in the zone. Close your eyes. Take slow, deep breaths, and mentally go to a calm, peaceful place—a river valley, a mountain glade. Experience it with all your senses and let the tension melt away.

Sequester the judge. Give your inner critic the day off and let ideas flow.

Be patient. This isn't *Jeopardy!* Take your hand off the buzzer and your eyes off the clock. Take as much time as you need to tap your longings.

Open wide. To the extent you can, temporarily suspend your analytical mind and material desires. Open yourself to a deeper source of wisdom. Sure, lofty profits and business awards are worthy goals. But you don't stand a chance of fulfilling your destiny if your mission is grounded purely in egotism and material desires. As Carl Jung wrote:

> *Your vision will become clear only when you*
> *can look into your own heart. Who looks*
> *outside, dreams; who looks inside, awakens.*

ASK THE RIGHT QUESTIONS

Take a deep breath, Clark Kent. You're about to duck into a phone booth. First, ask, *What was I sent here to do?* Yep, a broad question, one so often obscured by daily stressors. Narrow your focus by applying the question to life's most important quarters: *What was I sent here to do for*

my spouse?   *my children?*

my parents?   *my extended family?*

my friends?   *the world?*

my career?   *my colleagues?*

my community?   *my country?*

the earth?   *my spirit?*

The only mission you can trust springs from your heart, mind, and soul. Strip away everything that has limited you—money, age, health, family, geography, and, the mother of all bugaboos, other people's expectations. Forget all that. Concentrate solely on your destiny. Now jot down your thoughts. Your mission is a collection of simple guideposts, like *Maintain physical health through proper diet, exercise, and self-care.* Don't worry about measurable goals—*Lose ten pounds by next birthday*—quite yet. To spur your thinking, ask, *What can I do every day to fulfill my purpose?* Here's what I came up with.

- Nourish myself with more spirituality.
- Build my communication skills.
- Ignore distractions that impede growth.
- Care and love more.
- Guide people one-on-one and in groups.
- Model healthy living and well-being.
- Tap my Higher Source for wisdom and discipline.

Now imagine that one of the cool things you discover when you die is that you get to eavesdrop on your funeral. What will your friends and loved ones reminisce about? What do you *hope* they'll reminisce about? Are the answers to those two questions different? What parts of your personality would you like to stand out? What deeds would you like to define you? Here's what I jotted down after pondering, *How would I like to be remembered?*

- He was a loving son, brother, and mate.
- He was the best father he knew how to be—a friend and mentor to his sons.
- He shared wisdom that helped friends get what they wanted from life.
- He tried to find the goodness in everyone and to bring people together.
- He shared his blessings.
- He had a sense of humor, lightened the load of people around him, and had fun.
- He was caring, loving, and gentle with himself.
- He stood up for his beliefs and challenged power in the name of community.
- He supported organizations that shared his values.

PUTTING IT ALL TOGETHER

After harvesting all these ideas, I sifted them around and mixed in a few more I plucked from my suddenly fertile imagination. Voila! My mission practically wrote itself. It's a living document, but here's my latest:

1. To evolve toward an enlightened and loving state.
2. To strengthen connections to my Higher Power, family, and friends.
3. To grow via education that integrates body, intellect, psyche, and spirit.
4. To develop my knowledge and communication skills.
5. To build nurturing environments that contribute to the growth of family and friends.
6. To contribute to colleagues by helping them develop their talents and productivity.

7. To teach leadership skills to organizations that improve the world.
8. To tread lightly on the earth so future generations inherit a healthy planet.
9. To help people achieve their missions.

Next, working draft in hand, set aside ten minutes here and there over the next few weeks and revise. Keep turning ideas in your mind as you garden, golf, or rock on the porch. If you can, get quiet and ask yourself whether there's any more information. Be still, listen. Keep a notepad ready.

When you think you've got it, repeat your mission statement out loud a few times to burn it into your consciousness. But don't just say it. Display it. Frame it and hang it on your office wall, or put it on your desk next to family snapshots. Make a wallet-size copy so it's always in reach. But remember: Just as you can't live in a house that exists only in blueprints, your mission can't produce anything until you grab a hammer and nails and start pounding away.

CHAPTER 44

TRUTH OR CONSEQUENCES

Pitfalls of Unethical Behavior

Sure, your mission statement is a thing to behold, with the potential to light up the world. But it isn't the Mona Lisa. You can print it out in fancy fonts, frame it up, and hang it. It's still not a work of art unless it inspires you to embrace the art of working and living ethically. Your code of ethics—the moral standards you use to relate to the world—bridges the distance between *listing* your ideals and *living* them. Ethical living, consistently choosing to do what's right, is its own reward. Admittedly, it's easy to resist everything but temptation—to paraphrase Oscar Wilde. Lots of things may look fun (and they are) and some things may also look harmless (but they aren't). Immoral behavior has lethal side effects for your business, employees, and yourself. Before you sidestep your conscience, consider the consequences.

You're being watched. Put aside for a moment the nanotechnology that makes cameras the size of pushpins. Look around. The people who report to you are watching your every move. Our natural competitive impulse finds us keeping an eye on one another. So often we raise the bar higher for others than we do for ourselves. One slip and we're instant grist for the gossip mill. But it's worse for the boss. Employees model their leaders like children model their parents. Swipe a few pads of Post-it notes and people will think that it's open season on the supply cabinet. That's why I gave my assistant, Dorie, an ongoing kitty of $100 to pay for personal expenses like snacks and postage. I obeyed every rule and received the same discount on tires and car repairs as everyone else.

You'll know it. Some people fold themselves into logic pretzels to justify dubious decisions. But deep down, where the best part of them lives, they know better. *New York Times* columnist William Safire explained it well:

> *The right to do something does not mean*
> *that doing it is right.*

Take the time my company car's lease expired. I upgraded to a more expensive model; however, profits were below expectations and the entire company was in belt-tightening mode. Even if nobody so much as raised an eyebrow, it didn't feel right to force the company to take the hit for my higher car payment. So I asked human resources to take an extra $300 a month out of my paycheck. Each year I also asked HR to compare my compensation against our CPA firm's national CEO market survey to ensure I was in line.

Those rare occasions when I did compromise, my conscience wound up costing me, often in subtle ways—I wasn't fully present around others, or the lump in my stomach wouldn't go away. That led to polluted thinking and bad decisions. "Guilty feet have no rhythm," as the song goes.

Do you sense you have an employee feeling guilty about a past decision? Tell them they're not alone. To the extent that you can, speak broadly about forgiving yourself for past errors. Tell them they know better now and they can resolve to avoid making the same mistake. Tomorrow is a new day with new opportunities to act honorably. We already know that it's deeply rewarding to do what's right for the sake of doing what's right. So take the high road—there's less traffic.

You're gambling with your good name. When news broke that Arthur Andersen had shredded Enron documents and committed other crimes and misdemeanors, the Big Six accounting firm's reputation was tarnished for good. It wasn't long ago that the overnight collapse of a global Goliath was unimaginable. Now there are days when the business section of the newspaper reads like a rap sheet.

We live in a transparent age. Corporations have glass walls. Disgruntled employees can e-mail incriminating documents faster than you can say, "Not guilty, Your Honor." If you bend the rules even once, you're asking for trouble. Same goes for your personal life. After the sale of Tires Plus to Bridgestone/Firestone was made public, I received an unsolicited call from a well-known accounting firm that I had never engaged. They told me I could save several million dollars in taxes by setting up an offshore account. But they added, while the loophole was legally defensible and wasn't likely to ever face a court challenge, it wasn't for the faint of heart. I don't like paying a penny more in taxes than I have to. But I do feel it's important to pay my share to recognize the opportunities that this country gave me to earn a good living. When I hear "offshore," I walk the other way. I've worked too hard for too long to run the risk of staining my reputation. It's not a question of faint-heartedness; it's a matter of right-heartedness. The dollar amount was irrelevant. You can't put a price tag on a good night's sleep, or a good family name.

CHAPTER 45

READY, SET, GOALS

Turning Dreams into Destiny

It's pretty darn hard to get from here to there without a roadmap. Laying out your goals bridges the gap between who you are today and the person you sketched out in your mission statement. Yet when I ask people all over the country whether they write up their goals each year, barely one in ten say they have. But that 10 percent gushes over how spelling out their goals transformed their lives.

Why the disconnect? Lots of reasons. Chronically impatient people think goal setting is a waste of time. They wonder why they should spend hours writing down what they want to do when they could be out there actually doing it. These are the same people who prefer driving around lost for an hour before stopping for directions. Others are wary of introspection, a prerequisite to pinpointing what they want from life.

Some folks actually fear success because living the dream might cause them to sacrifice their suffering. Personal demons trap certain folks into thinking they don't deserve happiness and financial security. Then there's fear of failure, a particularly acute malady for fragile egos that just can't take the blow of another disappointment. Any of this sound familiar? If so, read and reread the self-coaching section. It'll help lift these obstacles.

Herding your goals into one place—a digital file, a legal pad, a planner— is deeply satisfying, clarifying, and deceptively powerful. In his 1951 book, *The Scottish Himalayan Expedition,* W. H. Murray explained:

> *There is one elementary truth, the ignorance*
> *of which kills countless ideas and splendid plans:*
> *that the moment one definitely commits oneself,*
> *then Providence moves, too. All sorts of things*
> *occur to help one that would never otherwise*
> *have occurred. A whole stream of events issues*
> *from the decision, raising in one's favor all*
> *manner of unforeseen incidents and meetings*
> *and material assistance, which no man could*
> *have dreamed would have come his way.*

GETTING STARTED

With your personal mission statement in one hand, writing down your goals with the other is as easy as filling out a job application. The five steps for crafting your mission statement also apply here—find a quiet place, relax, don't judge, be patient, open up to a deeper wisdom. Once grounded, take a minute to review your mission. Let it sink in. Now jot down what you'd like to get out of life's big departments during the next twelve months:

Family	Romance
Business	Finances
Friends	Physical fitness
Social life	Spiritual fitness
Intellectual fitness	Recreation
Emotional fitness	Community service

Looking to boost sales by 20 percent? File under *business.* Want to get your temper under control? File under *emotional fitness.* Ready to start working

Wednesday evenings at the soup kitchen? File under *community service*. Before starting, consult these guidelines:

Have fun. Choosing what you want from life shouldn't feel like homework. For me, it's like picking out fruits and vegetables at the farmer's market. Or, think back to the childhood excitement of paging through holiday catalogs and making out a wish list. *You* decide which goodies you'll get.

Make it user-friendly. Arrange your goals in an easy-to-read, easy-to-modify format—perhaps a bulleted list of items or research-paper outline.

Be specific. Clarity and precision make goals measurable, whereas vague, moving targets are difficult to hit and easy to abandon. Where possible, add a measurable metric (a profit target, a number of sit-ups) and a timeline (vacation departure date, weekly visits to the gym). The more details the better. Which goal do you think is most likely to produce action: "Lose weight"? "Lose ten pounds"? or "Lose ten pounds by May 15"?

Shoot for the stars—or not. Goal setters fall into two camps. The dreamer likes to hang a humdinger of a target—your company making ten million bucks, date a supermodel, play polo in the Hamptons—knowing he'll fall short but looking forward to the adventure. The pragmatist, on the other hand, motivates herself with challenging, accessible objectives. She's disappointed if she can't put a line through everything on her to-do list. Which camp are you in?

Examine your motives. Don't just identify *what* you want but *why* you want it. After getting in touch with my mission, I discovered I wanted to build a successful tire company to brighten our customers' day and provide opportunities for teammates to grow in a healthy environment. Had I wanted to grow my company purely for ego gratification—which was a primary driver early on—the results would've been markedly different. Our company didn't shift into higher gear until I did, too.

Walk the tightrope. Life is a daily balancing act. A lot of people zero in on their career and tune out everything else. I can relate. All the late nights and weekends I worked exacted a toll (cancer, divorce). The world is full of hardworking moms and dads who would gladly return the extra money they earned if they could turn back the clock and cheer at a couple more Little League games or boost their kids up a few more jungle gyms. The ultimate gift of time is the moments when you're fully present, without the faintest thought of anything but what's in front of you. Yet, success is impossible without hard work. Nothing is easy. Indeed, sometimes circumstances legitimately demand an obsessive focus on work during an extended stretch. Operating out of balance occasionally can help you achieve a better balance in the long run. Trouble is, lingering too long in the red zone can lead to burnout, health problems, bad relationships, and ill-advised decisions. Or, at the very least, a vague feeling of emptiness and a life that just doesn't work very well.

Mix it up. Blend together short-term goals that you can hit in a few weeks, medium-termers that you can reach in a few months, and long-term goals that may take a year or more. Spacing out goals produces a sense of ongoing accomplishment and keeps you motivated. It's also not a bad idea to find a mix of long shots and chip shots. Envelope-pushing projects test your abilities, but an agenda full of them may set you up for failure.

Make it your own. Some goals will find their way onto your list out of your sense of obligation. Just make sure the majority spring from you rather than somebody else.

Be gracious in defeat. No matter how bold your effort, uncontrollable circumstances may intervene. That's okay. Look at what you did accomplish—knowledge, relationships, confidence—in the pursuit. If at least part of the goal is still doable, recycle it for next year's list.

FINISHING TOUCHES

Once you're satisfied with your list, sign and date it. Treat it like the important document it is, a compact with yourself. But there's always room for amendments (and they shouldn't require an act of Congress). Review and revise your goals every few months so they're up to speed with life's twists and turns. You may need to adjust your exercise routine in the wake of a promotion that demands more time or travel—a development that could also impact financial, social, and relationship goals. If you happen to slow down to a trot, tweaking your goals sparks a renewed dedication to dig in your spurs and start galloping again. Caveat: Don't overuse revision. It can become an excuse for giving up on what you wanted.

Your list of goals is a companion to your mission statement. Keep them both conspicuous, at work and at home. Don't lose sight of why you get out of bed every morning. Carry an easily accessible copy in your BlackBerry, planner, or wallet. A quick glance now and then helps me keep my goals top of mind. Sure, you can skip all this. None of it is convenient. But it's better than being a human Ping-Pong ball—always in the middle of the action but getting smacked in so many different directions that you're lucky to wind up where you started the year. Unappealing, huh? As former General Electric CEO Jack Welch put it, "Control your own destiny, or someone else will."

CHAPTER 46

WORK THE PLAN

Linking Goals to Action Steps and Schedules

Jim Pascale was just twenty-seven when we hopped into my car and took off for Iowa. It was our first market outside Minnesota, and I'd just promoted Jim to Iowa regional manager. Speeding out of Minneapolis and down I-35, I asked to see his schedule. Gripping the wheel with one hand, Jim grabbed his planner from the backseat and handed it over. I was a little shocked by what I saw. "Do you have a copy of your goals with you?" I asked. Jim froze and shot me a deer-in-the-headlights look. "Pull over," I said. "I'm driving." Back on the interstate, I told Jim to write down everything he wanted to accomplish for the year, from career and financial goals to travel, health, and relationships. He listed the categories and wrote things like, "Hit my bonus target," "Pay off personal debt," "Visit my parents in Chicago." Then I told him to list the action steps they required. Finally, I asked him to set deadlines.

When Jim finished, I congratulated him, but cautioned that it was only the first step. I told him to rewrite his monthly schedule by finding homes on his calendar for what was personally important. Next, he added mandatory work meetings. Then he added other high-priority tasks and appointments.

"As I entered each item," Jim recalled, "I began connecting the dots between my goals and my daily activities. To hit my personal financial goals, I had to hit my bonus targets. To hit my bonus, I had to fix up my stores and hire good people. It was obvious those things were related, but I hadn't been working toward specific, measurable goals in such a step-by-step way." By the time we hit Iowa, I sensed something in Jim had shifted. In the months that followed, he was more purposeful and disciplined. Two years later, he was named vice president of franchise operations, and had doubled his salary.

Do what you've always done and you'll get what you've always gotten. You can conquer the summit of any mountain—if you set your mission in motion with action plans. Eloquent mission statements and lofty goals are a good start. But without deliberate deeds, they fade like yesterday's paper. The last trace is a vague sense that you'd once been at the doorstep of something big. As Will Rogers said, "Even if you're on the right track, you'll get run over if you just sit there."

FIRST CREATE, THEN INTEGRATE

An action plan is just what it sounds like—a list of what must be done to change a goal's status from "To do" to "Ta-daaa!" In 1998, I renewed my commitment to deepen my relationship with my parents, who are divorced and live far from my Minneapolis home. My mother, Elizabeth, eighty-nine, lives in southern Indiana, and my father, Bill, eighty-six and now living in an Indiana nursing home, lived for years in southern California. Here's how I linked that goal—and its action steps—to my mission. (The same drill works for business goals.)

Personal Mission Statement (relevant portion): To build nurturing environments that contribute to the growth of family and friends.

Goal Category: Family.

Goal: To enhance my relationship with my mother (I created a separate plan for my relationship with my father).

Action plan:

1. Call Mom three times a week.
2. Take a weeklong vacation with her wherever she wants to go.
3. Spend six long weekends at her Indiana home.
4. Host her in Minneapolis from Christmas to New Year's Day.
5. Send cards on her birthday, Mother's Day, and other holidays.
6. Financially assist her so she lives a comfortable, active life.
7. Consistently check in on her feelings and her life, and leave nothing unsaid. Regularly express that I love her and appreciate all the love she's given me.

Writing action plans is invigorating but, like your mission and goals, they're still just words on paper. Transferring your action plans over to your schedule and to-do list is the critical link. Just be sure to mind your priorities—schedule your personal life first and plan business around it. Meeting personal goals paves the way to success at work. Lay important family dates on your calendar like primary coats of paint—birthdays, Little League, family outings, vacations. Sure, something will come up at work, you may have to miss a game or two. The point is, if you don't schedule them, you'll miss a whole lot more.

It's actually easy to integrate action plans into daily life. After calling my mother to discuss what dates worked for her, I typed everything—the weeklong vacation, long weekends, holidays, annual financial review—into my Microsoft Outlook calendar. I also added send-a-card reminders three days ahead of each birthday and holiday. As always, "Call Mom" anchors the top of my Task List. It's a joy to lace my action plans—business objectives, financial planning, physical exercise, spiritual growth—into my daily life. I know it improves the chances that I'll do what it takes to hit my goals.

SCHEDULING BREEDS SPONTANEITY

I can hear the snickering: *Whoa, does this guy's calendar tell him when to brush his teeth? If I wanted that much structure, I'd join the military. Where's the flexibility?* Look, I'm not suggesting you become a lean, mean scheduling machine. Block out plenty of breathers and get spontaneous within the boundaries of your schedule. It's foolish to pass on serendipitous opportunities simply because you've got an appointment, especially one you could easily reschedule. Enjoy the freedom to improvise; just don't put off things *you* made high priority.

Productivity gets cranked up by connecting the dots between your mission, goals, action plans, and schedule. You'll find you're more relaxed and spontaneous because the parts of your life that really matter are (generally) on track and accounted for. For me, that means I'm free to live fully in the moment. With everything in sync, my mind isn't cluttered with the debris of a million to-dos: *Oh, no! I was supposed to meet George for his one-on-one two hours ago! I forgot to send a birthday card to my brother!* That kind of spontaneity I can do without.

Think of action plans as suggestions and reminders. Careful not to pack 'em in too tight. Time was when my days were wound so tightly I made every meeting only if my schedule worked like a Swiss watch and I didn't hit an ill-timed red light. No matter how much I rushed for the next meeting or the next flight, I was like Wile E. Coyote chasing the Roadrunner. After tiring of the adrenaline rushes that produced, I finally built some cushion between appointments. That gave me time for a few deep breaths and let me catch up on minor tasks. I still find myself in an occasional tight spot, but now it's an exception rather than the rule. Bottom line: Schedule your time or it will schedule you.

Keep in mind Professor Cyril Northcote Parkinson's tried-and-truism: "Work expands (or contracts) so as to fill the time available for its completion." That is, the more air you build into your schedule, and the more time you allocate for doing something, the longer it will take. That limits the number of goals you hit. Eventually, if you're discipline-challenged, you'll feel like a helpless bystander watching your life pass by with nothing to show for it but gray hair and regret. The solution? A middle ground where scheduling is less an obligation than an art. It takes practice to find just the right blend of flexibility and structure. But once you're in the zone, you'll sense when you can push off appointments without causing too many ripples.

TAKE YOUR EYES OFF THE PRIZE

As I work toward a goal, I often visualize what achieving it will feel like. But to actually get there, I need to focus on a series of short, easy steps. As poet M. C. Richards wrote:

> *A knowledge of the path cannot be substituted*
> *for putting one foot in front of the other.*

Let's say you want to land the big Acme account. Sure, it's fun and inspirational to visualize the handshake in Technicolor detail—whooping it up at signing, pumping up the team, adding it to your portfolio, and watching things snowball. But the lion's share of your focus must shift to what it takes to accomplish the goal. That calls for an action plan. Ask yourself, *What's the smallest step I can take right now toward my goal?* Then ask, *What's the next smallest step?* Then look for the one after that. Keep going till you've written down every step you can imagine. Perhaps your list will look like this:

Goal: Land the Acme account.

Action Plan:

1. Research the company.
2. Hone sales skills by reviewing my last refresher course and scanning sales books.
3. Ask colleagues why previous shots at Acme had fizzled.
4. Prepare for upcoming sales call by analyzing the fizzle's cause and spelling out our company's enhanced pricing package and service commitment.
5. Introduce myself via a letter to the decision maker at the parent company.
6. Follow up a week later with a phone call to set up an appointment.

Now weave the steps through your schedule and to-do list, and start crossing them off. Take five minutes each morning and fifteen minutes at week's end to review progress and priorities—with market conditions in flux, a goal that seemed essential six weeks ago might be meaningless today. If you think of other steps, update your action plan, schedule, and to-do list accordingly. Then dig in again, and keep shoveling until you hit pay dirt.

CHAPTER 47

TIME WISE AND ORGANIZED

Embracing Enlightened Efficiency

So many leaders have the efficiency equation only half right. Take the business owner who's enlightened but inefficient. He's like the absent-minded preacher, late to the pulpit with lines of a great sermon running through his head—some written on scraps of paper in his pocket, the rest scattered around his office. His heartfelt attempts to inspire only confuse his flock. Then there's the unenlightened but efficient boss man. He's more like the world-class surgeon with arctic bedside manners. His skill would save more lives if he didn't submarine his patient's will to live by describing the progression of her disease as if it were a mutual fund chart.

A leader who's both enlightened *and* efficient is like a trusted family friend. She deeply cares about the personal education and well-being of people under her watch, while tirelessly challenging them to be productive and disciplined. To her fans, she's like a double shot of espresso.

Enlightened efficiency isn't an end in itself. Without it, however, you stand little chance of getting what you want and ultimately living out your mission. Steadily ratcheting up your efficiency lays the groundwork for handling future challenges. It's the tipping point that can take you from frustration to fulfillment. As one of my favorite sayings goes:

> *The will to prepare to succeed is more*
> *important than the will to succeed.*

I CAN'T BELIEVE IT'S NOT CLUTTER

Shooting for efficiency without first getting organized is like trying to break the speed limit on a highway under construction. Potholes and roadblocks will fling you into a ditch before you get out of first gear.

Organization paves the way to enlightened efficiency and reaching your goals. Can you be productive with a messy desk and chaotic files? Sure, anything's possible. But it's easier to get it done without the clutter. Especially when you add a personal digital assistant (PDA)—BlackBerry, Palm Pilot, Clio, Treo, Mio—to the mix to keep mission-critical data at your fingertips. The idea is to conserve time and adrenaline.

I'd be lost without my BlackBerry. Before I leave the office, I sync it with my PC's address book and to-do list. On the road, I update and revise on the fly; I stay connected in an airport or doctor's office through phone, Web access, and wireless e-mail. Then I upload everything back into my PC once home. (Caveat: Prioritize people over PDAs when out with friends and family. I pocket my BlackBerry, otherwise I'd glance at it so often that I couldn't follow the conversation. If you must check e-mail, take a trip to the restroom or step outside.)

I prefer a PDA to paper planners because it's compact and reduces redundancy (plus, it's a wireless wonder—when I update my calendar on my Black-Berry or PC, the other device automatically updates). But there are as many planning systems—digital and manual—as there are personalities. PDAs also help capture those firefly thoughts. A microcassette recorder or good old pen and paper also do the trick. Even if you're driving, don't let a good idea get away. In the car, paper and pencil are impractical (if not lethal), so I leave a voice mail for myself with my hands-free cell phone or pull over and tap on my BlackBerry.

Cleaning up the clutter begins from the inside out. Internal clarity naturally stirs desire for external clarity, and makes your personal and business life flow smoothly. Changes unfold subtly, but the day will come when you stop in your tracks and marvel at how a heady concept like enlightened efficiency has become as natural as breathing.

ALL THE TIME IN THE WORLD

It hurts to see people who've yet to balance efficiency with perspective. A few years ago, after a keynote address to Students in Free Enterprise, I judged a national student-business competition. Later that day, I chatted with a supplier manning a convention booth. By coincidence, his daughter had given one of the forty-five-minute presentations I had judged. I asked how he'd enjoyed it. "Oh, I had to stay at my booth," he said. "There's business to get, you know." My heart sank. *You poor soul and your poor daughter,* I thought. Here his daughter was competing in a national contest and he couldn't spare forty-five minutes? Imagine the message that sent her. What clouded his judgment and twisted his priorities?

Sorry to say it, but I know the answer—fear. In my lean early years, I was so scared about making payroll that I felt that every meeting, every resignation, every sales dip—everything was a white-hot priority. Even when business clicked into place, parting with the mind-set was a challenge. Any problem could whisk me back to the bad old days, and off to the races I'd go.

If twenty-four hours in a day seems to shortchange you, you're not alone. A recent *Wall Street Journal*/NBC News poll showed that 80 percent of us describe our lives as busy or busy to the point of discomfort. More telling: Surveyors had to call 31,407 phone numbers to find 2,001 Americans with enough time to answer their questions. The I-don't-have-enough-time mantra becomes a self-fulfilling prophecy—you don't have enough time because you never believed you would. Enlightened efficiency demands that you consciously choose to experience time differently. You replace the old mantra with a new one: *I have all the time I need to do everything I need to do.*

Something magical happens when you add purpose to your life by identifying your goals, breaking them into action plans, and building your schedule and to-do list around them. Time. Slows. Down. It's easy to explain. The smarter you are with your time, the more of it you have. Still, no matter how sharp your focus, time-wasting traps lurk in every office. We covered The Meeting, which can rank among the deepest black holes, in chapter 26. A few other time traps to avoid are:

Trim the talk. Imagine. If you have thirty conversations daily, each running four minutes longer than necessary, you lose two hours a day. Zeroing in on the matter at hand and cutting just a little fat goes a long way toward reclaiming your schedule. Saving ten minutes here and fifteen minutes there ultimately frees you up for those times when people need you most. Three talk trimming tips:

- **Push your purpose.** Be cordial, of course, but clip the small talk. Prior to longer conversations, I list the questions I want to ask and the points I need to make. Just one minute of prep makes for a productive and punctual exchange.
- **Bottom-line it.** Our people had a gentle way of cutting off ramblers. We'd respectfully interject a phrase I learned from efficiency guru Edwin Bliss: "Bottom line?" Without fail, the rambler cut to the quick (if a little sheepishly) and made his point. A softer variation sounds like this: "Sorry, I'd love to hear more, but I've got an appointment. Can you bottom-line it? Or we can talk later." Remember that bottom-lining is a business move that works only if it's caring rather than demanding. Also it is not a shortcut for personal matters.
- **Do it digitally.** Whenever possible, handle the matter via e-mail or text message. I send and receive dozens of messages a day to inquire, inform, and build consensus at lightning speed.

Get dialed in. The telephone is either your greatest ally (an alternative to writing letters and memos) or your worst enemy (a font of interruptions). Making cell-phone calls during out-of-office downtime—with a hands-free headset, without sacrificing family time—is a good first step. Here are two more ways to avoid getting hung up in the phone zone:

- **Appoint an auxiliary gatekeeper.** My outgoing voice-mail message was a trusted sentry at Tires Plus, unfailingly repeating: "Hi, this is Tom Gegax. Please leave a message detailing your needs and desires so either the appropriate person or I can get back to you in a more helpful way. Thanks for calling, and make it a great day." The upbeat message worked because it prompted callers to say *exactly* what they needed. It stopped them from simply leaving their contact info, the first serve in a maddening game of telephone tennis. It also saved my executive assistant, Dorie, a ton of time.
- **Leave precise instructions.** When you can't reach your contact, leave a thorough message and ask him to respond on *your* voice mail. Voíla! You've eliminated phone tag and done some business. It's the same asymmetrical communication that made e-mail a business revolution. We don't always need a two-way. When you do, say as much in your voice mail, detailing when and where you can be reached. Caveat: There are many times when reaching out to an employee or customer demands more high-touch than high-tech.

Be upfront, not uptight. For longer conversations, presentations, and informal meetings, be clear about how much time you've got. Nothing forces people to condense their points better. A saleswoman once told me she needed an hour. I told her I could afford only fifteen minutes and suggested she pack her points into three five-minute stages: sales pitch, questions, decision discussion. Recognizing that fifteen minutes was better than zero, she talked fast, hit the high notes, and wrapped it up at minute fifteen—with an occasional gentle nudge when she drifted off course. I was polite and friendly, but firm. Value your time and others will, too. Sound too tough? Would you rather miss your kid's soccer game because you didn't have time to complete that day's priorities? I don't think so. It's easy to get consumed by whatever's in front of you at the moment. Keep reminding yourself to be mindful of whom you're with, why you're with them, and how the encounter fits into the larger picture of your day, your career, and your life.

BATTLING BRUSH FIRES: THE SIX *D*'S

When's the last day you *didn't* have a high-priority phone call, an urgent e-mail, or a stressed-out colleague begging for attention? Getting pulled off course is in every entrepreneur's job description. I call my strategy for dealing with daily interruptions the Six *D*'s. When something pops up, rather than robotically just doing it, I start with the first option. If that doesn't apply, I move to the second. I keep cruising down the list until I reach the appropriate action.

1. Don't Do It. Seriously, some things will simply go away if you ignore them. As you grow more focused, you'll also grow more resilient to the tug of minor things that try to pull you off your path.

2. Delay It. Some interruptions disappear if you simply delay them. Think of all those urgent voice mails, e-mails, and memos you returned to after vacation. You never knew about them, yet they invariably cooled.

3. Deflect It. Some flare-ups only get hotter when they're delayed. If something belongs outside your work group, don't let it clutter up your desk. Pass it on.

4. Delegate It. Enlightened entrepreneurs don't do things other people are paid to do. You're not hiring the right people if you're thinking, *If I want it done right, I have to do it myself.* Delegate whatever you can. Otherwise, mindless minutiae will slam the brakes on your business's development. (Delegation is so crucial that chapter 40 is devoted to it.)

5. Do It Imperfectly. Don't automatically shift into perfectionist mode when you realize a task is something only you can do. You'll burn huge chunks of your schedule and brainpower that belong to worthier enterprises.

6. Do It Really Well. Some brush fires demand your full, immediate attention and need all your effort. But it's a lot easier to find the time and energy for big challenges when you've doused other flare-ups with the first five *D*'s.

CHAPTER 48

MIND-BODY BALANCE

Bringing Your Inner Team into Alignment

Would you sit back and twiddle your thumbs while a competitor poached your customers and employees? Would you blow off network security until a vicious virus crashed your computer system? Doubt it. When it's business, some of us are laudably proactive. When it comes to personal issues, however, too many of us have upside-down priorities. We wait until a crisis body slams us before contemplating the possibility of making better choices.

Case in point: The triple trauma that struck me at forty-two also flattened my assumptions about health and wellness. Divorce and a business cash-flow crisis crumbled my psychological and spiritual foundations. Then cancer forced me to rethink physical fitness. Those ordeals poked gaping holes in my theory that a shrewd mind was the only arrow I needed in my workplace quiver. Six painful months of self-analysis revealed the barriers I'd erected between life's four essential elements—body, intellect, psyche, and spirit.

Not only were the four players on my "inner team" incommunicado, they had never been formally introduced. My intellect was calling all the shots, my body never looked beyond its next run, and my psyche and spirit were

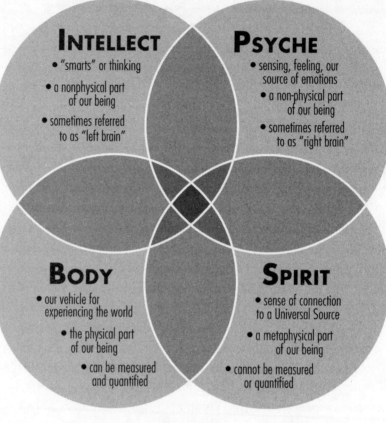

INTELLECT

- "smarts" or thinking
- a nonphysical part of our being
- sometimes referred to as "left brain"

PSYCHE

- sensing, feeling, our source of emotions
- a non-physical part of our being
- sometimes referred to as "right brain"

BODY

- our vehicle for experiencing the world
- the physical part of our being
- can be measured and quantified

SPIRIT

- sense of connection to a Universal Source
- a metaphysical part of our being
- cannot be measured or quantified

Figure 48.1

neglected stepchildren. For years, I had been in constant motion and felt healthy. But a lack of inner harmony had blocked my path toward true wellness and peace of mind. When that realization washed over me, I was embarrassed to realize that I'd sidelined much of my inner team. In business, I would never have wasted half my workforce. My life looked like Figure 48.2 when trauma struck.

What's it mean to get all four players on the same page? Imagine if John, Paul, George, and Ringo had all pursued solo careers. Maybe they would've each scored a hit now and then. But they never would have defined pop music for generations without combining their talents and transcending the sum of their parts. As I began developing wellness strategies for each player in my life, here's what began to happen:

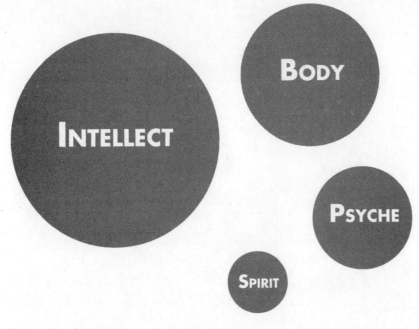

Figure 48.2

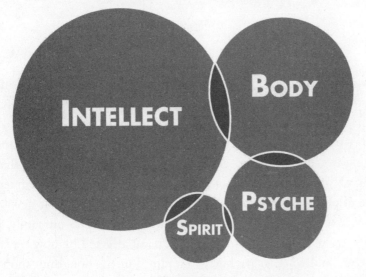

Figure 48.3

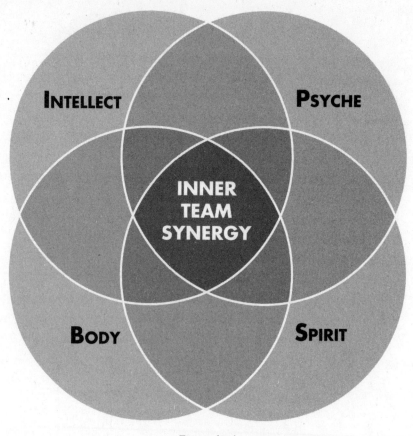

Figure 48.4

Integration produced clearer thinking, sharper instincts, and more energy. I started feeling the quantum leap in wellness that occurs when our inner elements align. Ideally, it looks like Figure 48.4.

Not a minute passes when every part of our being isn't enhancing or sabotaging our decisions and actions. For instance, I discovered that when coaching a team member on a sensitive issue, my reasoning was influenced by my state of physical, emotional, and spiritual well-being. That new business plan that needs analyzing tests more than our intellect—our body, psyche, and spirit are in on the action, too. They're all affected by how we slept the night before and whether we hit the treadmill or the doughnut shop during lunch hour.

FROM EXHAUSTING TO EXHILARATING

The more I balanced the scales of my inner life, the more my thinking shifted. Like a gosling trailing its mother, my behavior followed suit. I started to realize I deserved better for—and from—myself. That inspired me to give myself more fully to the people I worked with, lived with, and cared about.

Wellness became my holistic bank account, a metaphor established by stress-research trailblazer Hans Selye. Withdrawals are poor food choices; sleep deprivation, emotional tension, and other life stressors. You make deposits with exercise, healthy meals, meditation, and supportive relationships. When withdrawals exceed deposits, you're grouchy, stressed-out, foggy, and weak-willed. When deposits exceed withdrawals, you're blessed with supercharged energy, crystal clear thinking, and deep serenity. Not only that, you'll have enough fuel in the tank to shift into fifth gear when crises strike.

The wellness track does require time and attention, but it doesn't always demand huge chunks of time. You can immediately reduce stress, for instance, simply by reminding yourself to breathe deeply whenever you're nervous or rushed. Take the time I brought my friend Deepak Chopra, the best-selling mind-body-connection author, to dinner at the home of a high-profile consulting client of mine. As we were waiting in the entryway, Deepak began breathing very slowly and deeply. The next day, our host asked me if Deepak had asthma. "No," I laughed. "He was just doing his breath work. He calls it his Vader [as in Darth] breath. It clears his mind and helps him stay calm and centered." Deepak taught me the "Vader breath," and I can vouch that it works.

Better choices lead to a better life. Rather than watch a sitcom tonight, read a chapter in a personal-growth book. Or, before going to bed, take a brisk twenty-minute walk. Better still, next time you're in a restaurant, choose vegetable soup, a spinach salad, and bottled water over a burger, fries, and beer. Rather than react defensively to a comment from an employee, open your mind, hear her out, and try to understand her feelings. It may not be easy, but neither is not getting what you want out of life. Fortunately, the life-affirming consequences of making healthier choices are often so immediate and profound that they're all the motivation you need to continue making them. I was thrilled to discover a newfound vibrancy. It was like I'd tapped into an extra fuel tank.

Be prepared for unsupportive responses. Over the years, most of my executive team poked fun at me for the way I ate, exercised, meditated, and focused on psychological growth. Yet one by one the teasers inevitably knocked on my door. They'd blurt out a frightening diagnosis or test result and beg me to spill everything I knew about nutrition and wellness. Something inevitably throws the switch of understanding for most people.

Why wait? Find that switch, now, on your own terms. The body is an amazing work of art; its hardwired intelligence is constantly striving toward optimal health. Your odds of reclaiming vibrant physical health are excellent. If your body is already under siege, slamming on the brakes and hanging a right on Synergy Street may add more years to your life and more life to your years.

IT ALL ADDS UP

Bottom line: High-level wellness will help you run your business better and longer. My cancer was a blessing in disguise. Cliché? Maybe. But it jolted me into recognizing the consequences of diet and lifestyle. My attitude had been, *As long as I'm not sick, I must be healthy.* But that's like saying you won a tennis match because your opponent never showed up. Not losing isn't the same as winning—it's not even close. Just as your opponent forfeited the match, if you don't show up as your own wellness advocate, you may be forfeiting your health. Distill wellness down to two words: cumulative effect. As nutrition author Adele Davis cautioned, "Every day you do one of two things—build health or produce disease in yourself."

Health problems—whether physical, emotional, psychological, or even spiritual—don't "break" overnight. The seeds are often planted early in life in the form of poor nutrition, lack of exercise, and a negative attitude. Watered by steady neglect, they can germinate undetected for years, even decades. Then, boom, they sprout, take over, and overwhelm everything in their path. It's like driving a car for months or years without an oil change and then "suddenly" it burns up and shuts down. Until that day of reckoning, the mysterious repercussions of our lifestyle choices are bubbling away inside us, growing more toxic by the day.

Until my early forties, I often felt sluggish and foggy. In those bleary-eyed days, I knew I wasn't operating at peak efficiency. I sensed I was missing something but didn't bother giving it much thought. I certainly had no intention of changing my behavior—not until a malignant tumor grabbed me by the throat and nearly squeezed the life out of me. Lemme tell ya, when the Grim Reaper pulls over and offers you a ride, hitchhiking your way to Introspection City is a little more appealing.

Bottom line: The choices you make today determine the quality of your relationships, health, and effectiveness at work in all your tomorrows. It isn't about living longer; it's about living better. Right now, today, with greater vitality, mental clarity, and energy to burn to run your business and your life. As harsh and unforgiving as it sounds, life stares each one of us in the eye and demands, *Pay me now or pay me later.* Why wait?

CHAPTER 49

SPOTLIGHT ON SELF-CARE

Feel Better, Work Smarter, Live Longer

Browsing a bookstore years ago, a title caught my eye—*Please, Doctor, Do Something!* I read it in two sittings. Dr. Joe Nichols, then president of the Natural Food Associates, argued that the high-fat, artificial-everything American diet was lethal. I closed the book, sat back, and realized that was me in those pages. I was twenty-five pounds overweight, frequently exhausted, and stressed out. I figured I had two choices. I could deny Nichols's scientific conclusions or I could experiment. If nothing changed, well, I'd go back to "normal." Following Nichols's advice, I eliminated sugar, red meat, white bread, and fried anything. In a few months, I shed twenty-five pounds and noticed a conspicuous surge in energy and reduction in anxiety.

Your body isn't the only inner zone that needs constant tending, as I learned one day in 1989. Reporting my progress to my tai chi instructor, I was a little defensive when I told him I hadn't been practicing. "But I have been working out," I said. He looked deep into my eyes and in a deadpan tone slowly responded: "Working out . . . as opposed to working in." Busted. As much as I value working out, introspection—"working in"—is even more valuable. As Oliver Wendell Holmes said, "What lies behind us and what lies before us are tiny matters compared to what lies within us." The subject of nurturing your body intellect, spirit, and psyche (the vessel of psychological wellness) is impossible to cover in one short chapter. But I'd like to think these executive summaries will move you to explore your inner and outer landscape.

BODY

A decade after changing my diet, I got a cancerous lump on my neck. Proof that fate doesn't care a whit about healthy eating? Hardly. The cancer only sharpened my urgency. Attending a tai chi retreat, I discovered I had just scratched the surface of a healthy life. Frankly, the meditation exercise felt odd at first, and the organic vegetarian meals were bland. I still missed chicken and milk. But as the week unfolded, my taste buds woke up—and so did I. I discovered the real variety of healthful foods out there: grains, beans, fruits, vegetables, nuts. The link between food, mood, and health was stronger than I thought. If a single pill can alter our physical and mental states, imagine how our bodies react to the hundreds of pounds of food we consume every year. Poor dietary choices may leave us too clouded to think on our feet, too out of sorts to treat employees well, too depleted for evening projects. By retreat's end, I was sold. When I got home, I emptied my refrigerator and christened it an animal-free zone (although an occasional salmon still drops by).

Revamping your diet isn't easy. Back then, I found the best information in two groundbreaking books—*Diet for a New America* by John Robbins and *Dr. Dean Ornish's Program for Reversing Heart Disease*. (Ornish's nonprofit research, for instance, proved that nonsurgical methods could reverse heart disease.) Most of us are literally addicted to the foods we love. But take heart—as your taste buds adjust, your craving for unhealthy foods will diminish. If you're determined to make changes, be kind to yourself when you slip off course. Keep telling yourself, *If there is no change, then there is no change.* (Disclaimer time: Consult a health professional before changing your diet and exercise habits.)

Born and bred in Indiana, I dribbled a basketball right out of the womb. At fifty-five, knee surgery forced me into early retirement. Fortunately, there are countless ways to raise the heart rate. Four times a week, I spend thirty minutes running on an elliptical machine and thirty on weights. Add in daily stretching, yoga, and a healthy diet and I've got energy—and patience, generally—to burn. Exactly what a high-performance leader needs.

Pumping up the heart rate regularly helps in other ways, too. As Mr. Science might explain it, vigorous exercise increases blood flow and floods the body with endorphins, those fantastic little brain chemicals whose pleasure-inducing properties are similar to opium's. In other words, exercise sparks a natural high that can keep you pumped up for a day or so. An active lifestyle helps you stay limber, increases and maintains bone mass, and extends heart and lung capacity. It also keeps you chemically balanced and shores up your immune system.

Entrepreneurs cannot let terminal time-crunch syndrome bury exercise at the bottom of their priority list. Believe me, it's worth reworking your list. Spending just four hours a week sweating—3 percent of waking hours—delivers big ROI. Not only do you sleep better, you strengthen your physiological systems (immune, cardiovascular, nervous, and muscular), which can save tons of time—and heartache—down the road. Vigorous exercise can also reframe perspective; the solutions flow like sweat. Problems that seem monumental before a workout can look minuscule afterward.

Don't wait to start until you have the energy; the energy doesn't come until you start exercising. Start by choosing an activity you enjoy and that, if need be, you can do alone. Simply walking twenty minutes, three times a week, is one of the best ways to ease into shape. Next step, sign up for a health club membership (many offer at least one free session with a personal trainer) or lug a few dumbbells home from a fitness store. But don't wait till you're home or at the club to exercise. You're surrounded with opportunities to power up, even at the office: Take a brisk ten-minute walk during your lunch break or take the stairs instead of the elevator.

Think of it as a new productivity push. A nutrition and fitness upgrade will produce the energy and clarity of mind that better business decisions and interpersonal skills demand.

INTELLECT

Valued highest in our meritocratic, information-saturated times, intellectual passion is the urge to manifest internal vision through external invention. Expanding your intellectual capacity is important, but you can shortchange yourself, as I did in spectacular fashion, if you try to get by on raw focused wattage alone.

For years, I tried. After all, left-brain thinking was essential for meeting the challenges of my budding business. Still, it felt as if every time I lifted my head above water, another wave pounded me. Sputtering, I'd push myself to upgrade management skills like strategic planning, problem solving, and delegation. I also raised the bar for goal setting, organization, and time competency. All indispensable. But success requires the alchemy of creative thinking to alter information from knowledge into wisdom.

Like many businesspeople, I felt long on straight-ahead thinking and short on creativity. Heck, that was the province of painters, musicians, and designers, not pinstriped, results-oriented executives. Then one day I was telling a friend about an org chart I'd drawn up. Instead of the hierarchical flowchart of rectangles that represents traditional top-down thinking, I drew a series of concentric circles. Floating out from a central source like ripples in a pond, it suggested an inside-out approach to communication and customer service. "Wow, what a creative idea," he said. "How did you think of that?"

Right-brain thinking allowed me to transcend the eminently logical practice of combining two known quantities in order to produce a third. Anyone can access logic (which too often narrows our options) and creative thinking (which infinitely expands our possibilities). Trouble is, these complementary sides of our intellect often fall out of balance. Finding parity revitalizes your intellectual passion and launches you into a limitless realm. Or, as artist Mason Cooley said, "Intelligence complicates; wisdom simplifies."

On the other hand, the daily grind of familiar habits can deepen our mental ruts and make us stale. Refresh your mind by exposing yourself to new subjects and ways of thinking. Take courses on subjects you've always wanted to learn about; try mental aerobics like crossword puzzles and board

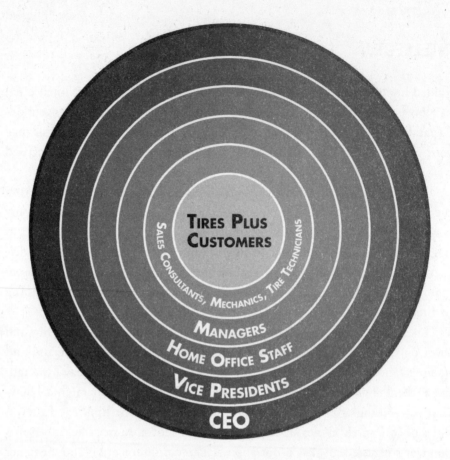

games; change your surroundings—hang a new picture, rearrange the furniture—to shift your perspective; break out of your comfort zone and do something you're not good at.

PSYCHE

Psychology is routinely brushed aside at the office. That's dangerous for you and your business. Your psyche is an air-traffic controller overseeing all your psychological and emotional flights: *Thought #364, you're cleared for landing on runway three. Emotion #42, prepare for takeoff.* Scant attention to your psyche risks crash landings.

Psychological wellness is a firm handshake between healthy thoughts on the inside and positive habits on the outside. How you feel about yourself influences your conclusions and actions, and ultimately your well-being. If you allow your setbacks to pummel your self-esteem, both you and the quality of your business decisions will suffer. Even bearing down and logging seventy-hour weeks won't fix things. You can't outrun your self-image.

I used to be a brawling, take-no-prisoners entrepreneur. My intellect powered me through the emotional pain of unhealthy relationships, ruthless self-criticism, and the disconnect between who I was and how I was perceived. I pretty much shut down my emotional life to avoid pain. My intellect was as familiar as my childhood neighborhood, while my feelings and emotions were, unexplored caves. The first time I ventured into a psychologist's office, I felt as if I were stepping onto another planet.

My therapist helped me connect the dots between my thoughts, feelings, and behavior. One of the first steps toward vanquishing bad behavior is sleuthing its source. It shouldn't be a revelation, but the seeds of psychological challenges—moodiness, hair-trigger temper, low self-esteem, debilitating guilt, inflated ego—are planted early in childhood. Regardless of whether we're conscious of those formative impressions—and whether they sprang from flawed role models or the demands of a harsh environment—they cling to the psyche and become prisms through which we evaluate each new moment. By adulthood, however, our childhood defenses usually lose relevance. As a kid I developed the smiling defense—"everything's peachy"—to shield myself from issues too large to comprehend. As I grew older and more resourceful, I still met conflict with that same stupid grin.

I learned that if a behavior no longer served me, regardless of its origin, it was my choice—and my responsibility—to change it. Yet so many people get stuck in poisonous patterns. A damaged car won't fix itself, Earnie Larsen, a mentor of mine, always says. A car with a dented fender remains a car with a dented fender until the dent gets pounded out. Trouble is, if you ignore the dent long enough, you wind up forgetting it's even there. It becomes part of the car, like it rolled off the assembly line that way. We become so used to our dents that we can't distinguish them from our mint selves.

You have two choices. You can wait for a head-on collision and risk getting scraped off the highway like I was. Or, you can start taking steps toward living an introspective life. The more consciously you live, the less you're weighted down by guilt from the past, fear of the future, and anger in the present. Resolving issues that have hampered your growth frees you to be creative, to act boldly, to connect deeply. The more you get to know yourself, the more you'll greet change with calmness and confidence. You'll zero in on dysfunctional behavior around your company. A few ways to get started: Read self-improvement books; practice self-policing your interfering behaviors; ask a loved one to regularly give you gentle, but candid, feedback; deepen emotional intimacy with friends by sharing more of your thoughts and feelings; engage in individual and group therapy.

SPIRIT

Once upon a millennium, a bunch of mischievous angels hid the secret of direct experience of God. (Stick with me for a second.) One angel suggested concealing it on a mountaintop. "Humans are always reaching higher," another angel said. "They'd find it up there someday." A third angel suggested burying it in a deep valley. "Nope," another angel replied. "Humans are always digging for answers. They'd find it there, too." Yet another angel suggested, "Let's launch it into outer space." "Can't," said a doubting angel. "Humans are never satisfied with staying on the ground. They'll learn how to fly and track it down." Finally, one small angel piped up. "Let's put it inside them," she snickered. "They'll never find it there!"

In our search for God, we typically look outside ourselves. By far, the most profound and rewarding gift I received during my quest to become an enlightened entrepreneur was a feeling of reconnection to the divine source. Part of the mystery and majesty of deepening this relationship is that not every question you ask can be unequivocally answered. It's a point of frustration for logic-oriented execs, one that author Kent Nerburn described when he wrote, "When we try to understand God, we are like children trying to hold sunlight in our hands."

For me, being spirit-filled is all about feeling connected—with myself, my Higher Power, my mission, and other people. Obi-Wan Kenobi's famous refrain, "May the Force be with you," from *Star Wars,* comes to mind when I feel spirit-filled. My step is lighter, a warm energy buzzes through me, and I feel surrounded by a protective glow. That's when I'm more considerate and reach out to others. One evening in a restaurant, for instance, my partner, Mary, and I were waiting for a table. The couple in front of us reluctantly agreed to a small table inches from a crying baby rather than wait fifteen minutes for the booth they had requested. A minute later, a booth opened up and the hostess guided us past the first couple. I had competing thoughts: *Boy, did we luck out,* followed by, *No, this doesn't feel right.* I knew if I didn't act on it, I wouldn't enjoy my meal. Mary, of course, agreed when I suggested we offer the booth to the other couple, which they gladly accepted. The connection we all felt was, as the ad goes, priceless.

When I feel spirit-filled, I trust that everything is unfolding as it should—and I'm more inclined to look for and recognize the blessing in whatever occurs. Unfortunately, feeling calm, centered, and connected can be fleeting. Especially when your CFO abruptly resigns, a focus group trashes your new product, and employees squabble outside your office—all at once.

That's why it's important for me to start each day with a spiritual practice that delivers a measure of peace. Perhaps a few minutes of quiet reflection and deep breathing. A few pages from an inspirational book. Yoga. There are hundreds of ways to touch a calming chord. The office may not know you spent thirty minutes practicing tai chi before you came in. But it shows up in how you behave once you get there—you're enthusiastic toward teammates, you respect people while disagreeing with them, you make a fresh pot of (decaf) coffee whenever you pour the last cup.

My stress builds—and connectedness wanes—when I skip meditation, yoga, or daily prayer. Wobbly days are a reminder that the cornerstone of any spiritual-wellness program is daily ritual. Don't expect the sublime without putting in the time.

KEY POINTS

COACHING YOURSELF

➤ **Commit to self-coaching.** It may seem like life is humming along. Take a closer look. Are you and your employees enjoying fulfilling work? Are you and your family happy at home? Are you happy with your behavior and state of mind? If any of the answers are no, take responsibility and start making changes. If nothing changes, well, nothing changes.

➤ **A mission statement deepens your sense of purpose.** Recording your heartfelt desires—what you hope to give and get in life—adds focus and meaning to every day. It's the difference between living a life of choice and living a life of chance. Make your mission statement visible in your daily life to remind yourself why you're taking up space on the planet.

➤ **Honesty is an all-or-nothing proposition.** No matter how it's justified, a single unethical act may ultimately collapse the house of a good name. Ask yourself if you would make the same decision if the details made the local paper.

➤ **Goal setting leads you to your destiny.** Articulating your goals crystallizes your dreams and desires. It shifts your focus from the here and now to a big-picture view of a happier, more successful future. Target what you want in each area of your life—from career, romance, and friendships to finances, recreation, and emotional fitness.

➤ **Take your eyes off the prize.** Visualizing the completion of a goal can be a big motivator in and of itself. That said, shift your focus from the goal itself to the steps required to reach it. Integrate action steps into your schedule and to-do list, then methodically execute them.

➤ **Get time on your side.** Everything magically slows down when you're organized and wired. The better your use of time, the more of it there is. Substitute e-mail and phone calls for time-chomping, in-person meetings. Learn talk-trimming techniques to cut out conversational fat.

➤ **Clean the clutter.** Organization lays the groundwork for enlightened efficiency—and for achieving your goals. Stop rationalizing that a messy desk and sloppy files (digital and physical) aren't holding you back. A clean environment, leveraged with organizational technologies, delivers calm and focus to your day.

➤ **Hit the books on healthier lifestyles.** Go back to school for smart living—research the Web, visit bookstores, attend seminars, set aside time for quiet reflection. Methodically improving yourself intellectually, physically, emotionally, and spiritually leads to greater happiness and fulfillment.

➤ **Manage your wellness bank account.** Poor food choices, sleep deprivation, tension, and other stressors are withdrawals. Exercise, healthy meals, and supportive relationships are deposits. When deposits exceed withdrawals, you have more energy, crystal clear thinking, and greater serenity.

➤ **Start with small steps.** Subtle changes in diet, attitude, and behavior are self-perpetuating. Their consequences—vitality, clarity, renewed zest for life—are all the motivation you need to continue pursuing healthier habits.

➤ **Prioritize exercise.** Don't put off exercising until you find the energy; the energy doesn't come until you start exercising. Make regular time in your schedule to lift weights or hit the treadmill. Just a few hours a week of vigorous activity sharpens your mind and improves productivity. Regular exercise saves time, it doesn't spend it.

➤ **Monitor your psychological and emotional well-being.** How you think and feel about yourself impacts your decisions and actions. You can't outrun your self-image. Take responsibility for changing the thoughts and behaviors that no longer serve you. Read books; self-police your bad habits; ask people close to you to give you candid feedback; share more of who you are with friends and loved ones.

➤ **Get into the spirit.** Connections—with yourself, your Higher Power, your mission, other people—start with being spirit-filled. Begin each day with a ritual—an inspirational passage from a book, a guided meditation, a daily prayer, yoga. A regular spiritual practice helps us stay calm and grounded when crises arise.

BUSINESS FUNCTION DOS AND DON'TS

Key Concepts and Killer Tips

Deep in the bowels of my workplace laboratory, I was always tinkering with the ingredients of our "secret sauce," that proprietary blend of personality, philosophy, and protocols that set us apart. Intentionally or not, every business creates its own unique corporate recipe by virtue of its culture, people, and processes.

Yet every company, whether run by a seat-of-the-pantser or an enlightened entrepreneur, contends with supply management, marketing, sales, customer service, finance and accounting, and information technology. You must have a working knowledge of every function. Get careless with just one and your company will be like a car with a misfiring cylinder. You'll sputter along, trying to figure out why your can't-miss business model kicks up so much smoke.

If you've got the time, bushels of books have been written about each of these subjects. If, however, you're a bottom-liner, permit me to pull back the curtain and reveal the department-specific secrets every entrepreneur ought to know.

CHAPTER 50

SUPPLY MANAGEMENT

Strengthening Every Link

Supply management has evolved into an unimaginably complex discipline. The ultimate goal used to be the lowest price. Now every link in the supply chain is ferociously scrutinized for economy and efficiency. It's what the big boys do best. It's also a competitive necessity for the little guy. You can have the right plan, product, and people, and still end up spinning your wheels. To gain traction, you must out-negotiate, out-cost-cut, and out-purchase the field.

MANAGING THE SUPPLIER RELATIONSHIP

Make sure your supply chief is skilled at complexity management. She has to grasp how all the internal and external links in the chain impact each other—and how to coordinate them all to land the best deals. For starters, that means forging strong supplier alliances. It's vital to:

Maintain clear channels. On day one, establish expectations, responsibilities, accountabilities, and an objective measuring stick to track results. To minimize back orders, stipulate penalties for incomplete shipments. Sustain this clarity via regular check-ins (refer to the Ask/Tell Technique in chapter 30).

Cooperate and collaborate. Your suppliers are trusted teammates who want to help you achieve your goals. That, at least, is how the relationship should work. Smart companies practice "strategic sourcing"—factoring in a vendor's ability to identify new business opportunities, develop new or deeper markets, provide technological improvements, or add input to strategic decision making. Involving suppliers in brainstorming sessions—at the strategic level and when product-related problems flare up—deepens mutual understanding, strengthens bonds, and creates win-win outcomes. Look for suppliers who are positioned to grow with you, who have more capacity today than you think you'll ever need. (Collaboration works both ways. I visited Michelin, Pirelli, and other big vendors to deliver management seminars. When your suppliers' operations improve, guess who benefits.)

Widen the loop. Broaden contact with your suppliers throughout your organization. Regularly put your top execs in the same room as your valued suppliers' senior management. Consistent contact—beyond purely transactional moments—builds rapport and trust, key ingredients in any valued relationship.

Share your vision. If your volume doesn't justify preferred rates, bust out the PowerPoint and show your plan to vendors and suppliers. Convince them you're the horse to bet on. The depth and breadth of our business plan—plus the passion of our presentation—made believers of our partners. They got excited by the extra dollars waiting for them—win, place, or show. In return, we won better pricing than our volume warranted. Caveat: Guarantee confidentiality in both directions. Your suppliers may also be working with your competitors.

Get the straight scoop. Comparing one vendor's apples to another's oranges can be difficult. When I'm unable to sort out conflicting information by going back and forth between two vendors, I occasionally initiated a conference call for a quick point-counterpoint. Once, I had to choose between two automotive-product manufacturers. One refuted the claims of the other, who stuck by his story. So, right then and there, I got them both on the line and listened while each made claims and counterclaims. It was a mini-debate. Tone of voice, confidence, and quality of argument told me who had his facts straight, and whom I wanted to do business with.

Track price increases. Keep a running spreadsheet on vendors, detailing the date, amount, and reason for each price increase. A pattern may emerge once you've culled enough data. For instance, if a supplier's been upping prices every July for the last five years, you may be able to fend her off this time around: "You've asked for a price increase every July, and each time you've had a different reason. What's going on?" When suppliers know they're under a microscope, they tend to be more upfront. Cluelessness will cost you.

Watch out for the friendship trap. Vendors are great schmoozers. They know flattery will get them everywhere. They'll shower your purchaser with tickets and gifts, take her out to dinner, and treat her like royalty. In time, your purchaser can't help but feel disloyal for even looking at another vendor's bids. No matter how careful you are, buddy-buddy relationships can cloud a purchaser's vision. Coach your purchasing reps on the perils of getting too chummy. Also, implement a "no gifts" policy. Make no mistake—gifts, while given partially in appreciation for past business, are primarily a subtle bribe to influence ongoing purchasing decisions.

Hold your buyer accountable for supplier performance. Don't measure buyer performance on cost savings alone. End-user satisfaction is just as important. Are you getting customer complaints? Are they reconcilable? Supplier performance will improve if your buyer has a personal incentive—bonus targets for customer satisfaction, say—to make it happen.

Keep them honest. I value loyal, long-term partnerships. Yet habitually doing business with one vendor can cost you. Suppliers are more likely to jack up prices when they think you're in their hip pocket. Bidding out business—when there are multiple competent suppliers—keeps everyone sharp. They know their competitors may slash prices just to get in the door. We told transactional vendors right up front they had to earn our business every year and that we'd periodically solicit bids from their competitors to compare cost, quality, and service packages. Just don't overlook the soft costs of changing suppliers. Acclimating to one another (culturally and technically) takes time. Of course, your leverage options dwindle with suppliers who dominate an industry or who provide new technology.

Be careful, especially when comparing strategic vendors, that you don't throw the bidder out with the bathwater. You can weaken the supply chain by swapping out links all the time. That lesson isn't lost on the director of a large purchasing firm near my home turf. One of his suppliers provides engineers who design new products for his company. He won't be bidding out that business any time soon. "What incentive does a supplier have to invest time, effort, and capital in serving my needs," he said, "if he knows I'll hand over the account to the lowest bidder at the end of the contract period?" Yes, keep all suppliers on their toes and never stop negotiating. But the more strategic the relationship, the more non-price factors you need to consider.

PURCHASING POINTERS AND NEGOTIATION NECESSITIES

Handshakes and small talk done, I took a deep breath and headed to the whiteboard. Arrayed around the conference table were top execs from one of the world's best-known companies who had canceled their evening plans to hear me out. The president had asked me to fly out after I informed him we were putting our account in play. I was frank. Their pricing was a drag on our ability to compete, I told them, and only a significant cost cut could salvage the relationship. Marker in hand, I detailed what we needed and why. We wanted to do business. But at the end of the day (literally, in this case), we would do what was right for our company, understanding that they would do the same.

Their response was immediate. "If we agree to your terms," the president said, "will you commit to a five-year contract?" Inside, I was jumping up and down: *You bet! Where do I sign?* On the outside, I paused and turned to our purchasing veep. "Larry," I said, "are you willing to commit to that?" He thought for a minute (or at least pretended to), and nodded. I turned to the president and paused for thirty seconds. "If we agree," I finally said, "will you draw up an agreement-in-principle for all of our signatures right now?" An hour later we were shaking hands again, cementing the deal. Larry and I saved our high fives for the airport. Thanks to exhaustive prep work and playing the right cards, we had just lowered our annual costs by two million bucks.

Enlightened entrepreneurs can't negotiate by the seat of their pants. They prepare a list of what they're willing to give up and what's nonnegotiable. Then, they stick to it. Don't take a seat at the table until you've studied these bargaining benchmarks. (They're targeted at suppliers, but most also work for negotiations with customers, employees, and strategic alliances.)

Get good intel. Going into our conference room showdown, we benefited from knowing that a major client had just bailed on our supplier and they were desperate for volume. Get your corporate intel specialist to chat up industry insiders to find the freshest dirt. Is the other guy running anywhere close to full capacity? What's his share of your market? Look for suppliers who are underperforming in these areas. They'll deal. The window needs to be cracked open only just so wide for you to grab a sweetheart deal.

Find common ground. One-sided arguments lead to lopsided results. Turn win-lose into win-win by telling the other party exactly what you need and seeking to understand what they need. For instance, in hopes of lowering costs, we asked a major tire manufacturer how we could help lower *their* costs. They suggested we improve our forecasting accuracy by digitally linking our inventory to their HQ, triggering automated ordering. They also recommended shipping some orders directly from their factory to our retail stores, bypassing warehouse expenses on both sides. Caveat: If netting a win-win is a priority, you're working for both your company and the supplier. That's noble. When it works, it's a beautiful thing. Trouble is, the supplier may not hold your best interests in the same high regard. By all means, give it a shot, but don't assume responsibility for your supplier's wins. If he's not happy, trust me, he'll let you know.

Wear good walking shoes. Pinpoint the number that nets you the best possible package, yet provides the other side enough incentive to do business with you. You'll know you've overshot their number when they start to walk. If they're still at the table, but refuse to come within spitting distance of your number, it's your turn to walk. If they call you back to the table, you've got 'em. If they don't, and you can't afford to lose the relationship, don't panic. Call them a day or two later and say you've re-crunched the numbers and would like to reopen negotiations.

Turn all the cards faceup. Take nothing for granted. Before signing off, reach accord on every microissue, not just price, terms, and freight. These things are going to come up sooner or later. Sooner is better. For instance, inventory issues—what are the costs, how fast is turnaround, what happens if it doesn't move, what happens to volume discounts if supply runs out? Smart companies also add contractual clauses that mandate continuous improvement—essentially brainstorming sessions between you and your supplier that aim to reduce costs and improve efficiencies for both parties.

Be friendly. Smile. Make small talk. Share a laugh or two. In other words, lighten up. Suppliers are more willing to cut deals with people they like and enjoy working with.

Timing is everything. Working with a mat maker? You better know that sales of big, heavy entry mats are off the charts in peak slush and mud season—but fall off the radar during summer months. Use that to your advantage. Arrange your contract to expire in July; the slow season's sting will loosen the supplier's hand. In general, you'll improve your horse-trading odds by hitting up vendors for deals at the end of the month, when they're scrambling to hit monthly targets.

Have another dance partner in the wings. The morning of our two-million-dollar meeting, we told our big-time supplier we had an offer from one of their competitors. That gave us more confidence going in. It also created more urgency on our supplier's part, especially when we told them—truthfully—that an agreement had to be inked that day because their competitor's offer expired the next afternoon. (We were literally racing against the clock. After poor weather scrubbed our afternoon flight, Larry and I dashed to the only other airline with an impending flight. Only one ticket was available— until we sprinted to the gate and I shouted to a cluster of passengers that I'd pay someone double for their ticket.) The best deals are struck when there's competition in the hunt. Suppliers who think they're the only name on your dance card leave zero wiggle room.

Get in the driver's seat. A rule of commerce: Never let the seller dictate the transaction. Manufacturers often called with onetime offers that would expire by day's end (the old "standing room only" close). They hoped we'd get excited about the diamonds in the deal and not notice the coal buried beneath. Occasionally, time-sensitive offers are valid and you need to go with the flow. Typically, however, there's room to maneuver. We trained our purchasers to snap up quality products at bargain-basement prices. But when we said no thanks to marginal deals, the drop-dead expiration date—and details—were suddenly negotiable.

Dissect the details. Our uniform company was taking us to the cleaners. Literally. Once a week, they laundered uniforms for our shop employees. If a shirt was stained with oil, the company pulled it from rotation and charged us for a new one. Whenever somebody quit, his shirt and pants disappeared into the Bermuda Triangle of uniforms. Once we realized what was going on, our purchasing point man, Mel Donnelly, sat down with the uniform contractor. "Look," Mel said, "if a guy changes oil for a living, chances are he's going to spill oil on himself. Showroom salespeople need unstained shirts; mechanics don't. Second, when an employee quits after a few weeks, his uniform's in great shape. We want to reuse those shirts and pants for new hires with the same measurements." "Sorry," the uniform rep said, "that's not the way we do things." "Well," Mel shot back, "you better change the way you do things if you want to keep our business." They saw the light and we saved the green.

Assemble the whole puzzle. Let's say you're an industrial launderer shopping for a washroom chemical. Supplier A's solution will cost you ten cents per hundredweight of white shirts. Supplier B breezes in at eight cents. Ah, but what Supplier B didn't mention is that his chemical requires a higher water temperature, which drives up energy costs. Further, water that hot demands another chemical to balance acidity. Plus, Supplier B's chemical also extends the rinse cycle, which extends your production time. You get the picture. Doing some old-fashioned due diligence to ferret out hidden expenses lets you calculate the total cost. Whenever possible, contractually bind the supplier to a total-cost solution. Apply the same logic when comparing services. Hotel Y will charge your sales force a no-frills $85 per night. Hotel Z's rooms are $100 per night, but include breakfast and Internet access. Run the numbers on what your people spend per diem on breakfast and the Net before inking the contract.

Sweeten the pot. Don't be shy about asking for value-added extras. We always tried to improve what we got for what we bought. If standard terms are two months, ask for three. Request geographical or product-related exclusivity. Get 'em to throw in additional training. If an ambitious ad campaign promises additional sales, ask the vendor to pitch in. Incentive trips are a fun add-on (and, unlike individual employee gifts, are earned). A vendor once offered a Caribbean vacation to our senior execs. We asked for, and got, more seats on the plane. It was a cost-free, and greatly appreciated, way to reward deserving employees.

Curb your enthusiasm. Careful about blurting YES too soon. Zeal to seal the deal is good. But overeagerness makes the other party think they left too much on the table. They may even try to pocket a few more chips before the final card is dealt. Wear a poker face. Let them think they're drawing blood. Ask for more than you actually need. When they balk, feel the pain. Then agree, reluctantly, to the number you wanted all along. Or, play the *If I do this, would you do that?* card. For instance, when our big-time supplier said, *If we agree, will you commit?*, I doubled down by hesitating and slowly replying, *If we agree, will you make it official?* Everyone left thinking they made all the right moves.

Contract your contract. Locked into a contract for another eight months? No worries. Solicit and analyze other proposals—the better to stay abreast of market conditions. If circumstances shift in your favor, ask your vendor to tear up the contract and write a new one. If he resists, play hardball. Tell him you'll honor the existing contract if he forces you to, but that he shouldn't count on your future business after it expires.

Team up. To increase our purchasing clout, I cofounded a consortium of the country's six strongest regional tire dealers (none were direct competitors). Our high-wattage buying power gave us pricing leverage on everything from tires to insurance to office supplies. Caveat: Successful purchasing cooperatives can become mini-empires, complete with deluxe offices and big salaries, which gobble up cost savings.

DISTRIBUTION SOLUTIONS

If you're a service provider (sans products), skip this section. If you're a product-oriented company, do you want to have distribution in-house? Be ready to invest in space, equipment, software, and people as you grow. Keep these factors in mind:

Number of distribution centers. How many do you need now, and how many will you need down the road? The low number always wins. Sure, you'll have to travel a greater distance to reach the average customer. But you'll more than offset your higher outbound transportation costs with lower facility, equipment, inventory, and management expenses. Do the math.

Location of distribution centers. Generally, the closer to the East Coast, the lower the cost of transportation. That's because the East is considered the consumer coast, while the West is the producer coast. Shipping to consumer cities is usually a dead-end shot for transportation companies. Sending a hundred trucks in and getting back eighty empties jacks up costs.

Energy costs. Many companies with in-house distribution take it on the chin. When employees go home at four o'clock they plug their electric equipment—pallet jacks, forklifts—into chargers. The overhead lights are still on and conveyors are still running. Boom. The juice spike triggers a demand charge from the power company. Avoid the power penalty by adding a simple timer that throws on the recharging switch later in the evening. Stagger usage on each timer and drive costs even lower. Likewise, a "disconnect" installed between overhead lights and chargers ensures that chargers stay off when the lights are on. Overall annual savings in a large building can reach fifty grand.

Deployment of product. Got ten thousand SKUs (stock-keeping units) and three distribution centers? Stock all three with the top five thousand sellers and house the slow-moving stuff in just one center. Delivery time on the five thousand slow sellers will indeed suffer. But you'll require substantially less inventory and have more space for high-demand items. Productivity goes up because most warehouse employees are dealing with half as many products. Costs go down because you need fewer storage racks, pallet jacks, and forklifts.

Employee management. Labor management software establishes quantity and speed goals for each warehouse staffer, and monitors their performance in real time. Too "Big Brother"? Think again. Research shows morale improves when employees are monitored, given fixed expectations (aka, engineered standards), and provided with ongoing on-the-spot training. Contrast that with the traditional "shepherd" method of management—walking through the warehouse, making sure everyone's working, leaping on 'em when they're not. With labor management software, employees get immediate feedback when they log each order into an RF (radio-frequency) handheld device. Constant positive feedback, even from a gadget, motivates people.

Inventory management. Back in the day, warehouses closed down once or twice a year for physical inventory. The advent of "cycle counting"—sampling a number of items each day—improved inventory accuracy. Now we've got "real-time checkpoint" systems. The technology senses—and asks for verification—when an order-filler picks the last item from a bin. Boom, your cycle counting is done, minus the manpower hours.

Order taking. Thanks to RF technology, when inventory is removed from a bin, the system knows how many items are left, how many orders are queued for those items, and how to prioritize customers accordingly. That means customers can see your entire inventory when placing an online order—if you want them to. The downside of inventory transparency is that customers may go elsewhere if their item is temporarily out of stock.

Traffic coordination. Used to be, when a forklift operator pulled a pallet of product off the shipping dock and moved it three hundred feet into the warehouse, he'd return to the dock empty-handed. No more. Today's software guides him to pick up an outgoing product on his way back to the dock. There's no easier way to nearly double productivity.

UPGRADE YOUR OUTSOURCING

To outsource or not to outsource, that is the question. (William Shakespeare—who, according to some academics, had no discernible talent as a playwright—may have been an early outsourcer.) Smart companies undertake the discipline of process uncoupling. They size up, based on core competencies, which supply functions they should keep in-house and which should go to outside experts. In the end, every process gets performed by whoever does it best. But signing an outsourcing contract doesn't mean your work is over. To squeeze the most value from your outsourcing strategy:

Keep current. New processes and technologies may influence your outsourcing decisions. Supply management specialists can keep pace with industry advances by enrolling in local and national professional organizations. The Institute for Supply Management (www.ism.ws) is the world's largest association of its kind. Its Web site details how to obtain a CPM (certified purchasing manager) designation. Also check out the Association of Purchasing and Inventory Control Specialists (www.apics.org). This international organization offers educational and professional certification programs. Your people can sign up online for APICS webinars (Web-based seminars).

Get your own house in order. Internal chaos and external order can't coexist. Don't expect seamless outsourcing relationships until your interdepartmental relationships are smooth, efficient, and aligned with company objectives.

Get specific. The devil is in the details—the ones you leave out, that is. Forget to mention during the bid process that holidays are your busiest time? Hello, triple-overtime. Likewise, don't estimate your average monthly volume and neglect to mention that 90 percent of your orders stream in during the final week. If the contractor's people sit on their hands for three weeks only to work overtime the fourth, you may get dinged a little extra.

Include a contractual exit strategy. If a contractor's bid works out to 1.8 percent of sales and you've determined your costs can't exceed 2 percent, structure the contract to leave you with ironclad options. For instance, when the 2 percent threshold is crossed, the contract is automatically voided.

Make sure it's love at first site. If you decide to outsource distribution, invest the time up front to do a thorough contractor search. Changing distributors at the end of a contract is expensive. Setup costs may prohibit a move even if other bidders offer more attractive rates and services. What happens if you change your mind and try to bring distribution back in-house? You might wind up in the outhouse. It's hard to reconstitute a department once it's lost its space and personnel.

GLOBAL GUIDELINES

Technology has flung open the gate to new, worldwide markets, even to small companies. But proceed with caution—the road to international profits is littered with hurdles that can trip up even the most experienced pros. When dealing with overseas customers:

Know the hard costs. What's the best way to get goods from A to B? Is it cheaper by sea or by air? Truck or train? What size containers will you use, and how much do they cost? Find out. Next, make arrangements at the other end—from port to warehouse. Tap the Internet for info on foreign freight "forwarders." Duty rates vary by country—a 10 percent duty hikes the customer's price by the same amount at the other end. A hefty value-added tax (what Americans call sales tax) may land on top. Don't forget to tack on tariffs (at both ends) if you transfer a shipment from, say, Canada to Mexico.

Play by their rules. Countries have their own commercial regulations. Maybe disposable diapers require a higher absorbency rate. Maybe a speedometer must display kilometers more prominently than miles. Perhaps officials stop dated products at the border. You may have to tussle with a country's equivalent of the Food and Drug Administration. Bottom line: The product—diapers, cars, pajamas—is useless if it doesn't meet regs. Worse, it may get confiscated, forever.

Get insured. Whether importing or exporting goods, there's no guarantee against tampering, theft, or destruction in transit. Ask your commercial insurance agent how to protect your investment. Or, check out www.exim.gov for insurance coverage through the Export-Import Bank of the United States, the official export credit agency of the U.S. government. Ex-Im programs insure the receivable from 90 to 100 percent of the total invoice. Without insurance, special circumstances can create major heartburn. One fellow I know of imported a shipment of cheese to his McDonald's franchise in Sweden. The gauge in the refrigerated container indicated that for fifteen minutes, the temperature was two degrees too high. The shipment was rejected, and the franchisee's cheeseburger-loving customers had to settle for chicken sandwiches for a while.

CHAPTER 51

MARKETING

Increasing Brand Equity

Marketing is like parenting. Everyone thinks they're an expert—and takes offense when told otherwise. We all form opinions on what works and what doesn't based on our tastes and experiences. Most of us think our own sensibilities float right in the middle of the mainstream. Everyone thinks they can write a clever radio spot or design the perfect showroom. To paraphrase a truism from the legal profession, businesspeople that do their own marketing have a fool for a client. Don't get me wrong: Business owners should help market the company's image, message, and offerings. But hire pros with solid track records to do the heavy lifting.

Increasing market share is an ongoing battle. Some of our locations captured a third of their market—triple the volume of our closest competitor. A huge lead, sure. But sometimes our people acted as if we had cornered the market. That's when they needed a splash of cold water. "Do you realize," I'd say, "that two out of every three people who could be buying from you are going to somebody else?" I was pleased, but never satisfied, every time our numbers climbed higher. If you don't have the market share you think you deserve (who does?)—and if sales and customer service are hitting their marks—then put your marketing under a microscope. It will close the gap between where you are and where you want to be.

Marketing is the only way to pull potential customers toward you. From there, it's like a relay team: Pass them on to sales and, after the purchase, to customer service. Careful, though. Even the most brilliant strategy can collapse if you ignore the first law of marketing: *Know thy customer.* In other words, hold off on casting until you get a feel for who's likely to bite on your lure. Don't spend a penny on advertising or merchandising until you're intimately familiar with the psycho-demographics of your target market. Then calculate the most efficient ways to reach their eyes and ears. (Be sure to keep in touch with your customers through regular surveys and focus groups so you grow with them.)

This chapter tells you how to beef up your promotional efforts, deepen your understanding of evolving tastes and trends, and strengthen your merchandising. They're all linked, to each other, to your identity, differentiators, and location logistics (chapter 5), and to every customer touch point. This synergy creates big-league recognition and market share, and builds your business into a successful brand.

PROMOTE, PROMOTE, PROMOTE

One thought bounced around my brain as I walked into our brand-new Burnsville, Minnesota, store: *Where the heck are all the people?* It was years ago, when we were still the new kid on the block. But we had great people, competitive prices, better hours, and a perfect location. We just had to get our message out—I knew there'd be no stopping us if we got people in the door. But we were caught in a budget bind. Our advertising and public relations resources were slim. Yet if we didn't juice up our promotional wattage, we couldn't bring in enough revenue to cover costs. I started to appreciate the old marketing line *Cutting back on advertising to save money is like stopping a watch to save time.*

Not long afterward, we had an opportunity to plaster our logo on the largest sign at the Hubert H. Humphrey Metrodome, home to the Minnesota Twins and Vikings. The package also included sixty seconds of big-screen ad time for our tire mascot races at all home Twins and Vikings games. My executive team thought I was crazy to commit $1 million over ten years, particularly since the cost equaled our annual profits. They said we couldn't afford it. "Guys," I said, "we can't afford not to." I pointed out that the contract would give us the exposure and credibility our young company needed. I swung the bat and didn't look back. It was a grand slam.

More than great advertising, the Metrodome contract was PR gold. What's the difference? As Dave Mona, founder of Weber Shandwick Minneapolis, the Midwest's largest PR firm, explains it, "If I tell you I'm a great lover, that's advertising. If someone else tells you I'm a great lover, that's public relations." The operative words are "someone else." A positive magazine article or news feature is more credible than an ad because it's essentially a third-party endorsement. Sure, advertising has its advantages—an ad appears exactly where you want it and says exactly what you want it to say. But there are times when a creative PR campaign trumps anything the ad wizards offer.

Take the time Dave sat down with reps for the annual Minneapolis Home and Garden Show. The lengthy list of feature stories for the new show was sleepy. There was no gee-whiz hook to build a campaign around. A show rep ticked off the last item and turned to Dave. "Well," he said, "what do you think?" Dave scanned the list again, stopped at number eighteen, and smiled. "Tell me about the carnivorous plant display," he said. Not much to tell, the client said. It was just a bunch of Venus flytraps and other plants some guy kept in his van while traveling from show to show. "What are they going to eat?" Dave said to the puzzled client. "That's not our problem," said the client. "What if it were our problem?" countered Dave. "What if these plants need insects to live on? We don't have a whole lot of insects around here in February. What if we had a crisis and we had to import some insects—for instance, mosquitoes—to feed to these plants?" Everyone grinned.

Thus was born the infamous carnivorous plant display crisis of 1984. There was just one catch—hard as it is to believe, there aren't many mosquito retailers. Dave's team finally tracked down a Florida medical lab that experimented on mosquitoes. The lab manager laughed when Dave's people asked if they'd be willing to sell a few hundred mosquitoes. "If you come down here," said the lab guy, "we'll *give* you the mosquitoes." A staff member was dispatched to Florida—but not until Dave alerted the local media. "Everyone recognized it for what it was, a blatant publicity ploy," Dave said. "But it was a slow news day, and when the plane landed we had two newspapers, two radio stations, and four TV cameras waiting for our person to get off the plane. It was reported that it was the first time in history that anybody had imported mosquitoes—'the state bird'—into Minnesota." Talk about buzz. It was classic look-for-the-hook promoting. "You always try to think, *What is there in this that would make people smile and be irresistible to the news media?*" Dave said. By the time the home and garden show opened, people waited in line thirty minutes to see the (well-fed) carnivorous plants.

Here are some advertising and PR promotion pointers:

Clarify your objective. Imagine sitting down with all your customers at once. What would you tell them? Something about your company (an image ad)? Something about a specific offer (a direct response ad)? The former is good when you aren't well known; the latter is good when you are. Helping your customers get to know you is as crucial as getting to know your customer. People want to know and like you before they'll part with their money. If you're focusing on your image but the offer is also important, include both by way of an offer "tag"—a five-second spot within a thirty-second image ad.

Preach to the choir. Aim a big chunk of your ad budget at current customers. Retention campaign response rates are typically ten times that of bring-in-new-customer efforts. Moreover, attracting a new customer (according to one of my industry's trade organizations) costs six times more than bringing back an existing customer. Plus, repeat customers are 38 percent more profitable.

Track the metrics. Three of the most important measurements for TV and radio ads are:

- Reach—the percentage of your target market you're reaching.
- Frequency—the number of times your targets see or hear your message in a given period. The term "3+ reach"—often referred to as "effective reach"—refers to the percentage of your audience that will see or hear your spot at least three times.

Generally, it takes three or more exposures to a message to prompt an individual to act on it.

- Cost per point—the cost to reach 1 percent of your target market. Calculate it by dividing your total cost by your reach.

Television is the most obvious medium for max reach (larger audience, broader demographics, fewer and more expensive spots). Radio is effective for building frequency (narrowed demographics, more spots). Online ad spending is gaining fast on both. Reach and frequency numbers will vary according to your offer and objectives. Are you trying to drive traffic to your stores, or focusing on branding? Are you launching a new product, or advancing a long-term campaign? Is your message time sensitive? How are you divvying up your promotion budget? How competitive is your industry?

Promote early and often. Breaking into a new area? Launching a new service? Open up the floodgates and saturate the market. Upfront expenses can be amortized over time, and offset by extra revenue from both the initial campaign and its carryover effect. For first-year markets, we upped our advertising and PR budget from 4 percent to 8 percent of sales—that included our over-the-top grand openings (Jesse Ventura even hosted one). We scaled back to 6 percent in the second year before settling back to 4 percent in year three.

Match the new kid's noise level. Brand loyalty ain't what it used to be. Don't let a new competitor—or your current foe, touting a new product—outgun you. Not even for a second. Pump up the volume before, during, and after the competition's campaign. Try a customer-appreciation promotion to remind your customers why they've always found you attractive—and why the new guy is just a pig in a wig.

Dare to be different. Global insurance giants and talking ducks go together like peanut butter and mustard. That is, until AFLAC took a quack at it in a hugely successful ad campaign. The company's agents thought management was crazy—until new business started pouring in. It takes guts to veer out of the mainstream.

Send a news release to media outlets. TV and radio news producers, magazine publishers, and newspaper editors are always scouting for story ideas. Make your news release stand out by keeping these tips in mind:

- **Create a wish list.** These are the publications and shows your customers read, watch, and listen to.
- **Do your homework.** Check out a publication's editorial calendar to find out if your product or service dovetails with upcoming themes.
- **Cultivate a relationship.** Call the producer or editor (Google for names and contact info) and introduce yourself. Tell her why your business is a good fit for her show or publication and ask if she's open to story ideas.
- **Put on your editor's hat.** Brainstorm with your staff to come up with a hook that readers or viewers would find interesting. You may love your plant's new jumbo press—but an editor will just yawn and delete your e-release from her in-box or toss your paper release in the trash. She may, however, find it unique that you deliver flowers and candy with every order. How to begin? Ask yourself, *What separates us from everyone else?* Then build on it.
- **Write a straightforward headline.** Convey the thrust of your release in a handful of words—*Customers get flowers and candy with every print order.*
- **Write in "inverted pyramid" style.** In other words, lead with the most important information (the broad base of the pyramid). The first paragraph should tell the whole story—who you are, what you're doing, and when, where, and why you're doing it. Each successive paragraph provides additional info in order of descending importance. Limit it to less than one page.
- **Stick to the facts.** A news release is just that—news. If you even start going down the *Here's why our company is so wonderful* road, you blow your credibility out of the water.
- **Focus on people, not things.** If possible, add a human face to

your story. If your news is product-related, what will your customers' perspectives be? Attractive photos are a great lure.

- **Don't go it alone.** Sprinkling in quotes and facts from industry authorities adds credibility.
- **Customize it.** Tailor your news release to each publication or show. If your story isn't in sync with a magazine's or newscast's personality, you're wasting everyone's time.
- **Anticipate the final product.** When you release information, you lose control over placement and perspective. Have your team comb over the release in search of positive and negative spins. Heads-up editing improves the odds of getting the coverage you want.
- **Build news releases into your strategic efforts.** Leverage an article or news segment relating to your business in multiple ways. Send reprints to customers and prospects, and reference or excerpt it in your advertising.

Do it yourself. A founder or chief exec is sometimes the best person to sell the company's story. Lee Iacocca pioneered it at Chrysler. He paved the way for Victor Kiam of Remington ("I liked the shaver so much, I bought the company"), Steve Jobs of Apple, and Richard Branson of Virgin Group. I took the publicity plunge at my company and did our TV and radio ads for five years. I figured if I could talk to prospects on air as well as I did one-on-one, I could persuade them to give us a chance. It worked—our same-store sales trended due north. Caveat: For every leader who makes a successful spokesperson, there are ten who are god-awful. Don't try it unless you have some natural charisma and can express yourself powerfully before a camera or microphone.

Communicate internally. You have to create internal excitement before you generate buzz out there in the real world. Whether you're launching a new service, rekindling your brand, or changing your product, rev up your employees first. Hang posters. Throw a launch party. Customers expect to hear the same enthusiasm from your people as they hear in your promotions. Get your sales staff and others to kick in ideas for promotion design (management and sales may have completely different ideas about your product). When a promotion's set, brief your sales team and support staff on every last detail—what, why, where, when—through meetings and e-mail blasts. You don't want anyone to drop the ball when it's thrown his way.

Find the right media mix. You gotta know whether to rifle (narrow market) or shotgun (broad market). Ad agencies and PR firms hike up the quality of your promotions; just make sure their loyalty is to you and not the media they purchase. Your promo options are:

- **Television.** More and more evidence suggests that TiVo and other digital video recorders are blunting the power of commercials. Plus, younger generations are spending more time with a computer than a TV, and baby boomers are diversifying their entertainment options. Still, for now, nothing beats TV for searing your brand into the consciousness of the market. Thanks to the proliferation of cable channels, lasering in on a niche has never been more possible—or more complicated. Channel fragmentation may have lowered ad rates, for instance, but are they cheaper from an efficiency standpoint? Does a thirty-second spot on the Dry Cleaning Channel really garner an efficient cost per point? Find a freelance media buyer who can navigate the numbers, find deals, and negotiate for you.

- **Internet.** Countless moms and pops have beaten expectations thanks to Google's AdSense and similar ad vehicles at Yahoo! and Microsoft. The Web sites charge advertisers only for surfers who click on their ads. In other words, you only pay for qualified buyers who sought out your product or service, and it's entirely quantifiable. At least, that's the way it works in theory. Keep an eye out for the latest news on click fraud, perpetrated by rivals who are so desperate to drive up your costs that they'll pay a third party to manually click on your ads hundreds or thousands of times.

- **Radio.** An economical sixty-second radio spot offers more ear time—compared to a pricey thirty-second TV ad—to sell your brand *and* your offering. Radio offers more flexibility than TV. You can swap out creative content in minutes and digitally send spots to a station at the eleventh hour. Radio also delivers a captive audience—listeners are typically sitting in their vehicle or office, and they channel surf less than TV couch potatoes. We took advantage of catching consumers in their cars, where they were particularly sensitive to a tire pitch.

- **Newspaper.** Papers work best for direct response, as opposed to brand building. Place ads where your target market will see them (our customers were sports fans). Page three of any section—above the fold—catches readers' eyes first. The next best are other right-hand pages. Ask an ad rep what sections and days of the week make sense for your offer. Whatever the plan, grab 'em with big headlines—otherwise, you'll lose 'em to the funny pages. Roughly 80 percent of your headline words should be five letters or less for quick reading and retention.

- **Yellow Pages.** Still a must, even with online search engines and multiple books to choose from. Make sure your ad is larger than your competitors'. Figure out where users may look for you and place smaller ads in those categories that direct them to your primary ad—the one with the screaming headline.

- **Direct mail.** Best way to hit a bull's-eye? Zero in on targeted criteria like ZIP codes, household income, age, or gender. Tap an experienced list broker for quality addresses at pennies per name. Done right, direct mail delivers big-time—ever-rising mailing costs be damned. Make sure your creative content delivers a quality brand message—clip art on a postcard isn't going to sell a lot of new homes. Test price points, headlines, envelope copy, and anything else you can think of; track results and keep refining. The newspaper-headline rule (80 percent of words are five letters or less) applies here. Don't forget the call to action—ask customers to act in a way that nets them something. It could be stopping by your store for a free gift or tax-free purchase. Print overruns of your mailing and leave them wherever potential customers cluster—grocery stores, malls, coffeehouses.

- **Trade publications.** Decision makers count on industry rags for news and trends. Best bet: Submit an article with your byline. A published article delivers more credibility than an ad, and it'll position you as an industry expert. Writing the article yourself (use a first-rate ghostwriter) also gives you more control of the content and saves the editor time.

- **Consumer magazines.** Whether local, regional, or national, match the demographic of the readers—age, lifestyle, income— to your customers. Who else is advertising? Call them and ask if their ads are working.

- **Sports marketing.** Our ads and promotions with the Twins, Vikings, Green Bay Packers, and Kansas City Chiefs were big winners. We also generated word of mouth with JumboTron tire mascot races at NBA games. (Our mascots—Sporty, Tuffy, and Classy—were also hits at parades and other community events.) Fans can't help but associate your name with warm feelings for the home team.

- **Out-of-home marketing.** Brand loyalty has been waning for each successive generation since World War II. People, especially the under-forty set, don't watch as much TV (when they do, they're more likely to TiVo out the commercials). They listen to satellite radio; they don't read the paper. Hunt down the elusive twenty-five-to-forty demo and get creative. Slap ads in restaurants, theaters, bathroom stalls, or on bus stop benches. Turn your truck into a mobile billboard, or use the stationary variety—but for heaven's sake, limit copy to a handful of words that are large enough to read in a quick glance.

Spread the virus. My son Trent was in a trendy Greenwich Village cigar bar in the mid-1990s when the woman next to him started talking up her Hennessy martini. "Hey, Paul," she finally yelled to the bartender, "would you please bring us another Hennessy martini?" She lingered on every one of the brand's syllables, and patrons took notice of the mysterious call. Before long, the drink was on everyone's lips. Mission accomplished: The curvy, charismatic brunette worked for Hennessy's ad agency. Call it building buzz, or "viral marketing"—it gives your grassroots branding effort a heaping dose of fertilizer. It takes other forms, too, from new restaurants that tell callers there's a month-long wait for a table, to lounge owners who pay models to drink and dance on their bars. Pretty soon, everyone's talking about that drink, that restaurant, that bar. The buzz seems organic, but it's every bit as natural as AstroTurf. Blogs, on the other hand, can keep the buzz real. Build your own in minutes. By and for aficionados and experts, blogs form communities and influence the influencers. Blogs, viral video clips, and buzz generators create a virtual watercooler for consumers to gather around to gossip about your product.

Wow them on the Web. Your digital presence has to be more than "brochureware." So often it's your Web site that introduces you to prospects. Every aspect should reflect your brand—the look, the feel, the text, the forms. Best bet: Install a professional Web designer on your team of external partners. Here are some ways to stand out:

- **Connect marketing partners.** Collect your Web and marketing experts in the same room to ensure your promotional efforts are consistent and interdependent.
- **Get "sticky."** Regularly update resources, offers, news, or data to give users a reason to stick around and come back. That holds regardless of your site's purpose—retail, lead generation, info hub.
- **Drive traffic via all channels.** Feature your Web site address on all marketing materials—direct mail, TV, print ads, and press releases.
- **Maximize e-visibility.** This isn't a do-it-yourself job. Partner with a specialist in search-engine optimization. You can have the greatest site in the world, but it's chattering in a vacuum if your target audience never sees it.
- **Be brief.** Users will read chatty paragraphs and concise bullets, but aren't likely to scroll through pages of boilerplate text. Enlist a professional Web copywriter to shape and spice the content.
- **Get specific.** Design your site with your target audience in mind. You have multiple audiences—consumers, wholesalers,

investors. Either develop separate URLs (uniform resource locators—geek-speak for Web site addresses) or cleanly split your site into sub-sites.

- **Sync with sales.** If your site is sales-focused, link a primary offer from your home page to an opportunity to buy. You also need an easy-to-use shopping section that takes advantage of opportunities to value-sell (aka, up-sell) and cross-sell, particularly at the "shopping cart" step.

- **Highlight the fresh stuff.** The "What's New" section on any home page is like catnip (especially if you add video). It keeps visitors up-to-speed on the latest products, sales, news releases, and events.

- **Lights, camera, action.** Audio and video podcasts get visitors to linger awhile. The operative word is "relevant." Posting extraneous clips can backfire.

- **Harvest qualified e-mail addresses.** Direct visitors to sign up for periodic newsletters, updates, and offers, and soon you'll assemble a golden address book. Install a sign-up button on your home page, at checkout, or both. For best results, consult with programming and list-management experts. Lists need regular pruning and sorting into appropriate categories based on customer preference.

- **Leverage e-mail.** Make a habit of mailing offers and updates to customers and prospects (auto-responders triggered by database settings can do this automatically). But exercise restraint—sending messages too frequently may annoy your audience. Important: Post an opt-out link at the bottom of your e-mails so people can unsubscribe. (Antispam laws require opt-out links on e-mail blasts.)

- **Secure affiliate programs.** Give affiliate partners unique URLs that link back to your site. Featuring these URLs on their sites and e-mails generates qualified Web traffic, improves your conversion rates, and improves your position on search-page results. If you're offering commissions, it's easy to chart the traffic and sales each affiliate generates.

- **Get in the feedback loop.** Web reporting, from your site host or subcontractors, produces all kinds of valuable metrics. Stay on top of traffic, visitors' origin (sites, affiliates), purchase patterns (conversion rates, frequencies), and other usage indicators. Another option: Use discounts or freebies to entice visitors to fill out surveys.

MAKE TRENDS YOUR FRIENDS

Volvo's plan to design a car for Gen X was stuck in neutral. The Scandinavian car company knew there were forty-four million consumers born between 1965 and 1977—but that's about all it knew. Enter Iconoculture, a Minneapolis-based leader in consumer-trend research and advisory services. "In order for Volvo's brand to appeal to Gen X, its car designs need to connect with the innate core values of the Gen-X consumer," Vickie Abrahamson, Iconoculture's cofounder and executive vice president of consumer analysis, told Volvo. Vickie's team put Gen X's cultural DNA under their "Macrotrend" microscope. They read their books, listened to their music, ate where they ate, shopped where they shopped. Iconoculture's observations led them to identify five key Gen-X Macrotrends—Artisan (one of a kind, personal style), Carpe Diem (passion, adventure), Torquing (style + high performance), Neo-Puritanism (traditional family values), and Great Expectations (luxury). The Volvo team translated those trends into concepts and designs relevant to Gen-X lifestyle values. The upshot? Five new interior prototypes and a stockpile of fresh promotional angles.

Business owners may try to pummel the competition, but if they don't leverage trends, they're like a boxer with a glass jaw. One good punch, and it's lights out. Maybe you have a sense of how customers relate to your product. But do you know how they live their lives? What are they passionate about? How do they view family, relationships, environmentalism? What defining events formed their belief system and values? (For Gen Xers, it's the first Gulf War, the fall of the Iron Curtain, and the Challenger shuttle crash.) What contemporary people, places, and cultural dynamics are influencing your customers? Enlightened entrepreneurs understand what makes each generation tick, from Boomers and Gen Xers to Matures (older than Boomers) and Millennials (or Gen Yers). Use that knowledge to create opportunities all across your business, from product development, brand equity, and positioning to sales, promotions, package design, and customer care.

Trend trackers think of themselves as immigrants trying to dial into the language and lifestyle of a new land. After all, trends are signposts for underlying consumer values. Understand those values—by getting in the heads and hearts of your customers—and you understand what drives their pocketbooks. Iconoculture's Lifestyle Trend Tracker Checklist translates your customers' needs, desires, and values into a healthier bottom line:

Open your media maw. Read every magazine and newsletter that touches your industry or your customers. Get a feel for where the two markets intersect. Don't worry about language barriers—it doesn't matter if you can even read Italian, you can still see Italian.

Look up. Customers in every economic class dream of reaching higher. Take it from a tire biz vet, you don't always have to reinvent the wheel. Consider carrying luxury products and services to the mainstream by reconfiguring and repositioning them to make them more affordable.

Look outside. Befriend your customers. Move beyond statistics and get to the point where you can finish their sentences. If possible, spend some time walking in their moccasins. Visit their stores, communities, and sporting events. You've gotta understand them where they live. Also, track trends outside your industry and expertise. You'll be surprised at how quickly you connect the dots.

Open your ears. Ask customers—in one-on-ones, focus groups, surveys—about their passions. Are they newshounds or sports buffs? Do their hobbies land them in the kitchen, the music room, the greenhouse? What brings their family and friends together, why, and how often? Great input leads to great insights.

Factor kids into the equation. Today's kids aren't shy about speaking up, whether the topic is wall colors or their first big-girl bed. Doesn't matter if it's a frozen pizza, a backyard playhouse, or the latest iPod—you're fooling yourself if you don't think kids are a major influencer in purchasing decisions. What Junior wants, Junior usually gets.

A WORD TO THE WISE: MERCHANDISE

The first Brunswick billiard table was built in a small Cincinnati wood shop in 1845. One hundred fifty-five years later, the company's selling channel seemed just as old. Most Brunswick tables were sold in mom-and-pop dealerships that cared little about the prestige of the brand. Many stores commingled brands and stacked tables on top of one another like cheap chairs. No surprise then that merchandising master Sandy Stein was summoned to Brunswick's headquarters in Bristol, Wisconsin. His assignment? Create a customer experience that would yield higher perceived brand value, create excitement, and separate Brunswick from the commoditized, low-end tables.

The solution? Sandy, founder of Minneapolis-based Stein Trending Branding Design, came up with the Brunswick Pavilion, a store-within-a-store concept that the company rolled out nationally. In a typical store, a dozen or more tables are positioned for optimal viewing, a processional-like entrance features history panels extolling the company's heritage, and backlit floor-to-ceiling fabric scrims display photos of additional table styles in various home environments. The result? A brand appreciation that transcends price and, more important, appeals to the "female factor." "The Brunswick Pavilion concept," Sandy said, "makes an emotional connection to women, typically the gatekeepers on large purchases. The showroom spurs the reaction, 'That's the way I want our room to look.'"

Sandy had racked up a big success, but now he wanted to run the table. Brunswick, however, passed on his idea to develop its own national prototype retail store. Convinced that the concept would change the face of billiard retailing, Sandy joined forces with a retailing colleague and invested twelve months' worth of spare time in writing up a business plan. Impressed, the company gave Sandy the green light, and the first Brunswick Home and Billiard store opened in Wilmette, Illinois, in September 2003. A consistently high revenue producer, it's the first billiard store to leverage cross-marketing.

The Wilmette store also serves as a laboratory that schools Brunswick dealers across the country in the art of merchandising.

Here are more entrepreneurial merchandising tips:

Provide a feel-good experience. Whether in-store or online, comfort is important. Emotions and feelings often drive purchases. Our store personnel were trained to treat guests like gold. Our interiors appealed to all of our customers' senses—beautiful showrooms, viewing windows into the auto bays, upbeat music, pleasing scents to offset the not-so-pleasant rubber smell, cappuccino, and a handshake greeting upon entry.

Make shopping intuitive. Presentation is everything. Target Corp. knows this. Its well-organized, visually appealing displays prompt customers to understand their options—good, better, best—and move smoothly from one category to the next. Differentiate yourself with an intuitive shopping experience.

Anticipate questions. Brunswick's lean, clean, in-store graphic imagery answers top-of-mind questions—"How big does my game room have to be for this table?" "What's the difference in height between a bar stool and a kitchen stool?" At Tires Plus, guests browsed displays that laid out our products and services alongside features, benefits, and prices. These quick-glance visual answers to frequently asked questions (put them online, too) empower customers to move further along into the sales process without feeling the hard sell.

Edit offerings. Too many choices can overwhelm the buyer. Some independent bar stool retailers, for instance, offer up to two hundred styles. That's confusing enough, but they're poorly displayed, too. By contrast, Brunswick's Wilmette store sports a well-lit "chair wall" featuring forty top styles and brands. Customers can stand in one area and leisurely select an ideal combination of style and finish.

Leverage the Web. The Internet fundamentally changed the way we shop. Customers are more savvy and more likely to shop unassisted.

Smart retailers offer intuitive online shopping experiences that seamlessly sync with in-store visits. But that's not the half of it. The Web is an avenue for building and reinforcing customer connections. Remember, relationships, not transactions, are the building blocks for long-term wallet share. Link your customers' core values (you've already done your trend research) to value-added propositions that appeal to a virtual community. This online community is a home where customers can exchange thoughts and information about your offering—and exchange instantaneous feedback with you. That puts you in touch with customers' thoughts about your products and services, and tells you how effective you are at solving their problems.

PRICE POINTS

Pricing is a key element of any offer. We were able to occupy the "low prices with niceties" niche by offering how-low-can-you-go pricing on commodity-like products and making a bit more on out-of-the-mainstream items, exclusive product lines, and premium products and services. Positioning aside, every company has to raise and lower prices periodically to meet marketing and margin pressures.

These are some pricing factors to consider:

- Adjust when necessary by continually monitoring your competitors' pricing and your sales volume.
- When commodity markets are rising, it's easier to raise prices in a B2B (business-to-business) environment than in a B2C (business-to-consumer). Corporate customers are more sophisticated and aware of rising material and energy costs. Besides, competitors are facing the same cost increases and will also be forced to adjust prices.
- Price hikes are sometimes unavoidable. In a B2B market, everybody shares the pain. Still, you need to finesse it by balancing two factors—how much to raise prices and how often. Let's say you're a supplier whose input costs have gone up 3 percent. You've got to raise prices by that much just to break even. Best bet: Build margin increases into your cost increases, and get past breakeven

on the widget. You'll stay competitive, and that extra little oomph will buy some breathing room.

- Raising consumer prices is sometimes touchier. Most retail customers don't track industry cost increases. Whether you sell to retailers or directly to consumers, presenting a price hike as a surcharge may work. When public awareness of market pressures (rising costs of gasoline, freight, steel) is high, they generally accept a pass-through charge.

- Lowering prices, on the other hand, is generally a matter of competition. It's done either defensively to match competitors' prices, or offensively to win market share. In a B2B environment, the key to lowering prices while maintaining profit margins is introducing new products. (This works for raising prices, too.) Here's an example. Let's call your flagship product Widget X. It's priced at $1,000. Rather than drop it to $800, create a new product, Widget Y, with a different value proposition—a few less features and a lower price point. Now you're differentiating yourself instead of devaluing your brand. This is how you sell to the big boys. Otherwise, staying with one product sticks you with an inevitable pricing arc—essentially a scheduled sunset of your margin structure (40 percent in the first year, 30 percent in the second, 20 percent in the third). Why? Big-box retailers relentlessly drive down prices. If you don't play by their rules, they'll find someone who will.

New products keep the sun from going down. Back to our example—Widget Y has different features, benefits, and price point. But it's structured to have a gross margin of 40 percent. See where this is going? In year two, Widget X drops to 30 percent but Widget Y starts out at 40 percent. In year three, Widget X falls to 20 percent and Widget Y slides to 30 percent. But then, out of nowhere, Widget Z captures a 40 percent margin. That's managing your margins (if not your alphabet). Most companies see their margins squeezed because they don't change their product set. Do the same thing over and over with the same negative result, and you'll either go crazy or out of business. Bottom line: Innovate or die.

GOING GLOBAL

Thanks to the Internet, companies of any size can become global players (97 percent of U.S. exporters are small and midsize firms). It's as easy for shoppers in Bangladesh to browse your Web site as it is for people in Baton Rouge. Perhaps you're already exchanging virtual handshakes with overseas partners. No? Just wait. Chances are you'll eventually sell and ship products overseas, purchase materials from overseas, set up an office overseas, or export jobs overseas (only as a last resort to stay competitive, of course). The world market is vast. Ninety-five percent of the earth's population—and two-thirds of its purchasing power—resides outside the United States. When doing business abroad:

Stay current. Even seasoned vets need to keep abreast of shifting geopolitical and global-financial dynamics. Start with your state trade promotion agency—most states have a small office within their commerce or economic development departments. It's a clearinghouse for federal, state, and local initiatives. Many offer export promotion assistance through workshops, seminars, and one-on-one counseling. Subscribe to *The Economist*. Or, see these Web sites for the latest hoops and how to jump through them:

- **Federation of International Trade Associations (www.fita .org).** FITA lists more than 450 independent national associations and provides links to seven thousand international trade Web sites. Sign up for *"Really Useful Sites for International Trade Professionals,"* a free e-letter.
- **The U.S. Government Export Portal (www.export.gov).** This site gives you the skinny on international-trade logistics and requirements. More important, it provides access to the U.S. Commercial Service, the global business solutions unit of the Department of Commerce. Through its 108 domestic offices and nearly 150 posts in 76 countries, the U.S. Commercial Service offers customized solutions to help small and midsize companies compete in the global marketplace.

- **International Chamber of Commerce (www.iccwbo.org).**
  ICC, the voice of world business, champions the global economy as a force for economic growth. Here, you'll find the home page for Incoterms 2000, thirteen international rules accepted by governments, legal authorities, and practitioners worldwide. Incoterms 2000 rules bridge communication gaps by spelling out buyer and seller responsibilities.

Set your strategy. Selling your product overseas? Bringing that function in-house could overtax people and processes dedicated to domestic sales—you may have to reallocate and add resources. Plan for complex travel arrangements, warranty repairs, and after-sales support. If you go with distributors to represent your product and manage post-sale issues, will you train them on their turf, fly them to your office for annual sessions, or do it all via webinars? Other options: Open an office in the foreign market, appoint an intermediary to find deals, or sign over your international development rights to a management company that will develop business in exchange for a cut. (Whatever the strategy, make sure you integrate step-by-step processes for overseas trading into your order-taking infrastructure.) Next, establish profiles of your ideal business partners. Perhaps you need someone who stocks warranty replacement parts and does on-site repairs. Another firm may offer twenty-four-hour tech support. Or, is it more important to have engineers on staff to do installs?

Appreciate cultural differences. There's always more to learn about countries you do business with. Go to school on their cultures, from business protocol to entertaining etiquette. Americans and Europeans, for instance, rely on meticulously detailed contracts, while the Japanese favor oral agreements or brief written summaries. In Japan, take a small gift if you're invited to someone's home. But don't wrap it in white paper—it's a symbol of death. Elsewhere, if you dive into a French or Saudi company's customer data before building the proper rapport, you'll get the cold shoulder. Standing too close to a Spaniard or too far from a Saudi suggests indifference. In some Asian countries—Hong Kong, Korea, Taiwan—triangular shapes are interpreted negatively. Germans and Japanese tend to be punctual, while time is more flexible in Latin American countries.

Habla español. It certainly helps to have employees who are fluent in foreign languages. But many growing firms can't afford the luxury. English, of course, is the lingua franca of business in most industrialized, non-Spanish-speaking countries. If you plan to do business in Latin America, learn Spanish. Or, hire someone who's fluent. South America might be a good market for factory seconds, but if consumers can't decipher labels and packaging, you may be forced to give steep discounts. Then there are advertising's linguistic land mines. Take Parker Pen. When it marketed a ballpoint in Mexico, its ads were supposed to read, *It won't leak in your pocket and embarrass you.* Trouble was, the firm thought the Spanish word *embarazar* meant "to embarrass." But owing to the word's context, Mexican consumers were amused when they heard Parker Pen's claim, *It won't leak in your pocket and make you pregnant.*

CHAPTER 52

SALES

Increasing Market Share

Asavvy sales pro knows how to turn yelling into selling. Before embarking on a family vacation, Tim, a sales rep for a Boston-based air compressor supplier, told his hot prospect that he'd drive back from Cape Cod on a moment's notice if that's what it took to close the deal. The customer promised he wouldn't nose around elsewhere in the meantime, easing Tim's anxiety. There was a lot more at stake than an order for a $30,000 air compressor. The prospect, a decision maker for one of the largest automotive companies in New England, had a dozen other outlets in need of product. The next week, back from vacation, Tim's phone rang. Sorry, the prospect said, turns out he placed a purchase order with another company. Steamed, Tim vented to Craig, his sales manager. The pair decided to make a last-ditch effort. There was nothing to lose. The prospect wasn't an existing customer, and besides, a man's word was his bond. "Yeah," the prospect said when Tim called, "I guess I can give you a few minutes tomorrow."

The next morning quickly deteriorated into a shouting match between Tim and the prospect. "Shut the *&%# up or I'll throw both your #&@ out!" the prospect roared at Tim after the shouting match escalated. "Whoa,"

Craig said, holding up his hand. "Let's all back up and take a breath." Craig turned to his hot-blooded sales rep. "I'll take it from here, Tim." After a series of clarifying, rapid-fire questions, Craig calmly explained the product benefits to the customer and described how his company would implement and service the compressor. He also offered a modest discount as a peace offering. In the end, cooler heads prevailed. The customer reversed his order and went with Craig and Tim's company.

Driving back to the office, Craig tutored Tim on all the Sandler Selling System (pages 342–346) rules he had violated. First, don't get emotionally involved—an out-of-control salesman is so worried about winning the argument that he'll lose the war. Second, give upset prospects a "mental enema" to flush out the anger. "You're not supposed to challenge the prospect," Craig acknowledged. "But if Tim had been passive, we would have lost the order. It's a fine line: You have to hold your ground, but in a respectful way." Craig's story gets better with time. Eight years later, that run-in has morphed into a half a million dollars in business. Whether you're selling software or industrial equipment, it's tenacity, passion, and resolving to do right by the customer that opens accounts and closes sales.

It's worth mentioning that the word "sales" needs a good slander lawyer. If Sales were a person, the image many would conjure is a chatty, slick salesman preying on helpless naïfs. My perspective was shaped by the wisdom of my dad, a lifelong salesman who taught me the value of ethical, win-win selling. To him, sales was a philosophy, an honorable relationship between buyer and seller in which value is exchanged. It's what bartering looked like in the grain-for-gunpowder days.

MANAGING THE SALES FUNCTION

There's a lot riding on how well you coach a sales team. Its performance determines whether your non-sales employees get bonus checks or pink slips. These rules helped us lead high-flying sales teams in our wholesale, retail, and commercial divisions.

Spend a bundle on a sales manager. Many a business owner studies subpar sales figures, scratches his head, and wonders, *What am*

I missing? A field general, that's what. A creative sales manager sniffs out the right slice of the market, trains and inspires rookies and veterans, and herds volatile personalities. Volatile? Salespeople tend to be mavericks. They're more impulsive than cube dwellers. On top of that, physically and digitally pounding the pavement armed only with traditional, unenlightened sales techniques can exact one heck of an emotional toll. Unfortunately, the way many sales departments operate is negatively self-reinforcing—a lot of leaders simply promote their best salesperson to sales manager. Good luck with that. There may be some overlap in expertise—people skills, for instance, and tricks of the trade. But management is a different animal. If your sales wiz doesn't have noteworthy leadership experience, his supervising stint may be a short one.

Track down the best salespeople. Your company team won't make the big leagues without an all-star sales force. The best are probably already employed—but don't let that stop you. Many are treading water, plying under adverse conditions—a mediocre product, poor merchandising, scant inventory, shoddy support. Those roadblocks are curbing their earnings and steering them toward greener pastures. Fling that window of opportunity wide open. Besides checking out the star-catcher methods in chapter 12, ask yourself, your people, and everyone in your Rolodex: *Has anyone knocked your socks off lately?* It's a fishing expedition that often nets great leads.

Be your own search firm. Ask yourself, *If I was a great salesperson, where would I work?* Then start dialing. Express interest in the company's offerings: "I want the complete picture, so have your best salesperson give me a call." When you get the star on the phone, tell her you heard she was a great rep and you figured she could refer you to other talented salespeople who may enjoy looking at new opportunities. If she gives you leads, great. If she asks for details, she's on the hook. Does she sound intelligent and experienced? Would you buy something from her? One more proactive move: Ask the firms you do business with for permission to pick their best reps' brains. To each one you get on the line, say, "Your boss says you're the best. I need a top gun, too. Where can

I find somebody like you?" If he expresses interest, take the high road ("Thanks, but I can't do that") and be satisfied with a good referral.

Go deep with your hiring MO. Salespeople are a unique breed. They need thick skin and a Kevlar ego to survive the battering ram of rejection. During the hiring process, ramp up your personality probing and role-playing exercises (chapter 13). Make sales aptitude and psychological testing mandatory (assuming legal issues don't pose a problem). Look beyond numbers when reviewing applicants' accomplishments. Did they build a territory from scratch or inherit it? Remember, you've gotta sell them, too—on your mission and vision for the company and the rewards that follow.

Offer seductive incentives. Dangle a fat carrot and you'll find salespeople racing around the track long after the nine-to-fivers have gone home. Big hitters prefer a generous commission arrangement with a get-the-bills-paid base. That's fine. Higher commission rates equal lower impact on your fixed costs. I always told salespeople I wanted nothing more than for them to make a lot of money because that meant the company was making a lot of money, too. In the retail world—Best Buy comes to mind—fair-market compensation without commissions also works. Commission caveat: Hire only ethical, caring people who would never sell anything customers didn't need. Preach incessantly that financial rewards flow naturally when they have the customer's best interests at heart.

Set performance goals. Settle on reachable, yet challenging, goals. Sit down together and analyze current sales, historical cycles, and the rep's track record. Benchmark her versus her peers. Make sure she walks away with goals she can call her own. There's not a lot of life in arbitrary numbers handed down from on high. Be patient with newbies—but not too patient. Build an exit strategy into your agreement ("If you fail to reach 70 percent of goal after four months, we'll shake hands and go our separate ways"). That helps cut your losses early and prevents uncomfortable terminations.

Train your force. Don't give up on your current players quite yet. With the right system (the Sandler Selling System is my favorite), even chumps can flower into champs. Invest in your salespeople by enrolling them in a great sales course. The cost is a pittance compared to the extra revenue it's sure to produce.

Build authority. Turn your sales team into doctoral candidates in their target industries. Demand that they understand everything from lingo to probable client pains so that they can put together the value propositions, price points, and solutions that work best. Every pain that arises should prompt a sales rep to tap three case studies— "Let's look at how I solved that problem in the past and go from there." Mastering product knowledge is just as crucial. Our retail, wholesale, and commercial personnel earned Ph.D.'s in Tireology at our in-house university. They pored over product and marketing literature until they could write the textbooks themselves, reciting nuances, features, and benefits for every brand. They knew how each product could cure customer pain. That's how you add value to every customer contact. The higher you rise above the pack, the more valuable you, and your brand, become.

Measure results. Where there's measurement, there's motivation. Our weekly e-mail reports ranked the entire sales force by various metrics. Sales folks are fierce competitors who love to see where they stand in rankings. They aren't satisfied being an Avis when a few more deals can land them in Hertz territory. Healthy—repeat, healthy— competition within the ranks leads to healthier profits for everybody.

Demand input from salespeople. As my dad used to tell me, "Appreciate and listen to your salespeople—they bring in the bucks that pay everybody else." Think about it. Your sales force is a direct pipeline to customers. They're the first to know when your customers' needs and desires morph—and they're an early warning system for what your competitors are doing about it. Require your sales manager to tap that rich source of intel via regular sales-team meetings and one-on-ones—and then work with other departments to incorporate adjustments on the fly. For example, I own a stake in a technology concern that hired two battle-tested salespeople with broad industry experience. Their former employer had completely tuned them out. So they were shocked when we treated their recommendations like sage advice and adjusted our product offering, training, and customer service accordingly.

Embrace "Big Brother." Weekly one-on-ones have limitations. The only way to ensure a salesperson is following protocol is to monitor her on a prospect call. Compliment her on what she's doing right and address her NTIs (need-to-improve areas) with the four-step Confucius Checklist (chapter 41)—tell her, show her, watch her do it and offer feedback, watch her do it again.

Advocate for your sales team. Drum up support for your sales staff via employee communication channels—e-mail blasts, executive meetings, employee meetings, one-on-ones. If it arouses resentment from the cubicles, nip it in the bud by encouraging empathy for the sales force: *Hey, man, it ain't easy hitting the bricks every morning and getting doors slammed in your face every hour.* Make sure your sales manager stays on top of technology trends so his team has all the hardware, software, and tracking reports it needs to stay dialed in and a step ahead of competitors.

Create material support. To present a first-class image, you've gotta have first-class business collateral. That's everything from business cards, stationery, and brochures to Web sites, newsletters, and trade show booths. Make sure they all deliver a consistent brand message. They're your silent sales force, at it 24/7.

MANAGING THE FUNNEL

Think of your sales funnel as a place to pour all your prospects, everyone from current customers to people unfamiliar with your offering. Our sales funnel (others call it a pipeline) report listed current and prospective accounts along with current or potential sales levels, goals, follow-ups, roadblocks, and solutions. Performance reports, filled with individual stats like the back of a baseball card, were e-mailed to everyone on the team daily, weekly, and monthly. The sales manager stayed on top of things through weekly one-on-ones with all his salespeople.

Constantly sift your sales funnel to separate hot leads from dead-enders. A good way to keep costs—and your sales team's frustration—down is to bring in savvy assistants to qualify the leads. Efficient above-the-funnel management keeps your rock-star sales reps happy and productive. Expecting sales pros to do their own cold-calling and lead qualifying is like asking Shaquille O'Neal to launder team uniforms. (Cold-call caveat: Mine isn't a one-size-fits-all strategy. It may indeed be worth sales reps' time to cold-call. Much depends on things like the size and maturity of the company and territory, the universe of available leads, the average account value, and the difficulty of reaching decision influencers.)

Rely on sales assistants. They qualify leads by getting prospects on the line—perhaps even arranging a face-to-face—and asking lots of questions: Would you like to lower your monthly widget bill by 30 percent?" "What are your company's biggest roadblocks?" "Gosh, how long has that been happening?" "How are you personally affected?" "How much is that costing you?" "What are you doing to fix the problem?" "How well is that solution working?" You'd be surprised at how prospects open up. Still, most leads won't pan out. That's okay. It's quality, not quantity, that counts—80 percent of your business comes from 20 percent of your prospects. They're the ones that get top billing on your sales funnel report. Stay on their radar with regular contact (e-mail updates work beautifully) and value-added offers.

SNIFFING OUT SUCCESSFUL SELLERS

The nature of the work demands that salespeople embody certain characteristics. Fine-tune your hiring and training processes to spot and develop these eight qualities:

1. Goal-oriented. Show me a five-star salesperson and I'll show you a go-getter with a track record of setting goals and achieving them. Real-world experience is the number-one predictor of sales success. Look for take-charge people who can rattle off case histories of how they set a goal, formulated an action plan, overcame obstacles, executed the plan, and got what they wanted.

2. Self-acceptance. Self-esteem is the best form of rejection protection. The greats don't take losses personally. They stay confident in their abilities and recognize that circumstances beyond their control sometimes influence outcomes. Take every opportunity to remind your reps they're great people, regardless of what the week's numbers look like.

3. Empathy. Great salespeople are great listeners. Customers sense the difference when a rep shifts from huckster to caring consultant. You can't fake it—the greater the suspicion, the lower the commission. Come to think of it, the term "sales force" is something of an oxymoron because a sale will fail if you force it. Bottom line: If your salesperson does right by his customer, he'll do right by himself (and your company).

4. Zeal. If your sales reps don't believe your offering is the greatest thing since e-mail, forget about revved-up customers. You got a guy missing passion for what he's selling? Help him connect the dots between what he's providing and how he's helping people. If he can't access his passion—and express it genuinely through verbal and nonverbal cues—he's dead in the water. Counterfeit enthusiasm kills off more sales careers than tacky menswear ever will.

5. Education-obsessed. The best salespeople settle for nothing less than complete mastery of their offerings. They consume every scrap of literature like it's a map to buried treasure. No nuance is lost on them. They know that customers are drawn to the magnetic pull of expertise.

6. Friendliness. It's human nature. People do business with people they like. Never underestimate the likability factor.

7. Doggedness. The yes a salesperson yearns to hear may be waiting patiently in line behind thirty-six door-slamming noes. Slogging through that cold-shoulder quagmire has broken the spirit of countless Willy Lomans. Top salespeople apply their batting average—for both number of sales and dollars per sale—to their goals. It's how they calculate how many at-bats they need to hit a home run.

8. Hunger. The best salespeople thrive on the thrill of the hunt. They're never complacent or satisfied. Oh, they celebrate when they score big, but only briefly. Then it's on to the next quest. There are always more prospects to find, more appointments to make, more people to help. Great hunters require only cursory coaching—just throw plenty of red meat their way and watch 'em run.

THE SANDLER SELLING SYSTEM

You've developed the mother of all widgets. Your can't-miss marketing strategy is locked and loaded. You've built a principled, outgoing sales force. But the cash registers won't start singing until you've plugged in the right sales process. I've seen and experimented with countless techniques. Hands down, the best is the Sandler Selling System (www.sandler.com), which has notched countless win-wins for me the past twenty-five years. No-nonsense and dignified, Sandler was founded on mutual respect between salespeople and clients. Sandler wins because it recognizes the two dynamics at work in the buyer-seller dance—the prospect's system and the salesperson's system.

Sales reps won't blossom until they catch on to the prospect's system. Over the years, through exposure to countless sales pitches, prospects have learned enough about the traditional selling process to thoroughly undermine it. Why? Because they feel they have something to lose—their money.

The four pillars of the prospect's system are:

1. Prospects Don't Always Tell You the Truth. Otherwise honest folks have no problem withholding information from, and even misleading, salespeople. They fudge the facts and hold their cards close, all out of self-preservation. Why? Prospects believe that while they're busy managing their daily affairs, salespeople are sharpening their talons. So they stay on their toes lest you finesse them into, heaven forbid, buying something. Precious little indication is forthcoming on how much they actually need your product or service because, well, that would play right into your hands.

2. The Prospect Wants to Know What You Know—for Free. Your prospect assumes you possess a secret for, say, improving productivity, or lowering costs. Why else would your firm invest in the marketplace? She knows your first goal is to generate interest in your offering, so she'll feign interest to pump you for information. She'll also try to secure your best price, but only to use as leverage against her current supplier. Unfortunately, unsuspecting salespeople often give insincere prospects all the free info and price quotes they want. That ultimately corrupts the marketplace, turning valued goods into cutthroat commodities.

3. The Prospect Commits To Nothing. Information in hand, she may imply she's close to committing. She'll dangle just enough hope to string you along as an unpaid consultant. You hang on, confident you've notched another win, when in reality you've got nothing. You may even get a gushing thank-you note. Might as well keep it; it's the only signature you'll ever see from her.

4. The Prospect Disappears. Overnight, it seems like she's skipped town. Voice mail and e-mail barriers spring up—salesman kryptonite. The relationship was terminated without your knowledge. Yet you continue following through because you've invested too much in chasing a phantom sale to admit you've been had. When reality sinks in, well, let's just say it's a bad day.

Now let's look at why the traditional selling system doesn't work. Whatever brand it goes by, its underlying structure is predictable. The salesperson must

- sell features and benefits
- withhold price and terms until value is established
- rely on presentation skills to gain agreement
- anticipate and handle objections
- employ an array of manipulative closing techniques

Sure, this system has survived longer than snake oil. But it's so widely used that savvy buyers see it coming. Worse, the manipulation it advocates contributes to today's adversarial sales environment that only hardens the prospect's system of defense. To top it off, each step is flawed.

- People don't want features and benefits; they want solutions.
- Delaying vital information wastes valuable time on dead-end pursuits.
- Presenting to blasé prospects wastes everyone's time.
- Focusing on objections gets the buyer's back up and makes the sale even harder.
- Your best pitches work about as well as one-liners at a singles bar.

In contrast, the Sandler Selling System frames the call as a business meeting among equals. The salesperson assumes the role of a high-end consultant, offering an honest exchange of information.

Here is the seven-step Sandler Selling System:

1. Establish Rapport. Stop acting like a salesperson. Shift your mind-set from *What can I get?* to *How can I help?* Be warm and genuine. That is, smile, maintain eye contact, use first names. Mention a tidbit you learned from your pre-meeting research. Forging a bond breaks down barriers that prevent you from understanding what she needs—and prevent her from appreciating what she has to gain. Continue building empathy and trust throughout the sales relationship.

2. Establish an Upfront Contract. Be clear on a few important ground rules. Establish the purpose of the visit, the prospect's agenda, your agenda, the length of the visit, and the options going forward.

For instance, cover all five bases by saying, "Hi, Jill, I've set aside an hour. Is that good? Great. What do you need to cover to make the best use of your time? Would it be okay if I ask a few questions first so I'll be in a better position to answer your questions? If it makes sense to go forward from there, terrific. If it doesn't look like a good fit, we'll know up front. Sound good?"

3. Uncover and Probe the Prospect's "Pain." People buy emotionally and justify intellectually. A prospect who doesn't have the tools she needs to do her job experiences emotional pain. Ask questions until you discover the issues causing that pain—and just how excruciating each one is. To move closer to a sale, the old adage is true—no pain, no gain. If the prospect is pain-free in your area of expertise, congratulate her and tell her she's good to go with her current vendor and not you.

4. Put Money Issues on the Table. Clearly deliver this message: The most important cost is not the price of the goods but what the prospect stands to lose if she does nothing. That said, determine the financial impact of the issues (the pain) you've uncovered. Then make sure the prospect's budget allows her to heal that pain with your cure.

5. Learn the Prospect's Decision-Making Process. Can the prospect make the final call? If not, ask for an appointment with the decision maker. If you first need to sell the gatekeeper, do it with the same respect you afford her superior. Before moving on, get clarity on all decision-related matters—*Who else has to sign off? To whose attention should you send additional information? What's a decision's typical timeline?*

6. Present a Solution that Cures the Prospect's Pain. Again, people don't buy features and benefits. They buy ways to avoid and overcome pain. Describe how you can fix her problem and heal the pain. Then measure her temperature using the "thermometer close." For instance: "Jill, you seem interested. Is that fair to say?" Follow up with, "Where are you on a scale of one to ten, with zero being 'no interest' and ten being 'sold'?" If the answer is five or less, you've got a problem. Retrace your steps. Probe deeper into her pain. If she answers between six and nine, say, "What do you have to see to get to ten?" After clearing each roadblock, repeat, "Where are you now?" until she gets to ten. Once there, say, "Great, what's the next step?" This erases pressure and places responsibility for the decision where it belongs— squarely on the prospect. Let her close the sale.

7. Reinforce the Sale with a Post-Sell Strategy. When a competitor realizes he's been cast aside, he may fight back with a lowball price or some trash talk. Shore up your sale before you leave by anticipating buyer's remorse and unearthing hidden objections. Thank her for taking your meeting, say you look forward to working with her, and add: "But could I ask, is there anything we haven't covered that may pop up and throw a wrench in the deal?" After addressing issues that crop up, ask what her next step is and what you need to do to keep things moving. Finally, thank her for trusting your solution and your company, and leave on an upbeat note.

Remember, business is won or lost on the sales dance floor as rapport is established. It's the moment of truth, when you determine whose selling system will prevail, yours or your prospect's. Without a strong system, you default to a passive role. Don't let that happen. The best dancers lead gracefully, always staying a step ahead of their partner.

CHAPTER 53

CUSTOMER SERVICE

Making Your Guests Feel at Home

I walked into a suburban Minneapolis Tires Plus store one day to find one of our young salesmen in a heated argument with a middle-aged customer. I stepped in and offered the older guy a cup of coffee. We sat down and I asked what I could do to make things right. He told me his car was late, and then confided that his doctor had just diagnosed him with terminal cancer. I told him how sorry I was, that of course I understood why he was upset. Fifteen minutes later, his car was good to go and he left satisfied.

Too many times there's a good reason for patrons to be on edge. Regardless of customer behavior, we banned our people from acting disrespectfully. No exceptions—that young salesman never battled another Tires Plus guest. If I found an employee fuming over a testy customer, I'd ask, "Ever have a day when everything went wrong and a minor incident set you off? Maybe the customer's child is sick or he's going through a divorce. If you're calm and caring and ask how you can help, he'll probably apologize when he snaps out of it. So don't take it personally and return fire."

Tires Plus customer service was legendary. I asked our people to add a touch of volunteerism to the job, to try to make each customer's day a little brighter. If we concentrated first on kindness and empathy, I said, healthy profits would naturally follow (as long as our prices and costs were in line).

Just a few words can forge customer connections. Some of my proudest moments came while reading comment cards. My favorite: A woman who said she had visited Tires Plus believing she needed new tires only to be told her old ones still had tread to spare. Our teammates reached across the corporate divide all the time. Our entire Coon Rapids, Minnesota, store signed a sympathy card upon news that a car had hit the dog of a longtime customer, George May. George was touched—and never bought tires anywhere else.

No one embodied this caring spirit better than Jake, one of our sales guys. One afternoon when Jake was new to the job, he noticed a customer was getting more upset with every delay. It couldn't be helped—mechanics kept finding problems and parts weren't in stock. Still, Jake sensed something more was going on. So he walked over to the woman and asked if he could help. Bursting into tears, she confided that she was a single mom and had just been transferred from a small town where all her family—and the only mechanic she trusted—lived. She was nervous about leaving work early to get her car worked on even though her boss—the only soul in town she knew—had recommended Tires Plus. Now she was trapped in our lobby, worrying that her young daughters would be stranded at a bus stop after school, unsure where their new home was. Jake took out his car keys. "Come on," he said, "let's go get your girls." When the four returned to Tires Plus and her car still wasn't done, Jake handed the woman his keys. "Take my car," he said. "I'll call you when yours is done." Two words: lifetime customer. That grateful mom never missed an opportunity to bring brownies for the store crew every time her car needed an oil change or new tires.

Why shoot for "legendary" customer service? As busy chief entrepreneurial officer, it's easy to lose interest and see customers as pieces on an assembly line rather than as human beings.

It keeps 'em coming back. Business owners spare no expense to get new customers in the door, yet often fail to provide a why-go-anywhere-else experience. Huge mistake. Customers are like spouses—take them for granted and they may go elsewhere to get their needs met. It's a vicious circle—businesses pour more and more resources into un-earthing new customers to replace the ones lost to neglect. This isn't rocket science. Showering attention on customers already in the fold keeps them there, so new customers become add-ons rather than replacements.

Take the time Pete Selleck, COO of Michelin Americas Small Tires, flew in to hammer out our partnership agreement. He asked for a store tour, so I showed him a few locations. In Woodbury, we introduced ourselves to a woman in the customer lounge and asked whether she had ever been to Tires Plus before. "You bet," she said. "My husband and I actually fight over who gets to come here with the kids." Surprised, I asked why. "My goodness," she said. "I'm sitting here watching a movie, sipping your cappuccino, and my kids are playing with toys on a clean floor." Pete was blown away. Later, I learned he shared the story with every tire dealer he worked with.

That's why smart companies focus less on trying to make unhappy customers happy and more on converting satisfied customers into "top box" apostles. What does that mean? Enterprise Rent-A-Car, which raced past competitors thanks to remarkable employee and customer loyalty, asks customers to rate its performance on a scale of one to five. The company grades itself solely by the number of customers who check the top box—"completely satisfied"—on the service questionnaire. Industry standards back up Enterprise's belief that "satisfied" just doesn't cut it. About 35 percent of "satisfied" customers will come back. Not bad. But a full 80 percent of customers who check "completely satisfied" will come back.

It pulls in new customers. Don't just satisfy customers. Astound them. Lay out the red carpet, and guests will rave to friends and family. That sends new customers to your doors and Web site—at no additional cost. Expect a dazzled customer to recommend you to two to three others. On the other hand, one rude encounter with an employee can torpedo every future purchase from that customer, his family and friends—and *their* family and friends. Expect a peeved customer to complain to three to eight others. Precious word-of-mouth buzz—free advertising—gets squandered whenever a customer has a less-than-excellent adventure.

It's the right thing to do. Back in 1986, David Wagner, owner of Twin Cities–based Juut Salonspa, was surprised when a regular showed up without an appointment just two weeks after her previous visit. She wanted her hair styled, not cut, so David assumed she had an important social engagement. Luckily, he had an opening. "I was in a great mood and I was really on," he recalled. "I gave her a great scalp massage and shampoo, and then styled her hair. We laughed and joked and had a lot of fun. When she left, she gave me a big hug that lasted just a little longer than usual." Two days later, David got a letter from her. He started reading, and froze. She explained that she had planned to commit suicide that day, and had come to the salon to get her hair styled so it would look good for her funeral. She changed her mind during the appointment because David had helped her realize life was worth living. She went home, confessed her plans to her sister, and agreed to check into a hospital.

David was stunned. "If you had lined up a hundred of my clients and asked me to choose the one who was considering taking her own life, she would have been last," he said. "She was gregarious, outgoing, and successful. I had no idea she was in such a dark place." David was grateful he had made a difference, and humbled by the experience. "I wondered what would have happened had I been upset or distracted when she came in and had just gone through the motions," he said. Something powerful shifted that day. David began feeling an enormous sense of responsibility. He wondered how many of his fifteen-odd clients each day were in crisis, and desperate for extra kindness and special attention. "I resolved then and there to treat every customer like I had treated my suicidal client," he said. David kept his promise, and wrote a best-selling book, *Life as a Daymaker: How to Change the World Simply by Making Someone's Day.* He defines daymaking this way: *To go about your life in a heart-centered, caring, and compassionate manner with a genuine intent to uplift others.*

He also decreed daymaking as the official "noble purpose" of Juut Salonspa's four hundred employees.

Here are six ways to win legendary customer loyalty:

1. Hire the Right People and Train Them Well. We showed everyone involved in hiring how to spot applicants who loved helping people and making their day. But that was only the beginning. Good employees also need training and inspiration. We enrolled new hires in a weeklong orientation where, among other things, I spelled out our mission—*"Deliver caring, world-class service to our guests, our community, and to each other."* The focus of countless meetings, talks, and training sessions, as well as big chunks of our employee playbook, dealt with how to treat our guests (we called them "guests" to inspire the kind of service you'd find at a fine hotel). You can't inspire daymaking service through occasional pep talks, memos, and meetings. It's gotta be walked, talked, and lived—day in and day out.

2. Treat Employees Right. If you leapfrog your people and focus chiefly on pleasing customers, you'll wind up with unhappy customers. Connect the dots, folks. Do you really expect employees who feel unappreciated to welcome customers with a big smile and a genuine desire to give them a positive impression of the company? Honor your people, concern yourself with their well-being, and respond to their grievances as if they were customers. They'll reward you with invigorated loyalty and new standards of performance and customer care.

3. Establish Clear Policies. No matter how attentive, bright, and spontaneous your people are, customer service should be as scripted as a political stump speech. Improvisation leaves too much to chance—even virtuosos rely on sheet music. In our business, guidelines were essential at three customer-care stages.

- **Initial contact.** Guests were greeted with WHENS—Welcome, Handshake, Eye contact, Name, Smile. We asked a series of questions to identify their needs. If appropriate, the salesperson walked outside with the customer to examine tire tread. He'd offer a solution, write up a work order, and invite the customer to relax in our lounge until her car was ready. Staffers also fielded phone calls according to a fun protocol I established in the early eighties: "It's a great day at Tires Plus. This is Jim. How can I help you?"

- **Warranty service.** Salespeople were trained to welcome returning, non-revenue-producing guests like they were new customers. The reason should be obvious—customers prefer to go steady rather than have a one-night stand. That means coddling. We had scripts prepared for every eventuality—fixing faulty repairs, replacing defective warrantied parts, servicing prepaid maintenance programs.

- **Customer complaints.** We welcomed them. No, seriously. They were opportunities to demonstrate we cared about our customers. We even deep-sixed the word "complaint" and replaced it with "guest opportunity." It's said that the value of a person's character is measured by how one deals with adversity. That's also true of the value of a company's character. Employees at every level need the authority to do whatever it takes to satisfy unhappy customers. Give guests the benefit of the doubt if there's so much as a sliver of gray. Does it work? You bet. Just as a broken bone comes back even stronger, we often scored more points by appeasing an upset customer than if the issue had been handled cleanly in the first place.

How do seat-of-the-pantsers handle complaints? My sister-in-law, Pam, had patronized a dry cleaner in Lexington, Kentucky, for fifteen years. One day I tagged along as Pam returned a pair of pants the cleaners had shrunk. The owner protested that it wasn't her fault, and implied that another cleaner had done the damage. She refused to make it right. Insulted, Pam never returned. Rather than spend thirty bucks to fix the problem, the dry cleaner lost a hundred times that in lifetime sales.

Enlightened entrepreneurs go from zero to hero by easing the tension in these five elements of customer complaints:

- **The Layers.** When a customer calls to lodge a complaint, will she reach a real person or a machine? Automated receptionists are convenient and save money, but they also elevate customers' blood pressure. When she is connected to a human being, will that person help her? Or, will she fall into a maddening maze? If they complain in person, is someone with authority on duty?

- **Listen and Determine the Problem.** A wronged customer may give you an earful of details, but she gets really angry when no one seems to care. Regardless of the actual resolution, a lot of customers will leave satisfied if somebody simply listens to them.

- **The Apology.** Two words solve most customer conflicts: *I'm sorry.* However, a forced apology only makes things worse. If it isn't heartfelt, she'll never come back—and bad-mouth you while she's at it. We used role-playing to get this across to our people. They practiced apologizing until their partner felt it was genuine. (Bonus: Employees told me this exercise also helped when they owed an apology to an angry spouse.)

- **The Duration.** The longer it takes to fix a problem, the more frustrated the customer.

- **The Action.** After gaining clarity, recapping the issue, and apologizing, we offered a tailor-made solution. If that was still unacceptable, we asked the customer what was fair. We granted all but the wildest requests. It's just smart business when you consider the value of a lifetime customer. As our playbook said, it's better to err ten times on behalf of an undeserving guest than miss satisfying a deserving one. The numbers don't lie. Profit on a customer's remaining lifetime purchases versus the cost of satisfying them? Not a close call. More important, its living up to your service promise.

4. Solicit and Act on Feedback. Create as many comment channels as possible. You can't get better without knowing what your customers think. For one firm, that may mean comment cards and follow-up phone calls. For another, it may be a Web blog. Dedicated complaint hotlines appeal to certain demographics. Some companies retain an outside service to conduct customer surveys, something Tires Plus did regularly. We also contracted a "mystery shopper" service—for both in-store and phone interactions—to get an objective, in-depth look at quality control.

Gathering information is pointless, of course, unless you act on it. We tweaked our store protocols all the time based on customer feedback. Every negative comment about an employee was routed to his manager's in-box (and cc'd to his district manager) so he could coach the offender back on track. When possible, we told customers about the fixes they inspired—and asked what we could do to win them back. If they said there was nothing we could do, we told them we understood because we had broken our promise. We also told them we hoped they were treated well by their new merchant because that's what they deserved. Our goodwill shocked some people and often turned them around. But that's not why we did it. It was a simple matter of decency.

5. Measure and Reward Performance. We had a customer-satisfaction metric called GEI (guest enthusiasm index). Applied to individual stores and the company as a whole, it measured the percentage of customers who would recommend us to friends. Below-average stores were targeted for extra coaching. It took a lot of sweat to pump up our GEI one percentage point. Darrel Blomberg, our full-time director of guest enthusiasm (that's not a joke title), labored two-and-a-half years to move it from 92.0 to 98.2. Personnel knew every smile counted—their compensation was partially based on a mix of store, district, region, and company-wide GEI.

Don't forget nonfinancial rewards like public ego stroking. Throughout the year, we'd receive a number of unsolicited customer letters praising employees who had been especially helpful. We printed those employees' names in our year-end holiday party program, and prominently displayed the letters. During the party, these customer service all-stars basked in a well-deserved round of applause.

6. Walk Your Talk. Entrepreneurs give a lot of lip service to their commitment to customer service. Are you among the ones who follow through? When you hear of a complaint, do you shake your head and joke about the odd-duck customer? Or, do you urge your people to look at the situation through the customer's eyes and do what it takes to make her happy? Do you shout, "You gave away WHAT?" Or, do you say, "Good for you, you remembered our values and did the right thing." Great customer service will wither on the vine without your heartfelt support. It wasn't uncommon for me to get emotional if we broke our promise. Our customers and employees knew it wasn't just an empty slogan.

CHAPTER 54

FINANCE, ACCOUNTING, AND IT

Beyond Bean Counting

We were sitting on hundreds of thousands of dollars' worth of unpaid bills when Jim Bemis joined us as chief financial officer in 1993. We couldn't mail checks because we didn't have the cash to clear them. In the previous twelve months we had added two locations in the Twin Cities and five in Des Moines, Iowa, a new market. Two of the new stores were seriously underperforming; Jim advocated pulling the plug. We shut down the stragglers and regrouped. In the short term, we decided to open stores only in the Twin Cities, where our brand was firmly established. Sure enough, every new homegrown store quickly turned profitable. Eight months after Jim joined us, the checks were truly in the mail.

Jim's financial leadership was pivotal. I was elated when he cleaned up our books and began delivering the P&L shortly after month's end. Even better, our auditors gave us high marks for the first time. Regrettably, many business leaders view "bean counters" as math geeks who're around only to clean up their messes. It's not a surprise, given that most entrepreneurs come from marketing or product-development backgrounds (present company included).

Had I read this chapter at the start of my career, my seat-of-the-pants days would've been a little less rocky.

CFOs AND THE FINANCE FUNCTION

Finance and accounting people are gatekeepers. They safeguard assets and make sure information is accurately captured, analyzed, and conveyed. Absent these controls, you open yourself to flawed decisions, theft, and embezzlement. That said, hire more than a checkbook holder or recorder of history. The CFO belongs on the executive team. The best ones are information hubs, providing the rest of the team with financial tools for running their departments.

Good CFOs provide monthly analyses and presentations to the executive team—that includes profit-and-loss statements within five to ten days after month's end. They challenge other department reps—querying marketing on overspending, hitting up retail over slow-turning inventory. Still not convinced of the CFO's value? I yield to Dave Cleveland, a forty-year banking vet and founder of entrepreneur-friendly Riverside Bank in Minneapolis: "If I could ever find a company where the owner paid the CFO more than he paid himself, I'd make that loan automatically."

No matter your take on the finance function, be careful not to hand over responsibility and power. After an early CFO repeatedly failed to produce accurate, timely reports—and resigned as a result—I challenged our CPA firm for not alerting me to his shortcomings. That's when I realized that the CPA firm's loyalty to the CFO may have colored its objectivity (he had selected them, after all). That was the end of that relationship; I helped choose a new CPA firm. From the outset, I made it clear to the new guys that their responsibility was to me as chairman and CEO. I also scheduled periodic one-on-ones with the firm's partner in charge. Bottom line: Get in the loop and stay there.

Every CFO's raison d'être is cost containment. No matter what pricing position your company stakes out, cost-cutting is an ongoing exercise. Ryanair, the Ireland-based no-frills airline that's revolutionized European travel, is an extreme—and extremely successful—example of how driving down costs drives up profits. Michael O'Leary, who heads up Ryanair, got religion on cost containment after visiting Southwest Airlines' Dallas headquarters in 1991. His motto now: A penny shaved is a penny earned. Like Southwest, Ryanair flies point-to-point to smaller airports and limits maintenance costs by using just one airplane model.

O'Leary also did away with preassigned seats, travel agent commissions, and frequent-flier miles. He even eliminated seat-back pockets to speed up cleaning. The strategy worked. Ryanair's average ticket price is more than 50 percent cheaper than its closest competitor. O'Leary wants to drop prices even lower, all the way to the ground. He hopes to someday give—yes, give—most tickets away and pull revenues from food, beverages, and other extras. By keeping costs low, Michael O'Leary is flying high—and definitely not by the seat of his pants.

You can always find more fat to trim, no matter how lean you are. Sit down with your management team and slog through the expense portion of your profit-and-loss statement. Line by line, ask two questions: *Does this add value to the customer experience? If so, can it be recovered through product or service pricing?* If the answers are no, eighty-six it.

These are some more waist-slimmers:

- Assume you're paying too much for absolutely everything, from your CPA firm to advertising to ballpoint pens (see chapter 50 for purchasing tips).
- Turn to your people for ideas to eliminate wasteful spending. (Our Profit Improvement Team included employees at all levels across all departments.)
- Weed out underperformers.
- Measure costs by department.
- Boost inventory and manufacturing efficiencies.
- Recalibrate compensation levels to reflect market conditions and organizational value.

BUILDING YOUR BUDGET

A consultant once told me about an anonymous client whose monthly reports showed he was meeting his budget. It left my friend scratching his head because the company was stuck in no-growth gear. He finally figured out his client was changing the budget whenever business conditions changed. The consultant's advice: Commit to an annual budget and live with it till death do you part (absent any major errors, of course). Relentlessly and cold-bloodedly measure your performance against your budget. Mess with the numbers and you'll have no idea whether you're achieving the goals you established at the beginning of the year. (Forecasts, on the other hand, should be updated regularly—and spending adjusted accordingly—to reflect actual results.) Your budget's influence seeps into every aspect of your culture. Hit the numbers and esprit de corps soars. Miss 'em through flawed understandings or bad budgeting, and morale tanks.

A budget is your strategic plan translated into numbers. Begin the budgeting process by viewing your strategic plan through the lens of financial considerations. Plan conservatively but think optimistically by sketching three scenarios—upside, base, downside. Why? Let's say you start the year by shoveling piles of cash into an ambitious new product launch. Six months later, the money's spent and sales are drying up. Panic Time. You scramble to salvage your business, not just for the fiscal year, but forever. Had you laid out a worst-case scenario—and run the numbers—during the financial planning process, you would have made more conservative management decisions. Budgeting forces you to ask the hard questions: *How much working capital will I need? How much labor will I need? What happens if I ramp up but revenue flatlines?* In 1519, Cortez, the Spanish explorer, arrived to conquer Mexico. Once ashore, he ordered his men to burn the ships that had carried them to the new land. It was a bold message—win or die. Cortez would have made a lousy businessman. Sometimes, retreat is the wisest call.

Here are some budget-building tips:

- Lay the groundwork for buy-in by involving all levels of management in the strategic planning process (chapter 23).
- Involve all managers—not just accountants—in the budgeting process. Get everyone on the same expectations page. Those who execute the plan will need help building it. Private agenda alert: Each participant's input may be tainted by the desire to protect their turf and maximize their financial gain.
- Begin the budgeting process in early November (or eight weeks before fiscal year end). At this point, your strategic plan objectives

have been set and you've completed your prep work, like building financial models and loading up last year's numbers.

- Start fresh with a "zero-based" approach. Begin with last year's numbers—but don't assume they'll remain constant. Analyze the origin of last year's business and what might change. Then build this year's numbers from the bottom up. Result? More accurate revenue forecasts and tighter expense control.

- Budget the "details." It's hard work, but if you don't do it, you'll miss a key assumption or expense and miss your numbers every time.

- Exercise caution. Estimate revenues on the low side and expenses on the high side (but not too high because people generally spend what's budgeted).

- It's okay to submit a more conservative plan with lower expectations to your bank. For instance, if your budget assumes 8 percent sales growth, the bank plan may assume 2 percent growth. Then, if you fall short of your internal plan, you still have a good chance of hitting the bank plan numbers and, more important, of meeting the covenants that the bank created based on the plan you gave it. No matter who your constituencies are (bank, analysts, board of directors), you can't go wrong with a strategy of UPOD—under-promise, over-deliver.

- Revise the budget quickly if you find a significant error—and immediately communicate all revisions to your bank. It's better to revise and report the revision than to miss a future projection.

MASTER THE METRIC SYSTEM

You're in the driver's seat, so keep an eye on the dashboard. Every business should track daily, weekly, and monthly metrics—receivables, payables, gross and net profit margins, sales, average sale, inventory. Enlightened entrepreneurs also insist on real-time measurements unique to their industry. For instance, three key manufacturing metrics may be:

- **Scrap rate.** Let's say you make die-cut labels. On any given day, the scrap rate is a hundred sheets. Suddenly, it shoots up to a thousand sheets. All that wasted material tells you some customer's order is going to be late. See that someone hits the floor to find out why. Maybe a machine broke down. Maybe somebody ran the job on the wrong paper. Whatever the case, if you ignore the scrap rate, a quality problem could slip by undetected—until you get a call from an unhappy customer.

- **Backlog.** Keeping orders flowing through the pipeline is vital. Too much downtime is murder on margins. (Have your CFO determine how to measure this metric.) Sales and manufacturing need to sync up to stagger orders and keep production rolling along—if every customer is promised next-day delivery, your plant better have a healthy stock of defibrillator paddles.
- **Equipment utilization percentage.** No metric screams "red flag" louder than this one. Too many entrepreneurs fall in love with equipment. One business owner I know had to have the latest toy but ran it only 20 percent a day. Idle employees passed the time watching wasted dollars—capital expense, depreciation, insurance, labor—swirl down the drain.

Numbers tell the story, but don't obsess too much about them. Entrepreneurs often succumb to analysis paralysis by studying too much—or the wrong—information. They whip out all sorts of spreadsheets but can't tell you their margins by customer and product. Ask yourself, *If I could have only eight pieces of company information every day, what would they be and why?*

Seat-of-the-pantsers often overlook the most obvious and important metric—cash. I found out how a cash crisis can sneak up on you when, one day in 1989, my CFO told me that we were $1 million in the hole and tapped out on credit. Financial statements may lead you to believe that you're raking it in, but next thing you know you can't meet payroll. The three biggest culprits are overdue receivables, slow-turning inventory, and growing too fast. All companies, particularly young ones, should keep close tabs on cash by forecasting their balances daily, weekly, and monthly—and then act quickly when projections fall short.

MANAGING RECEIVABLES

In the mid-nineties, an Arizona wholesale customer played us like chumps. They steadily grew into one of our largest customers, paying like clockwork. Then they placed a succession of huge orders that pushed them beyond their credit limit. Red flags flew, and they pleaded for our help. We made an exception because of their sales volume and sterling payment record. You know where I'm going with this. We got stung to the tune of five hundred grand. Lesson learned. My philosophy is simple. Not only do you have to get paid, you have to get paid on time. To optimize management of your receivables:

Get it in writing. Use a credit application to document mutually agreeable payment terms—date due, finance charges. Dot the *i*'s and cross the *t*'s—so you don't have to cross your fingers come collection time.

Know your customer. Don't rely solely on credit reports for information on commercial accounts—that info is often two years old. Call and get references to check pay histories.

Establish a personal relationship. It's not always practical, of course, but it can tilt the payment odds in your favor.

Walk away from large, suspect sales. If you're not completely confident an account can or will pay you on time—and the sale is large enough that not collecting the cash can hurt you—don't take the sale.

Use liens when appropriate. If you're selling certain property or services, be sure to document your lien rights. If you're selling inventory, for instance, your bank can help you file a lien on the property sold. A lien can be your best friend. (Why do you think banks always get paid first?)

Get strict with past-due accounts. Contact the customer as soon as your protocol permits. (In our company it was seven to ten days after a missed due date.) Wait until an account is ninety days past due and you may be too late. Do all future business C.O.D. (cash on delivery) until the customer is current again. No exceptions, no matter who the customer is or how long you've had a relationship. Get lax and the account may snowball out of control. Then there will be two companies in trouble.

Establish phone protocol. The first call to a past-due account is always a relationship-building call: "I'm just calling to make sure you received the invoice." The second is a problem-solving call: "I'm just checking in to see if there's a reason why we haven't received your payment." If there's a pause, don't fill it; wait for the customer's response. Subsequent calls should always be firm, fair, and professional.

Tutor customer-relationship "owners." School them (typically your salespeople) in accounts-receivable policies and procedures. Feed them clear, easy-to-interpret aging reports. Account-relationship decisions should be led by those who own the customer relationship. After all, they have a vested interest in the outcome. That said, final decisions regarding ongoing credit are the credit manager's call.

Meet regularly with your credit staff. At least once a month, review all accounts. Ensure action steps are pursued—phone calls, past-due letters, final demand letter, collection agency, legal action—to resolve past-due accounts.

Dealing with overseas customers? Be prepared to be resourceful, especially if you've never met the customer and credit references are impossible to come by. Skip Thaler, an old friend and importer-exporter, once sent a shipment of tires to Italy. The customer never picked up the order. As far as Skip knew, a UFO had scooped her up. Because freight and duty fees were too high to retrieve the shipment, Skip got on the horn, dropped his price, and found another Italian buyer. When determining a payment protocol for foreign customers, factor in these three primary risks:

1. Country Risk. Before you pursue an overseas deal, consult country risk ratings published by folks like Dun and Bradstreet, Veritas, and World Bank. Already shipped product to, say, Lebanon? Good luck collecting payment. Domestic problems weaken a country's currency, so governments often restrict hard currency from leaving their borders, which would raise inflation, interest rates, and exchange rates vis-à-vis the U.S. dollar. That's not to say you can't pry dollars out. You'll just need a really big lever.

2. Currency Risk. If, on the other hand, you agree to take payment in foreign currency, protect yourself against fluctuations by contractually specifying a minimum conversion rate. (Don't forget to include conversion fees.) It's not unheard of for currency rates to plummet 50 percent from the time you seal a deal to collection day.

3. Payment Risk. What's the cardinal rule of international trade? Know your buyer. Begin every business relationship by pricing your product in U.S. dollars and asking for advance payment. (Make sure your bank processes international wires.) Sure, it's a stern approach, and revenues may suffer in the short term. But it's better to lose one-time buyers than it is to expose yourself to ruinous risk. Up front, tell your trading partner that as your relationship matures, you can explore more equitable ways to share risk. In time, move from advance payment to letters of credit to documentary collections (they're less onerous than letters of credit). After building a solid history, settle into open payment terms.

BOND WITH YOUR BANKER

Your bank is a partner, not an adversary. Get your banker on board by communicating early and often. Habitually review your monthly financials together—bankers love it when you consider them an extension of your management team. Be especially forthcoming with bad news. It's human nature—nobody likes to tell the banker when there's a significant negative variance between projected and actual income. Some execs roll up their sleeves and quietly try to turn the situation around. A month goes by. Two months. Things get worse, and one or more of the loan covenants are blown. Sheepishly, they call their banker, who's none too happy to be the last to know. You're better off coming clean up front: "I thought I'd give you advance notice. We just calculated that, due to weather, we're not going to hit our November numbers." Chances are he'll waive the company's covenant before D-day. He's human, too—the last thing he wants to do is go to the loan committee with bad news after the fact. Avoid that scenario by committing only to loan covenants—current ratio, leverage ratio, debt-equity ratio, interest coverage—you know you can meet. (FYI, aggressively negotiating those covenants earns bankers' respect.)

One of the smartest things you can do is take a lender to lunch. Lay the groundwork by getting to know three key people in your bank—your relationship manager (typically an up-and-comer), her boss or her boss's boss (the closest thing nowadays to the traditional gray-haired banker), and, most important, the person who chairs the credit committee. It works like this. Your relationship manager goes to her boss. They decide whether to, say, extend your credit or amend your covenant. After a credit analyst reviews the request and writes up a report, it's taken to the credit committee, where your fate is decided. The credit chair's job is often drudgery—he's chained to his desk analyzing financial information all day. The big secret is he never gets invited to lunch. He has no idea who the companies are behind the loan requests. So, when your relationship manager introduces you to her boss, invite the boss—and the credit chief—to tour your company and have lunch. The credit guy will love taking a break from the dungeon. It's also a coup for you. The credit chair will have a better grasp of your business *and* you're no longer just another name on a loan request. Those two factors alone could make a big difference when your loan comes up for review or you need a covenant waiver. But it'll be too late if you wait for stormy weather. Do the meet-and-greet now, while the sun is shining.

MANAGING AND FUNDING GROWTH

Businesses are like sharks—their survival hinges on forward progress. Sometimes that means adding new stores, plants, or regional offices. In other businesses, it means selling more widgets to existing customers, creating new products, or raising same-store sales. Even if you're content to stay comfortably small, standing still isn't an option. Costs rise, competition lurks. Unless you advance—spreading escalating costs over an expanding revenue base—you'll gradually take on water. But there's more. Growth has a voracious appetite and sharp teeth—not just for capital, but also for people and systems. Focusing on growth growth growth rather than day-to-day necessities may starve the operation's core, the source of life-giving income.

Entrepreneurs are typically more "growth aggressive." Founders of companies tend to be builders all the way down to their DNA. They love to create products and expand capacity, and they're confident the business will justify the expenditures. Each new success emboldens an entrepreneur to take on even more risk. Trouble is, as a company gets larger, new layers of complexities arise and its risk profile changes, dramatically. Enlightened entrepreneurs upgrade their skills to meet elevated risk head-on, aware that adrenaline-fueled crapshoots too often wind up with somebody going bust. Here's where a board of advisers (chapter 7) is worth its weight in stock options.

In lieu of a board, find an outsider to ask you some tough, basic questions. Take the expansion-happy retailer whom I've consulted. I asked him five questions about his plans to branch from one location into three. "Are you a well-oiled machine?" I asked. Until you have airtight procedures, I said, running three locations will produce ten times the headaches. Second, I asked, "Is your offering unique, or are you just lucky?" If it's the latter, I said, don't count on duplicating your first location's success. Third, "Do you have a well-documented, cookie-cutter plan that lieutenants can execute?" You simply can't be in two or three places at once. Fourth, "How are you going to expand?" Essentially, it boils down to two options: company-owned stores or franchises. Last, "Are your pockets and fortitude deep enough to weather a harsh expansion, or system failures." Your original location often will suffer when your attention pivots to new stores. He was stumped on every question.

He didn't resist when I suggested he shelve his growth plans until he had five good answers.

Retained earnings are clearly the Wheaties of business growth. However, absent sufficient earnings and borrowing power, raising capital may be an option. The risk here is that selling equity is how many entrepreneurs lose control of their company. One CEO I know owned well over half his company—until his ambitious plans outstripped resources. He was forced to continually raise money and sell shares on the cheap. Ultimately, his stake shrank to 5 percent.

Avoid the oxymoronic death-by-growth nightmare by doing sound due diligence. Before adding all the ingredients—people, equipment, inventory, real estate—prepare revenue and expense projections to determine whether your plans are affordable. Sophisticated businesses and private equity pros run the numbers through capital investment formulas based on discounted cash flow (DCF) models and targeted internal rates of return (IRR). These calculations answer two basic questions:

1. How soon will the investment break even, so you can pay shareholders?
2. What will be the return on investment?

Nailing down these numbers takes a lot of the risk (but not all) out of the investment's "go/no go" call. To ignore crunching numbers in favor of going with your gut is to court disaster. The gut doesn't appreciate that "units"—equipment, storefront, salespeople—have to quickly support themselves (payback) and contribute profitability (ROI), all according to precisely targeted financial goals.

The best acid test for profitability is a "cap-ex," or capital expenditures, calculation. Scholars may laugh at my simplification, but all I care about is helping ethical, hardworking folks make the right choices . . . and money. Here's how you do it. Divide your expected cash flow from the new unit (a store, say) by its cost (initial capital outlays, inventory, one-time preopening expenses, and so on). Then divide the result by the number of years invested. Carry over the sums on a cumulative basis—if you add more capital equipment, for instance, increase the denominator accordingly.

For example, say the cost to open a store is $100,000, and its first-year

EBITDA (earnings before interest, taxes, depreciation, and amortization) is $10,000 in the hole. Your cap-ex calculation is:

−$10,000/$100,000=.10/1 year=−.10 (ROI is underwater by 10 percent)

Now, assume the second-year EBITDA is $60,000. The cumulative EBITDA becomes $50,000 (−$10,000 + $60,000). The new cap-ex calculation is:

$50,000/$100,000=.50/2 years=.25 (ROI is 25 percent)

The Really Big Question: When do you reconsider the investment? The Simple Answer: If you can't put money back into shareholders' pockets at the end of three years (ROI of 33 percent) or four, tops (ROI of 25 percent). A piece of equipment can often pay for itself in less than a year—an ROI of more than 100 percent. I watched a national fitness chain fail at the basics as it rolled out dozens of new fitness centers. While each one was profitable, it took more than seven years for the company to recoup its initial investment via earnings. Yet because the heavily trafficked centers required upgrades every seven years, the owners had to double down their capital expenses before they could turn a profit. It's like Sisyphus and his rock. Each time he pushed it up the mountain, it rolled back down again.

Leveraging your offering may be the gateway to growth. Small businesses often break into new markets by forming alliances with larger companies who're ravenous for breakthrough concepts and technologies. That's why San Diego–based Mitchell International, Inc., one of the three biggest providers of e-business solutions for the automotive-insurance and collision-repair industries, approached APU Solutions, a small midwestern company offering a Web-based, real-time way to buy and sell auto parts. APU (disclosure: I'm a part owner) swapped the use of its real-time estimating software for access to Mitchell's sophisticated infrastructure and customer reach. David-and-Goliath alliances are win-win. The Goliaths get game-changing ideas, technologies, and products, while the Davids gain credibility, market intelligence, and networking opportunities.

Growth through acquisition presents another set of challenges. Tires Plus marched into Kansas City and bought six stores that we immediately remodeled. Sixty days later, our signs were up and the stores were open. The transition was seamless because customers viewed the old locations as brand-new stores. Later that year, we acquired a dozen stores in Omaha. I'm still scratching my head over why we didn't follow the Kansas City script. Instead, we kept the stores open under the old name. We waited months to re-brand them, and remodeling took an entire year. We also took our time replacing employees who didn't fit our culture. It wasn't exactly a shocker when we fell a country mile short of our sales goals.

If you plan to acquire other companies:

- **Expect culture clashes.** Buyouts push employees out of their comfort zone, triggering an avalanche of emotions. They fear their jobs are in danger and the new owners could ruin everything. Remedy: Communicate early, often, and with empathy.
- **Weigh the pros and cons of organic growth.** Taking over an existing outfit inserts you instantly into the marketplace. But a lot of companies—especially big boys like Best Buy and Wal-Mart— like to start from scratch. Why? It's easier to retain complete control and ensure that reputation is built—and employees are trained—the right way.

LOSS PREVENTION

You could practically hear a TV announcer booming, "Smile, you're on *Corporate Camera!*" Shortly before we hired Eric Randa as head of loss prevention, he was handed The Case of the Vanishing Laptop. A digital camera and other pricey items had also disappeared from corporate offices. They were after-hours thefts, so Eric looked to the building's entrance camera for clues. Sure enough, an unfamiliar maintenance worker had been on duty. Eric directed his right-hand guy to stake out the parking lot. When the suspect emerged at the end of her shift, he nabbed her red-handed.

If only catching the bad guys (and gals) were always so easy. Employee theft is the culprit behind 30 percent of all business failures. Yep, you read that right, and the percentage is even higher for small businesses with scant margin for error. The U.S. Department of Commerce estimates that sticky-fingered employees steal upward of $40 billion annually from American companies. Collaring dishonest employees makes a dent, but the real cost savings is in prevention. Protect your business with these measures:

Scrub rather than screen job candidates. You wouldn't hand your house keys to someone you don't know and trust. The keys to your business are no different.

Question areas left blank on the application. It may be intentional. Gaps in employment history, while often innocuous, may indicate time spent in the slammer.

Conduct background investigations. The cost is negligible—especially with volume discounts—compared to the messes made by bad eggs. Verifying an applicant's Social Security number costs about ten bucks. County, statewide, and federal criminal-record checks cost about $20 each. Drug tests run about $40 apiece. At the very least, go deep into applicants who'd have access to assets, from a dockworker handling manufactured goods to an accountant with signature authority on bank accounts. Avert lawsuits by choosing a reputable sleuth.

Distribute an "ethical conduct agreement." In job interviews (chapter 13), stressing your zero tolerance for corruption is a good start. But not all employees, particularly younger ones, know where to draw the line in the sand. Require teammates to sign a form that explains what constitutes stealing and why they shouldn't look the other way if a colleague swipes company assets. Further, leave no doubt that controls are in place to detect theft and that the hammer of the law will fall hard.

Explain how theft can steal their jobs. It's easy to rationalize that lifting a few reams of paper won't hurt anyone. Your people may even feel they're just collecting the "bonus" you overlooked. Use memos, Web site postings, group meetings, one-on-one's—whatever it takes—to convince people that minor thefts combine for major hits on profits and paychecks.

Scan for red flags. Treat every cash shortage, missing asset, or inventory shrinkage like it's a four-alarm fire. The sooner you investigate, the more likely you'll catch the perp and minimize losses.

Eliminate temptation. As I've mentioned, Oscar Wilde used to quip that he could resist anything but temptation. Take note, and build in checks and balances. Require a countersignature on company checks, and don't allow the same employee to both approve and pay invoices. Desperate circumstances can warp decent people's scruples and lead them to "borrow" what they can never realistically repay. Regularly review accounts payable, and conduct annual, independent audits to police for irregularities. Don't allow financial records to leave the office. Buy a shredder. The more hurdles thieves face, the less likely they'll take that first leap.

Invest in physical security. An alarm system not only scares off bad guys, its electronic access codes record who enters the building around the clock. Review system-generated reports occasionally and follow up on comings and goings: "Hey, Sandy, are you really working so hard that you need to enter the building at 2:26 AM?" Alarms should sound when back doors are opened without keys, and building keys should be impossible to duplicate by anyone other than authorized locksmiths. Also, use clear trash bags—a favorite trick of the dark trade is to conceal company property in the trash only to double back later and retrieve it.

Get insured. Catching a thief doesn't necessarily mean you'll catch up with your stolen goods. Popular products like electronics, computer equipment, and power tools get fenced fast on the street. Get an insurance policy that reimburses for theft and fraud.

Guard against retail losses. You may have a great product, great marketing, and great locations. But you're still going down if your product disappears and your cash and checks don't make it to the bank. According to the most recent National Security Retail Survey, conducted by the University of Florida, the causes of inventory shrinkage broke down this way: 47 percent was due to employee theft, 32 percent to shoplifting, 15 percent to administrative error, and 6 percent to vendor theft. (Inform vendors up front about your inspection process.) Ready for another jaw-dropper? The average hit caused by a dishonest employee was $1,023, while the average shoplifter made off with $128. It makes sense. Employees have the opportunity to commit theft daily while shoplifters zip in and out.

How to minimize risk?

JOIN A NATIONAL THEFT DATABASE. ChoicePoint, General Information Services, and U.S. Investigations Services offer three of the best. Built by retailers for retailers, these databases share information on shoplifters and employees terminated for theft and fraud.

REVIEW REFUNDS AND VOIDED SALES. When a Montana lumber store cashier processed hundreds of refunds—many for big-ticket items—over a fifteen-month period, Gary Kasper suspected foul play. The company's loss prevention chief, Gary, went undercover after installing a hidden camera to monitor the cashier's register lane. He posed as a customer and bought a $500 tool, then "forgot" the receipt on the counter. Sure enough, the cashier pocketed it and later filled out a refund slip—all captured in living color. The cashier was prosecuted for $25,000 worth of fraudulent refunds.

PROVIDE EXCELLENT CUSTOMER SERVICE. Greet customers as they enter and repeatedly acknowledge them during their visit. Ask if they're finding what they need and whether you can escort them to a product. Shoplifters are edgy people who prefer to blend into the woodwork. If they can't, they'll likely go elsewhere.

MOUNT CLOSED-CIRCUIT TV CAMERAS IN PLAIN SIGHT. Surveillance deters shoplifters and dishonest employees alike.

CLIP ELECTRONIC ARTICLE SURVEILLANCE (EAS) TAGS ONTO GOODS. Beeping tags have thwarted countless shoplifters, and they pay for themselves. Thanks to the microchip revolution, better antitheft technology comes to market practically every month.

WAIT AND WATCH. Set aside time to monitor, from discreet vantage points, your employees over the course of a day. Look for suspicious activity during opening and closing "observations"—and during lunch hour, when lower-level employees relieve managers. Bird-dog an employee on a bank-deposit run. Even more important, use stakeouts to catch employees doing something right. Congratulate them for opening on time or for a by-the-book bank run. You'll boost morale and also send this subtle message: They'll never know when you're out there watching them.

MANAGING IT (INFORMATION TECHNOLOGY)

Purchasing, finance, and IT people rarely speak the same language. Techies get excited about new toys that bean counters don't have the chops to critique, and jargon-challenged purchasers are often at the mercy of tech-savvy vendors. That skills gap is difficult to bridge, leaving a big hole for IT investments to plunge through. Building that bridge requires three main pillars:

1. The integration of IT into the strategic-planning process.
2. The unqualified support and leadership of upper management (which should include the IT director).
3. The acceptance that IT investment is ongoing.

Building IT into strategic planning is the best way to align IT strategy with business strategy. Getting immediate buy-in from all departments is critical. Why? Because IT failures are generally rooted in business, not technical, breakdowns. It comes down to change management. Implementing an IT initiative starts a domino effect—every business process also changes. That's why upper management must own and manage an "IT project." Most people resist change—especially technological ones. Your IT staff can manage the technical side, but they can't mandate that users accept the change. If key users haven't had a seat at the designing-testing-training table, and don't view the new process as markedly better than the old, a project is doomed before it begins. You and your senior execs have to hammer home the point that promised returns will materialize only if everyone gets on board and adjusts the way they operate.

A big IT fallacy is that ROI will magically start growing like a weed. Don't count on it. Maximizing ROI demands that you keep investing in the solution. That means training both IT and users on technology, applications, and enhancements. It means budgeting money for help-desk support, process redesign, and upgrades. (The upgrade cycle of enterprise software is generally one to three years; each event can require up to four months.) Failing to fully invest in IT solutions is why many companies are using only 20 percent of the functionality they buy. How can that happen? Easily. A hot project plops in the lap of top management. They dutifully approve an IT purchase in line with the company's capabilities and projections. The bare-bones functionality of the IT solution get implemented, the hot project is complete, and everyone moves on.

That waste can be minimized—at least for nonstrategic IT solutions—by partnering with an MSP (managed service provider, aka, outsourced service provider or utility computing service provider). Thanks to MSPs, which deliver computing resources over the Internet like a power utility delivers electricity, management can now focus on IT's use and not its generation. Like other commodities, users are billed only for services they use. Bottom line: Most organizations' core competency isn't, and shouldn't be, IT systems deployment and management. Today's IT focus is on Web-based access, not assets. Asset-based IT—owning hardware and software—is going the way of the passenger pigeon. Look at the explosion of Salesforce.com. According to Gartner, Inc., the leading provider of research and analysis on the global IT industry, 80 percent of large-company IT investments now go to MSPs. Why the migration? Lots of reasons. Partnering with MSPs

- reduces your IT infrastructure and deployment risks
- allows you to quickly scale your IT infrastructure up or down
- lowers up-front costs as well as costs associated with excess IT capacity
- eliminates the need to staff up for peak demand periods

- allows your IT group to concentrate fully on strategic issues
- starts with well-defined and fairly generic applications—e-mail, messaging, connectivity, hosting, security, redundancy, storage, disaster recovery, stand-alone applications (like sales automation)

Here are more IT success strategies:

Cycle IT leaders throughout the company. Don't confine your senior IT people. Give them operational experience in other departments so they understand the business better and know what the company needs to succeed. Our Adopt-A-Store program required IT staff to spend time in stores each month to learn skills like store opening and closing procedures, receiving freight, doing inventory. We wanted them to understand the capabilities and needs of the people who used the systems they designed. Computer programmers are a different breed. They may be able to operate a system in their sleep, but that doesn't mean the average user can. Keeping the people who design your systems connected to other parts of the company ultimately helps both your internal and external customers.

Hold your IT chief accountable. It's every entrepreneur's nightmare—the break-the-bank software purchased two short years ago is obsolete. Make sure your IT head invests in flexible open architectures that allow your company to change with the market. Growth potential also needs to be taken into account—big investments should include volume price breaks for future users, computers, or servers. (An outsourced MSP solution might be your best bet.)

Embrace industry standards. That means not building proprietary solutions. Why? Highly customized software is like a drug. You get hooked and can't get off it. It begins to cost more and more. Before you know it, you can't switch dealers—er, vendors—because your cost to move off their solution is higher than the incremental cost of your next fix—er, upgrade. Mandate that IT solutions be compatible with other primary systems within the organization.

Don't create more problems than you solve. In the late 1990s, CRM (customer relationship management) solutions were all the rage. A lot of organizations coughed up big bucks for CRM software without specific plans for how to use it. The result? ROI was DOA. Software is a tactic, not a strategy. Develop a strategy first, then secure the tactics to support it.

Demand ROI from most IT investments. When a business unit proposes an IT solution, challenge your people to prove that it will directly benefit the company in measurable ways. Require the business unit, and IT, to budget it. Then hold IT accountable for the technology and the business unit responsible for results. Make sure your financial reporting is clear and transparent so results can be traced to specific investments. Caveat: There are exceptions. Up to 20 percent of your IT spending should be R&D related. Your IT staff needs to stay on top of advancements that can translate to competitive advantages. Without an R&D budget, all your staff can hope for is to stay afloat.

Be wary of big promises. Benchmark industry IT investment as a percent to revenue. You'll need it as a shield against slick-talking sales folks. Skilled IT vendors can construct an ROI model showing you can invest as much as your total revenue and still get a rosy ROI. Hello? If Wal-Mart—perhaps the smartest technology user in the game—can't squeeze more ROI past a certain percent-to-revenue threshold, what makes you think you can?

KEY POINTS

BUSINESS FUNCTION DOS AND DON'TS

➤ **Manage your supplier relationships.** Expect more than supplies from suppliers. Require them to add value by identifying business opportunities, developing markets, providing technological improvements, or contributing to strategic decision making. Find suppliers who are positioned to grow along with you.

➤ **Negotiate shrewdly.** Make a list of what you're willing to give up and what's nonnegotiable. Have a target number in mind, and don't budge from it. Hold firm on deal-breakers; good suppliers will change the way they do things to keep your business. Still, look beyond your own agenda—create win-wins by finding ways to help you both boost business. Find agreement on even the smallest issues before signing off.

➤ **Marketing is not a do-it-yourself project.** Hire pros to do the heavy lifting. But don't spend a penny until you've defined your goals and target customers. Then devise efficient ways to reach them. Pump up your team about the possibilities. Go to school on your online options, and don't overlook viral marketing.

➤ **Polish your pricing protocols.** Stake out your position on the pricing continuum. Then adjust when necessary by continually monitoring the competition's pricing and your sales volume. When costs rise, nudge prices as much as the market will bear, and hide margin increases in your cost increases. As an alternative to price hikes, consider introducing new products at more profitable price points.

➤ **Manage the sales function.** A top-notch sales manager is a must. The good ones endlessly study the market, train and inspire staff, and massage egos. Hunt down the best salespeople and sell them onto your team. Provide generous commissions—the more they earn, the more you do, too. Competitive intel? It's right there in the brains of your salespeople, who have direct pipelines to customers.

➤ **Study the Sandler Selling System.** Build rapport, establish an upfront contract, pinpoint the prospect's pain, determine that pain's financial impact, identify the decision maker, offer a solution, and follow up with a winning post-sell strategy.

➤ **Deliver legendary customer service.** Keeps 'em coming back for more. Customer replacement is wasteful and expensive. Good customer experiences lead to "free advertising"—dazzled customers spread the word to family and friends. Treating people well is also the right thing to do; a little kindness goes a long, long way.

- ➤ **Win customer loyalty.** Happy, well-trained employees are more likely to treat others right—and earn lifetime customers. Establish customer-care guidelines, solicit and act on feedback, measure satisfaction and reward results, and support solid service every way you can.

- ➤ **Land a great CFO.** Expect your CFO to provide monthly analyses and presentations to the executive team. He should consistently challenge other departments to raise their game, and lead the never-ending war on costs. The best CFOs are data hubs, providing the rest of the team with financial tools and metrics.

- ➤ **IT and loss prevention are key parts of the financial team.** Invest time, energy, and money—their impact will echo throughout the company.

- ➤ **Bond with your banker.** Your banker is a partner, not an adversary. Keep communication strong. Make her an extension of your management team by regularly reviewing monthly financials together. Be candid with bad news. Build relationships with key bank personnel, including the person who chairs the credit committee.

WEATHERING WORST-CASE SCENARIOS

When Bad Things Happen to Good Companies

FDR was wrong. Business owners have plenty to fear besides fear itself. At any moment, the unexpected can splinter your operations, rupture your strategic plans, and jeopardize your survival. I've spent many anxious days and sleepless nights worrying about nightmare scenarios. After fumbling a few pressure-packed incidents, I developed a crisis drill:

Ease physical tension. Jerked into panic mode, your muscles tighten and breathing grows shallow and fast. Take slow, deep breaths for a few minutes. Continue to breathe deeply while massaging your neck and shoulders.

Get a grip. "Worst-case" is a relative term. No matter how stressful and expensive a business challenge is, it's not in the same league as serious illness or a death in the family. Pull yourself into positive territory by looking for hidden opportunities and appreciating what you've got—family and friends, dedicated employees, a great product, loyal customers. Keep reminding yourself of what's truly important in life, especially when your mind races and queasiness bubbles in the pit of your stomach.

Create and execute action steps. Pick yourself up, dust yourself off, and start writing a bulleted survival strategy. Paralyzing anxiety dissipates the more you organize your thoughts and begin mapping your way out of the rubble. Then, start working the plan—every step moves you closer to regaining control. Here's a spur-of-the-moment action plan I wrote when a key employee resigned.

- *Place an ad in the paper.*
- *Network with professional contacts.*
- *Consult list of potential candidates.*
- *Interview and consider promoting Cathy and compressing her development schedule.*

Worst-case scenarios drop from the sky, sometimes right into your lap. Take the April day I opened a letter from my executive committee. "Dear Tom," it began, "we want to inform you that we, your entire management team, are resigning to form a competitive tire company. Hopefully, we'll be friendly competitors. Thanks for everything and we wish you well." It was signed by everyone who reported to me. For a moment I panicked—a mass exodus was my greatest fear—until I spotted the postscript at the bottom: "PS, April Fool's!" I looked up to catch everyone marching into my office and enjoying a big laugh.

Worst-case scenarios don't have to end up with worst-case results. Handled correctly, they can turn out to be blessings in disguise. When your feet are to the fire and you come out on top, you're stronger and more confident for the experience. One thing's for sure—you find out what you're made of. You also deepen your business knowledge, which makes you a better leader in the long run. The stories that follow can prepare you to turn worst-case scenarios into catalysts for growth.

CHAPTER 55

RELATIONSHIPS ON THE ROCKS

Rescuing Key People Who Jump Ship

SCENARIO #1: BOLTING KEY EMPLOYEE

Option #1: Let 'em go. It was an ordinary afternoon—until my CFO and HR chief interrupted a meeting in my office. "We have to talk ASAP," one said solemnly. My heart sank. I motioned them in and instinctively asked the dreaded two words: "Who's leaving?" Our IT head had resigned after a non-competitor lassoed him with a big offer. I convened an emergency session of our core executive team to consider our options. We brainstormed awhile but decided to sleep on it. It was a long night. A disruption in any of the multiple mission-critical initiatives IT was spearheading could prove costly. I practiced some deep breathing, focused on all the things that were going right, and began mapping out an action plan. By morning, I had regained perspective. While my philosophy was, *We don't lose anyone we don't want to lose*, we decided to make an exception, concluding that matching the offer would throw our salary structure out of whack. We named an interim head from within the department and, six weeks later, found a knock-your-socks-off replacement.

Option #2: Try to keep 'em. I was never resigned to losing a valuable employee. As long as she hadn't turned in her ID badge, I figured I had a shot at keeping her. First, I shifted my mind-set from *How will this person's absence make things more difficult for me?* to *What's best for this person?* I'd sit down with her and say, "I have mixed emotions, Jane. On one hand, I hate to see you go. On the other, if you think this is an opportunity you can't pass up, then good for you. You deserve the best. I'm not going to try to talk you out of it. I just wanted to thank you for your contributions. If you're open to it, we could brainstorm a bit to make sure you're making the right decision."

If she agreed, I'd sketch out a Ben Franklin balance sheet by drawing a line down the center of a whiteboard. In the left column, I'd list the pluses of the new company. In the right column, I'd list the pluses of staying with us. As the list grew, I duly recognized the positives of the new job. But I also objectively, with her best interests in mind, pointed out the drawbacks. For instance: "You'll have to work fifty-five hours a week? We can arrange for you to max out at forty-seven. A thousand dollars is all that separates us? You're scheduled for a raise of at least twice that at your next review." Depending on circumstances, I'd occasionally use a more sophisticated decision-making model called the "Weight & Rate." Its beauty is that it considers both the relative value of each decision point and the likelihood that either job will deliver it.

These exercises shed light, yet logic takes a person only so far. After reviewing the pros and cons and adding up the numbers, the wild card is the employee's gut feeling—and if your caring attitude hasn't turned the tide, all you can do is respect where she's coming from. My impromptu brainstorming sessions worked about half the time. The other half, I usually ended up agreeing that, yes, our analysis showed she was better off accepting the new position.

Burned Bridges. All bets are off if the departing employee poaches a key client on his way out. This threat causes more heartburn than a triple-decker meatball sandwich. It's particularly acidic for leaders of

WEIGHT & RATE DECISION-MAKING MODEL

In four steps, you can help an employee achieve clarity about her choices. In this example, one job promises an unbeatable schedule, while the other offers a much higher salary.

1 Write in the leftmost column the factors influencing the employee's decision. The list can be as long as she likes.

2 Ask her to weigh each factor's importance (column A in the example) by assigning it a number from one to ten, with ten being the most important. The same number can be used more than once. In the example shown, a chance for further education and a supportive corporate culture are both rated a six.

3 Now ask her to take her best guess at rating the likelihood that each job will offer what she wants (column B in the example). Again, use one through ten, with ten being the most likely.

4 Multiply column A by column B to get a subtotal for each factor, then add up the subtotals for your final result.

THINGS I WANT FROM A JOB	JOB OPTION 1			JOB OPTION 2		
	A Importance of this factor to me	**B** Likelihood this job will give this	SUBTOTAL	**A** Importance of this factor to me	**B** Likelihood this job will give this	SUBTOTAL
Flexible working hours	10 x	10 =	100	10 x	5 =	50
Sufficient money	9 x	4 =	36	9 x	10 =	90
Good benefits package	8 x	6 =	48	8 x	7 =	56
Chance to further my education	6 x	8 =	48	6 x	5 =	30
Supportive corporate culture	6 x	9 =	54	6 x	3 =	18
	TOTAL POINTS = **286**			TOTAL POINTS = **244**		

financial service companies, sales-driven outfits, law firms, and other organizations where clients value account-manager relationships over the business itself. The best strategy is to wake up before this nightmare begins. Odds are low that employees will skip out with clients (or colleagues) if you've won them over with a healthy culture that makes them feel trusted and valued.

Start knitting a safety net anyway. Make sure top execs—including you—and support staff go out of their way to build relationships with big clients. Any good CYA (cover your, um, behind) plan includes signing linchpin people to fair non-compete agreements (chapter 14). That said, do what you can to resolve the matter without lawyers. Try a little soft reasoning with departing staffers: "I know you need to do what you need to do. But how do you feel about having a mediator determine who's right here?" If you're turned down, your attorney counsels action, and the bolting employee endangers your team, tell him you have no choice but to take him to court. (That also sends a message to the rest of the company that your contracts have teeth.) Then focus on replacing both him and the lost sales.

Additional proactive strategy: Succession planning (chapter 42).

SCENARIO #2: BOLTING MAJOR CLIENT

The phone call couldn't have come at a worse time for Alexis Bloomstrand. The sole owner of New Morning Windows, she had just had surgery to fuse four vertebrae, and faced months of recuperation. She was in the midst of building a new house on the heels of divorce. She was also negotiating with her ex to buy the Minneapolis building that housed the business they had launched twenty-two years earlier. On top of all that, it was just a month after the 9/11 terror attacks. She had an inkling bad business news was brewing. Two weeks before going under the knife, she asked her flagship client, one of North America's largest window manufacturers, whether the rumors were true about its impending purchase of her competitor, a Canadian custom-window manufacturer nearly three times New Morning's size. No deal was in the works, her client assured her.

Four days after her surgery, the phone rang. The client had indeed purchased Alexis's competitor and was giving sixty days' notice that its strategic alliance with New Morning would be terminated. Overnight, revenues plunged from $8 million to under $3 million. Alexis managed to keep all seventy-five employees on through the winter holidays, but eventually cut the staff to thirty. The new year brought more bad news. A major lender acquired Alexis's bank and issued her a default notice. A few months later, referred by both her attorney and a trusted consultant, she looked to the Platinum Group, a Twin Cities–based turnaround firm. "I couldn't have gotten financing without them," Alexis said. Platinum tutored her in cash-flow models, inventory management, new production efficiencies, and cost-cutting strategies. Eighteen months later, New Morning's revenues rebounded, and then some. "In three years of hell," Alexis said, "I learned more about running a business than I had in the last twenty."

Losing your biggest client is traumatic. When revenues nose-dive, these proactive strategies can help soften the landing.

Build a stable of advisers. Panicked business leaders don't make good decisions. When one of New Morning's suppliers later hit a rough patch, Alexis suggested he pony up for expert advice like she had. It was an expense he said he couldn't afford. "I told him he couldn't afford not to," Alexis said. "Our legal and consulting fees were $200,000 one year. That makes me sick. But if we hadn't spent it, we wouldn't be here today."

Upgrade financial fluency. Working with consultants helped Alexis learn the nuts and bolts of cash flow and cash management. "I knew the basics," she said. "But they showed me the importance of mastering the financial end." She now knows how to build a financial planning model to prove the company's long-term viability and attract new financing.

Raise the performance bar. Forced to scour her labor costs, Alexis didn't like what she saw. Some veteran employees were coasting on inflated salaries built by automatic annual raises. She tackled productivity issues head-on by implementing education and training programs. She upped the ante on task-heavy job descriptions by spelling out challenging, but reachable, goals. Most important, she tied a large portion of salary to performance. For icing, she pledged to the staff an equal distribution of 15 percent of after-tax profits. Three years and three rounds of layoffs later, and with thirty-nine employees instead of seventy-five, morale reached an all-time high.

Contain costs—at any cost. Getting lean and mean is an ongoing discipline. It's what the big boys do best. Check out the cost-containment strategies in chapters 54 and 56.

Expand your customer base. Alexis recruited new sales reps to pursue new markets, an important part of her strategic plan. But don't overlook existing markets when you need to replace lost sales. When a wholesale customer dropped us, for instance, we called his strongest competitor and delivered a message that was hard to refuse. We could increase sales, we told him, because we understand the local market and carried brands with established name recognition—built courtesy of his competitor.

Think big. The more your business is fueled by synergy, the quicker the pieces will click into place. Alexis stepped up training and mentoring for employees at every level. She cleared communication channels and established a bonus plan to invigorate the culture and drive innovation. She streamlined operations and reorganized work flow to do more with less. Bottom line: Think macro, act micro.

Have a plan in place to change the client's mind. I'd pull out all the stops to win a customer back. I'd appeal to decision makers to—please, please—in recognition of our longstanding relationship, at least sit down and talk things through. (In a case like Alexis's, obviously, that isn't an option.) Together, we'd explore what our rival offered versus what we had. If we were outgunned, I'd be the first to admit it. More often than not, a few tweaks here and a few concessions there were enough to save the relationship.

Additional proactive strategy: Customer service (chapter 53).

CHAPTER 56

NATURAL DISASTERS

Coping with Catastrophes

SCENARIO #1: NATURAL DISASTER

When a 1981 tornado took out his biggest cash cow—the most profitable of his nine Sound of Music stores—Dick Schulze focused on possibilities, not pain. The storeroom, remarkably, was spared. So Dick held a Tornado Sale in the parking lot. Lured by steeply discounted stereo gear, thousands of Minnesotans swarmed the place. Police had to shut down traffic, so great was the frenzy stirred by the overnight best buy in town. Realizing he had stumbled onto something, Dick phoned his other eight stores: *"Bring over more hi-fi components and car stereos!"* Within two years, he had completely transitioned from average prices/average volume to deep discounts/high volume. It worked. Oh, he also slapped on a new name—Best Buy.

Message: When disaster strikes, force yourself to ask quality questions. Don't moan, "Why me?" Instead, think, *What can I do right now that will make things better?* or *How can I turn this setback into an advantage?* Asking positive questions shifts your mind into creative gear. Suddenly, you see ways to capitalize on whatever Mother Nature (or market forces) throws at you.

During 1997's Flood of the Century in Grand Forks, North Dakota, our employees asked themselves, *How can I help?* Flooding had begun seventy-five miles south in the Fargo-Moorhead area. Regional manager Mark Lessin rounded up his Tires Plus teammates and hit the streets. "The house of one of our Moorhead mechanics was about to get swallowed up," Mark said. "So we camped out in his driveway for four days and filled sandbags."

By the time the Red River's surge reached Grand Forks, it had risen out of control, threatening dikes and levees. More than fifteen Tires Plus employees—and their families—from Fargo, Moorhead, and Grand Forks reported for duty. They worked a shift at the store, then rushed to the dike to fill sandbags for another six hours. "It was a lot of long days and late nights, but we saved several communities," Mark said. We also stationed water trucks at our stores to supply residents with fresh drinking water. The overtime pay—everyone was on the clock throughout the ordeal—took a bite out of monthly profits. But our roots in the communities grew deeper, our bonds with employees grew stronger, and sales quickly trended upward. In the long run, we came out ahead. Bottom line: We did the right thing.

Proactive strategy: Pray a lot.

SCENARIO #2: PERSONAL CRISIS

It was an ordinary Monday night for Larry Dennison—except for the killer headache. Everyone else in his Farmers Insurance Group office had gone home, so Larry dialed 911. The one-time district manager of the year was lucky. Most aneurysm victims don't make it to the phone. One month in an intensive care unit and two surgeries later, Larry was left with unintelligible speech and double vision, and confined to a wheelchair. A doctor told Larry's wife, Gay, that her husband was months away from rehab. A nursing home, the doc said, was the best option. She shot back four words: "Over my dead body." Gay saw to it that Larry stayed put.

Larry filled the Farmers' leadership void by handing over temporary control to his daughter, Hayley, the agency's head of recruiting and training. Like an air-traffic controller guiding in an accidental pilot, Larry advised his daughter from his hospital bed (Hayley was one of the few who could decipher Larry's speech). Hayley wasn't about to let her dad down; she worked around the clock to meet the district's goals. Farmers was so impressed they featured Hayley in a company video.

Larry beat the odds. In October 2001, nine months after his aneurysm, he returned to work. His balance, speech, and vision were still severely impaired. His patient staff helped him operate his keyboard, and they weren't shy about asking Larry to repeat himself. He used a walker to navigate corridors. Month by month, Larry grew stronger. Today, I can understand almost everything my friend says. His handshake is firm and he walks without a cane. Once again, his district is one of the country's top producers. He even went on to win two more prestigious awards. Larry's recipe for recovery? He surrounded himself with good people. He expected the best and prepared for the worst. He picked himself up every time he fell, and never lost his sense of humor.

I faced my own personal challenge when, at age forty-two, a triple trauma of divorce, cancer, and cash-flow crises left me in no condition to run a company. I needed a few months to recover. But before I dropped out of circulation, I had to take care of business. I shelved the want-tos, divvied up the have-tos, and communicated, communicated, communicated. I drafted a letter to employees that offered some explanation. I asked for their patience and thanked them for keeping us afloat during my leave. Then, one by one, I told my key people exactly what I needed. Finally, I briefed our bank and vendors that I was temporarily releasing the reins. Over the next six months, I communicated sporadically with the office. If I did drag myself into work, I just lay on the couch in my office. After three months of vegging out and another three months of healing strategies—therapy, yoga, meditation, nutrition, self-help books, retreats—I returned to work rejuvenated.

Fortunately, Mark Sathe's 2000 odyssey also looks promising. Given a sentence of a year to live following diagnosis of malignant melanoma, Mark, at fifty-two, turned over control of his Minneapolis headhunter firm to a young exec. He crafted a stock plan that gave each of his six employees 1 percent of the company and incentives for more. Mark's plan, including diet and lifestyle changes, is working. He still endures chemo treatment, but it doesn't slow him down. "We're in the midst of our strongest year in company history," he told me in 2006. "We still have no turnover this decade, and employees now own more than 20 percent of the stock. I'm now a granddaddy, I work out regularly, and I'm looking good—or so everyone tells me!"

Not everyone gets advance notice from the Grim Reaper. That explains the growth of "key man insurance"—a life insurance policy that names the company as beneficiary (chapter 6). The payout helps it survive the blow of losing the person who made it work. These stories also underscore the importance of periodically consulting experienced tax and estate-planning attorneys.

Proactive strategies: Minimize potential health crises (chapter 49). Succession planning (chapter 42). Estate planning (chapter 6).

SCENARIO #3: PUBLIC RELATIONS CRISIS

A salmonella outbreak had sickened tens of thousands of Minnesotans. The culprit? Schwan's ice cream, state officials told the manufacturer's senior management during a conference call. Before hanging up, Alfred Schwan ordered his people to stop making and selling the company's flagship product. He cut his business trip short and caught the first flight home. The next morning, the media descended on Schwan's rural headquarters. Alfred was ready. When a reporter asked what he was going to tell customers, Alfred's reply revealed the depth of his character: "Don't eat Schwan's ice cream." The outbreak, he said, was unacceptable. He apologized to his customers and announced a recall of every last scoop. A week later, authorities nabbed the perpetrator. The salmonella was traced to a subcontracted trucking company that had carried Schwan's ice cream ingredients in the same tankers it used to transport raw eggs.

It was a flashback to the 1982 Tylenol scare twelve years before. Once again, aggressive crisis management prevented a sterling brand from being tarnished. Schwan's actually walked away with its reputation enhanced. "With the trust Schwan's had built through the years," recalled former Schwan's president Ken Noyes, "our customers forgave us a lot quicker than we forgave ourselves." He wasn't exaggerating. Some customers even refused to hand over half-empty cartons of ice cream when Schwan's trademark home-delivery trucks rolled up. "We said we had to ask for their ice cream as a precautionary measure and promised to give them free replacements when we got things resolved," Ken said. "They said, 'No, I like my Schwan's ice cream. I'm not giving it up.'"

Schwan's handling of its salmonella crisis should grace the pages of every public relations textbook. Every PR predicament, of course, has its own challenges. Perhaps you're closing a plant and offshoring production. Or, maybe one of your executives was arrested under embarrassing circumstances. When the media show up and thrust a microphone in your face, the experience will hurt less if:

You're prepared. Start now by identifying which employees would serve as front-line contacts should "the worst" happen. Crises rarely strike during working hours, so ensure that everyone has a contact list. Agree up front on the values and commitments that will drive the message of any crisis response—responsibility to the community trumps profit concerns, for instance. Planning beyond that may not be helpful. Most execs overestimate the value of a "crisis plan." They commission their team to spend all kinds of time putting together a three-ring binder that gathers dust and can't possibly foresee the situation that actually unfolds. When an incident does occur, its unique nature will shape the response. That said, your team should always include an attorney and a PR professional who can school your spokespeople in media relations. Also, identify your "publics" (employees, employees' emergency contacts, customers, investors, suppliers, bankers, retirees, neighbors), and know how to reach them. Quickly. News that used to take days to travel now ricochets through cyberspace in nanoseconds.

You've got the facts. Gather every shred of information from as many sources as possible. Then determine how much to release.

You apologize. First, be contrite. Second, be contrite. Third, be contrite. This is more difficult than it might appear. Look at the rogues' gallery of disgraced politicians, sports stars, and domestic divas who made matters worse by getting their back up. There's no better lifeline for a spiraling reputation than genuinely expressing regret, taking responsibility where you should, and patiently explaining what steps are being taken to ensure the incident won't happen again.

You're sincere. Step out of your insular universe and imagine what the situation looks like to the public. Empathize with their concerns.

You'll come off as a stooge if you or your people simply parrot a duplicitous party line.

You're honest. Never, under any circumstances, lie. Lying to the public will permanently damage your company's image, to say nothing of your personal credibility. It takes only one solid hit to knock off the crown of a good name. If you don't know an answer, say that you don't know, that you'll do everything you can to get that information. If a question is best left unanswered, pledge to address it when the full picture comes into focus.

Proactive strategies: Uphold the highest ethical standards (chapter 11). Coaching yourself to peak personal performance expands your capacity to lead during a crisis (chapters 43–49).

CHAPTER 57

IT'S STRICTLY BUSINESS

Dealing with Brutal Bankers and Cutthroat Competitors

SCENARIO #1: CALLING THE LOAN

I had the seven-year itch. After six years in business, it was time to expand our retail operation. Research had convinced me the future of the tire business was in retailing. Before long, tight margins would strangle wholesalers like me. So, I went for broke. In one year we doubled our store count, from three to six, and poured money into marketing, equipment, and personnel. The rub? That little matter of being woefully underfunded. Because our marginally profitable wholesale division couldn't support us, we were quickly up to our wheelwells in retail red ink.

One day over lunch, my banker and friend, Jeff Mack, dropped the hammer. "I'm sorry, Tom," he said. "Our auditors reviewed your financial statements, and they're telling me we should call your loan. You had a successful wholesale business and you blew it by expanding into retail." If I couldn't pay off the note, he added, the bank was prepared to collect its collateral—our company. Panic Time.

Clearing my heart from my throat, I said, "Jeff, hold on a minute. Let me show you what we're doing." I pulled out our projections and explained how profitable the new stores would be once they matured. I showed him our new business plan. "Please," I said, "give us two months and I promise you'll see a turnaround." Jeff took our plans back to the bank, met with the audit committee, and called the next day. "Okay," he said. "You've got sixty days. That's it." Flush with adrenaline, I challenged my team to execute our plan and do whatever it took (while still observing the law!) to maximize profits for two months. It worked. We got back in the black just in time to hold off the liquidators.

Consider bank skirmishes the cost of doing business. Eight years later, in 1991, I was fighting off yet another bank. Our local lender had been acquired by a faceless national bank. Soon after, one of the mega-bank's low-level henchmen called to inform us our business model didn't mesh with the bank's philosophy. "We're giving you sixty days' notice that your line of credit is being eliminated," he said. We had two months to come up with $2 million. Panic Time, the sequel. We approached every bank in town, including Riverside Bank in Minneapolis, the reputed last stop for desperate entrepreneurs. If I had to pick a low point in my professional career, being turned down by Dave Cleveland, Riverside's president, would be it. Word was if Dave wouldn't loan you money, nobody would. It was true—he didn't, and they didn't.

Once again, we scrambled to free up every dollar that wasn't nailed down. We met with suppliers and reminded them of their vested interest in our success. We told them if they wanted our business they had to help us out by taking temporary promissory notes instead of payment on inventory. Two suppliers agreed. Boom—there's $1 million. We cobbled together another million by extending other payables, reducing inventory, and offering discounts to wholesale clients for paying us ahead of schedule. By day sixty, the bank had its money. We also had a new bank. (To my sweet satisfaction, Dave Cleveland was in the audience four years later when *Inc.* magazine awarded me the 1995 Midwest Entrepreneur of the Year Award. He told me turning us down was the biggest error of his career.)

Now we were in the clear, or so I thought. Six months after that '91 bank crisis, I was in the Cayman Islands with my sons. Getting ready for dinner, the phone rang. It was John Berg, our new CPA at Coopers and Lybrand (now PricewaterhouseCoopers). He was finishing his first audit of Tires Plus and had serious concerns. We had turned a profit, but our rapid growth had backed us into a highly leveraged corner. We were pouring money into new stores faster than we were draining it from existing ones. John said approving our audited statement would, under auditing standards, be stating that we could continue as a financially viable entity. That, however, was turning into a difficult conclusion to draw.

For the next hour, I tried to persuade John to sign that statement. I patiently explained our strategic supplier relationships and budget projections. "John," I said, "you know the stores that have been open awhile are doing well, and that the new stores will mature. We have a solid history." Then I locked in on two important points: our track record of conservative accounting practices, and our heavy—and wise—investments in systems and people. Finally, he saw the light and signed off. A bit wobbly, I hung up and collapsed backward on the bed. I asked my boys to give me a minute. Then I put on a fresh shirt and we went to dinner.

When faced with a cash crunch:

Lower labor costs. Where appropriate, hire part-timers or try outsourcing. For sales, offer new hires straight commission or, if necessary, a modest draw. A differentiating product or service and sizable market will attract the right salespeople. If it's last-resort time, reduce compensation across-the-board, all the way to you and the senior management team. Sincerely explain it's only until the crisis lifts and ask them to hang with you.

Get concessions from suppliers. Share your strategic plan and growth projections. Smart suppliers will see where you're going and how long it'll take. They'll get darned excited—and loosey-goosey with terms—if you can convince them your business will triple in five years.

Ask suppliers for promissory notes. You sign a note for, say, $1 million. The supplier credits your account for that amount and "sells" you $1 million in inventory. If you hit your numbers and continue to grow, you never accrue interest. The note's just deferred year after year, like a self-renewing, interest-free loan. As long as everything follows plan, the extra inventory finances the growth necessary to generate the income to pay off the note. This strategy can save your bacon. But use it cautiously. It comes with two downsides: One, it uses up a chit—there's a limit to a supplier's goodwill. Two, you may be facing an uphill struggle in future negotiations. In other words, if the supplier is unhappy, it can "call the loan."

Speed up receivables. Do the math. If your credit line is maxed out, offer customers a 1-percent-per-month "anticipation discount" for paying cash immediately instead of waiting thirty days. In effect, you're borrowing at 12 percent annually (sky-high, but remember, we're in the crisis section) while benefiting in three ways. One, you avert a cash-flow crisis. Two, you fund growth without giving up equity (venture capitalists expect returns a whole lot better than 12 percent). Three, your invoice shoots to the top of your customers' "pay list," which shrinks your bad-debt ratio.

"Factor" your invoices. In accounting-speak, a factor is a third party who buys invoices, or accounts receivables. This is a good way for a fledgling business to generate immediate working capital. Factors commonly pay clients advances of around 80 percent of the invoice value. Once the factor collects on the invoice, he pays the balance, or "reserve," minus a factoring fee of between 2 and 4 percent. It's a nice tool for collecting money in a day or two rather than thirty to ninety days. Downside: Expensive money.

Extend payables. Ask suppliers if you can pay in sixty days instead of thirty (or ninety instead of sixty). Then pay on the very last day. It's interest-free money. The bigger you get, the more likely you'll get favorable terms.

Manage inventory. Thanks to technology, inventory management has never been easier. Good news, because just-in-time inventory is a competitive necessity. Turning stock every thirty days instead of every sixty days frees up boatloads of cash. Better still, with thirty-day turns and thirty-day terms, your cost of inventory is zero. Sixty-day terms are even better—collect in thirty, pay in sixty, and you get the use of your supplier's money for thirty days.

Additional proactive strategies: Supply management (chapter 50). Finance and accounting (chapter 54).

SCENARIO #2: THE COMPETITION ATTACKS

The day that an arm of one of the country's largest companies announced its intent to crush us was like my own professional Pearl Harbor. They had boasted in a video at a national media fest that they were going to enter certain new markets and turn regional competitors like Tires Plus into roadkill. (Our Twin Cities base was their number-one target market.) Overnight, we shifted into warrior mode to defend the interests of our employees, customers, suppliers, and shareholders. Like a football coach who posts an opponent's insults in the locker room, we used their braggadocio to whip our people into a competitive frenzy.

We had eighteen months to plan our counterassault. First, we chartered a plane for our top managers to scout the competition's closest market. The battle plan: Neutralize their every strength; exploit their every weakness. (It wasn't quite *The Dirty Dozen,* but we *were* on a mission.) At some of their stores, we posed as customers. At others, we made like fawning tire dealers from faraway markets dying for a tour of their finely tuned machine. We snapped rolls of photos and took pages of notes. Once home, we benchmarked their prices from dozens of newspaper ads and conducted thorough price surveys. In no time at all we had reams of data.

Next, our top people hopped a bus for a fourteen-hour tour of the five areas in our market our opponent was targeting. We wanted to see, through our customers' eyes, how we stacked up. With diverse backgrounds and representation from every department, we recorded what each store felt like and what was needed to stave off the big boys.

Finally, we brainstormed around the clock. Within weeks, we had a fifteen-page action plan. A full six months before the invasion, we were on war footing. We remodeled stores at each front, staffed them with our best people, lowered prices, and bumped up stocking levels. On the wholesale side, we blitzed commercial and fleet accounts in a five-mile radius of each threatened store. We even launched a mini preemptive strike, snatching a prime location our competitor was bidding on.

It was a healthy, spirited competition. We had great respect for the other side, even as we prepared for merciless combat. But all the (aboveboard) traps we had set turned our adversary's gung ho into a frustrated oh-no. They tried to build megastores right next to our locations, so close to the road they would've obscured our signs and buildings—a direct violation of the zoning laws we had scrupulously obeyed. They hired the best real estate attorneys. They retained former city officials who knew how to circumvent ordinances. When our competitor won preliminary approval in one city, we mounted a legal challenge. I also lobbied at city council meetings. We didn't ease up until we had secured a level playing field.

For months after opening, they slashed many prices to well below cost, telling the V.P. of pricing, I later learned, to "bring them to their knees." We matched 'em dollar for dollar—one tire free-fell from twenty dollars down to five bucks. I remember one teammate asking, "How can we keep doing this? It's brutal." "Hey," I told him, "we've worked our tails off for too long to let somebody waltz in and steal our market." We vowed not to rest until they hoisted the white flag. Less than three years later, they shuttered their stores and got out of Dodge.

Other competitors were smarter. They did their due diligence, saw we weren't vulnerable, and backed off. Home Depot, for one, tested tire retailing in our region. We girded for battle, they took notice. Six months later, they quietly abandoned the idea. Another time, a friend—the CEO of a national tire giant—asked for a store tour. He and his attorney flew in on his Learjet. The first thing he asked was how big he should make the check. I said we weren't for sale. Before the tour, my friend excused himself during lunch. In his absence, his attorney leaned in and said, "You might want to change your mind about selling because we're coming in anyway." I just smiled. Later, after touring our stores and taking in our locations and friendly personnel, I drove them back to the airfield. As my friend showed me his jet, he said, "You should be very proud of what you've built, Tom. We won't be coming in here any time soon."

Additional proactive strategies: Strategic planning (chapter 23). Marketing (chapter 51). Continuous systems improvement (chapter 27). Action plans (chapter 46).

KEY POINTS

WEATHERING WORST-CASE SCENARIOS

- ➤ **Don't lose your cool.** When a crisis shreds your plans, don't panic. Take slow, deep breaths to stay calm. Keep perspective; it's not the end of the world. Most important, start composing a survival strategy ASAP—solution-oriented thinking and positive action steps keep fear at bay.

- ➤ **A crisis may be a good thing.** Crises reveal character, and they're often growth catalysts. Handled right, a worst-case scenario can leave you stronger and more confident, deepen your business wisdom, and turn you into a better leader.

- ➤ **Don't let key people leave.** Avoid just shaking a valuable employee's hand and wishing her luck at her new job. Ask if she's willing to brainstorm some to make sure she's making the right decision. List the pros and cons, and show her why staying put gets her closer to her career and financial goals. If you can't match the offer, say so, and extend an open invitation to return if things don't work out.

- ➤ **Prepare for bolting clients.** Losing a big client is traumatic. Don't wait to prepare a safety net. Get out front. Build a stable of trusted advisers, upgrade your financial skills, keep costs low, streamline operations, expand your customer base, and prepare a plan to change the client's mind.

- ➤ **Face a personal crisis head-on.** Need a leave of absence? If possible, take care of business first. Divvy up your duties and spell out the situation to employees, vendors, and business partners. Your attitude can make or break you. Stay positive and take good care of yourself in every way possible.

- ➤ **Prepare for PR predicaments.** Avoid a public relations nightmare by identifying internal front-line contacts, agreeing on the values that will drive the simple message of a crisis response, and partnering with a PR pro who can school your people in media relations.

If the worst happens, get all the facts, apologize with contrition and, above all, tell the truth.

➤ **Anticipate financial dilemmas.** Faced with a cash crunch? Free up every dollar that isn't nailed down. Ask suppliers to accept temporary promissory notes instead of payments. Extend payables, speed up receivables, reduce inventory, factor invoices, and offer wholesale clients discounts for paying ahead of time.

➤ **Dodge bullets.** Under attack from rivals? Stay tapped into your network and industry news—the sooner you know what's coming, the better you'll handle it. Consider competitive pressures during strategic planning, regularly sharpen your marketing methods, commit to continual process improvement, and develop action plans for dealing with inevitable competitor challenges. Bottom line: Stay lean, stay sharp, and never surrender.

GROWING PAINS

Stepping It Up from Small Business to Midsize Company

Entrepreneurs are visionaries. Risk takers. Daredevils, even. They get through the early days on guts and adrenaline, lurching three steps forward, two steps back, living the dream. That works for a while. But inevitably, growth stalls. The dreamer who built a $5 million business from scratch is almost always ill-equipped to take it to $100–200 million. Reaching that rarified revenue range demands three big upgrades:

1. Upgrade Yourself. If your company steps up to the next level of growth, it'll happen either thanks to you or in spite of you. My career crossroads came nine years in. Our revenues were $12 million, but expansionitis had us gushing red ink. We couldn't find good talent fast enough, and our lightweight systems were imploding. Desperate, I hired Dean Bachelor, a turnaround consultant, to stop the bleeding. After exhaustive due diligence, he sat me down and looked me dead in the eye. "Tom," he said, "the biggest problem in your company is you."

My jaw dropped as Dean rattled off a laundry list of my transgressions and shortcomings. Our debt-to-equity ratio was four to five times higher than our bank's comfort range; I was Ivan the Insensitive with employees; our lame budgeting process was steering us toward a financial cliff; the absence of a strategic plan caused us to operate in continual crisis mode.

My head was spinning. I was the problem? How could I be the problem? I had to collect myself, swallow hard, and acknowledge that my company was growing faster than I was. I had been trying to do it all myself, which of course made me more frantic, less caring, and a lousy leader. Sure enough, I was a baby CEO at all of thirty-eight years old. But that mattered squat. I had to toss my ego out the window, roll up my sleeves, and get to work.

I committed to a regimen of continuous improvement—as a leader, coach, and manager of business functions. I had a feeling that if I didn't lead the way up, I'd turn into a lead weight carrying my people to the bottom. I told my executive committee that if my own skills couldn't keep pace, I'd do the honorable thing and bow out. As majority shareholder and chairman, I had the power to replace myself as CEO and president and was fully prepared to do so. In fact, many entrepreneurs choose to hand the reins to a new CEO and step aside, or hire a COO (chief operating officer) to clean up after them. I chose to *upgrade* myself rather than *replace* myself, and for the next fifteen years, persistence and stubbornness pushed me to keep up with the demands of leadership.

2. Upgrade Your People. That meeting with Dean Bachelor took us from $10 million to $70 million nine years later. But it took a lunch with Dick Schulze to set the stage for our next growth spurt. Dick, founder and board chairman of electronics giant Best Buy, was an important mentor to me. Over lunch in 1994, I casually mentioned that I was working harder than I ever expected. He asked how long my management team had been together. "Twelve years," I told him proudly. He nodded and said, "There's your problem."

I was stunned. Dick was right. We were reaching a lot of our goals, but our jackrabbit growth was noticeably outpacing the skills of some key execs. Back in my seat-of-the-pants days, I had masked my fears and insecurities by wielding an iron personality. Basically, I hired submissive people in constant need of my unerring guidance. My micromanaging had created a play-it-safe culture where people did just enough to get by. Now I was more hands-off, but still conflicted about how to handle loyal yet mediocre performers. Speeding back to the office, it hit me that my personal vow to be kind and caring could coexist—it had to coexist—with expecting outstanding results and holding people accountable.

One by one, over the coming weeks, I challenged the dozen members of my executive team. Half responded and tirelessly upgraded their skills. Wayne Shimer remembered it as a sort of near-death experience. "Tom sat me down," Wayne recalled, "and said, 'Wayne, you're just not giving the team what it needs. If you can't make it work in the next ninety days, we'll have to make a change.' I said, 'Fine, I understand. I'll either make it happen or I'm gone.' And I made it happen. That's the way Tom operated—tough, but not rough. I respected that."

Six other execs couldn't or wouldn't pick up their game (three were reassigned and three left). My corporate Darwinism was working, but our executive-team flowchart looked like a slice of Swiss cheese. So many open key positions stressed me out, but I knew that filling each slot with exactly the right person called for patience.

Patience wasn't my problem. Where I messed up was assuming that seasoned vets from Corporate America would have more knowledge and skills than people already on my team. Sure, sometimes it's necessary to recruit heavy hitters for a specialized slot like CFO. But big-company outsiders, particularly those prone to bloated, bureaucratic thinking—numbers over names, politics over performance, formality over urgency—often clashed with our caring, service-oriented, entrepreneurial culture.

Take the vice president we lured from a Fortune 500 firm. He floored me one day with a passing remark. "Oh, I forgot to tell you," he said, "Darren, the manager of our Richfield store, told me he wasn't happy about some things. I told him if he wasn't happy, he could find another place to work." "You've gotta be kidding," I said, barely controlling my anger. " 'Like it or lump it' is not the way we do things around here. That's a clear violation of our mission, vision, and values. Darren's a big-time performer and he's the last guy we want to lose. If he's got complaints, we need to hear him out." I called Darren as soon as I could. It was too late. He had just accepted an offer from another company.

Serves me right. I never should have hired that veep in the first place. I fell for big cred, charisma, and championship schmoozing. I even short-circuited our own rigorous hiring process to get him. Not that he lacked for talent. He could shuffle paper, crank out memos, and market himself like a Midtown Manhattan pro. It took me a year and a half to realize he never actually did any real work. After I asked for his resignation, I discovered that everyone else had seen right through him. Wiping the egg off my face, I promised myself I'd never flip-flop that old adage, "Hire slow, fire fast." Even as the gaping hole you're trying to fill grows wider by the day, don't panic. Be prudent. Plugging the wrong person into a key position is like applying a Band-Aid to an infected wound. By the time you realize you're in trouble, you may have to amputate.

3. **Upgrade Your Business Partners.** In the midst of our executive team makeover, I began applying the same high standards to vendors, suppliers, and professional services. Our longtime CPA firm was a midsize regional shop. I learned we were their largest consumer-based business client, so I interviewed more sophisticated firms that could jump us to the next level. I was astonished to see what we'd been missing. We treated each candidate like a potential hire and made sure they shared our vision. We ended up switching to a larger firm with invaluable retail-chain experience.

Our constant quest to upgrade our vendors and strategic partners propelled our growth, but cost a friendship. Almost from day one, we called on Jack McClard for our equipment—wheel balancers, alignment machines, hydraulic lifts. I loved Jack like a brother. But after ten years, big national vendors started taking notice. One of Jack's rivals offered us a package of product lines that would save us $100,000 annually, without sacrificing service or quality. I asked Jack if he could match the offer. He tried but came up well short. "I hate to do this, Jack," I said, "but one of our principles is to give the best value to customers and shareholders. I've gotta go with the other guy's offer."

It was painful for both of us. But there was more at stake than dollars. I felt the eyes of my people on me, watching to see if I would walk my talk. Afterward, Jack and I maintained a friendship, but it was never the same. Yet I didn't regret my decision. Doing anything else would've compromised our principles, and that would've made me feel a lot worse for a lot longer.

With *The Big Book* as your guide, growing your company can be just as exhilarating as those heady upstart days. I hope it provided the knowledge and wisdom that'll help you shed any remaining seat-of-the-pants ways. May it navigate your path to enlightened entrepreneurial leadership, and may the journey be fulfilling and profitable.

KEY POINTS

GROWING PAINS

- ➤ **Upgrade yourself.** Your business will jump to the next level because of you, or it'll leave you behind. Find a trusted outsider to help face your limitations, then go to school on them. If you can't make the jump, do the honorable thing and hire a CEO and move yourself to the president role.
- ➤ **Upgrade your people.** Management teams can get moldy, especially if you hire people who play it safe and cling to your leadership. Be kind, caring, and demand outstanding performance. Better to have empty key positions than keep them filled with underachievers, and resist the lure of charming all-stars from the outside.
- ➤ **Upgrade your business partners.** Apply the same high standards to vendors that you do to your employees. Do not hesitate to comparison shop, even if it means alienating a good friend. Doing otherwise violates company principles; and your people will notice and follow suit.

ACKNOWLEDGMENTS

'm indebted to the thousands of teammates who taught me a lot and helped me develop a company that made us all proud. Their willingness to listen, learn, and share their insights contributed to this book. Special thanks to Don Gullett and Larry Brandt, fellow principals in arms.

Special thanks to my life partner, Mary Wescott, for her steadfast support and encouragement in whatever I do.

Eternal thanks to my cowriter, Phil Bolsta. Few writers can command authority and authenticity about both business and personal enlightenment. As soon as we met, I knew he was the right person to help me turn my leadership system into a book. His vibrant style makes reading about business more entertaining than I ever thought possible.

Thanks to my assistant, Edie Sandmeier, whose dedication and multitasking are the stuff of legend, and to Jason Goldberg, who helped shape *The Big Book*.

Many thanks also go to T. Trent Gegax, an eleven-year *Newsweek* magazine vet, who provided chapter-by-chapter editing. His active, edgy style grabs me like that of no other business book I've read.

To my mother, Lib, thanks for a lifetime of unconditional love and modeling a meaningful, active life at the age of eighty-nine. Thanks to my son Chris, who, like his brother, Trent, continues to enlighten my personal and professional lives. Thanks to my two daughters-in-law, Samara Minkin and Heidi Gegax, who heighten my awareness in so many important areas of life. And thanks to my brothers, Gary and Tim, and their wives, Pam and Allison, for their love and support.

I'll always be indebted to my business mentors: Dick Schulze, Curt Carlson,

Carl Pohlad, Dean Bachelor, Tom Macintosh, and John Berg.

Numerous friends, colleagues, and industry experts sacrificed substantial chunks of time to refine *The Big Book* or to help in other meaningful ways. My thanks to Matthew Abbott, Scott Bakken, Doug Barber, Romaine Bechir, Anil Bhatnager, Bruce Birkeland, Alexis Bloomstrand, Rinaldo Brutoco, Jim Bundick, Terry Childers, Larry Dennison, Roger Elias, Sherri Engstrand, Mari Fellrath, Kirsten Finstad, Brian Freeman, Mark Gassedelen, Pam Gegax, Terry Gips, Vivian Glyck, Joe Goldberg, Bob Hauer, Don Hays, Bill Hibbs, Marcia Hines, Andrew Humphrey, Ron James, Ryan Kanne, Gary Kasper, Elizabeth Kautz, Tom Kieffer, Ed Klemz, Gregg Kloke, Mike Koenigs, Ann Krzmarzick, Tom Kuhn, Bea La-Monica, Charles Lukens, Jim Lynum, Dave Mona, Patricia and Craig Neal, Greg Nemec, Gregg Newmark, Ken Noyes, Donald O'Connor, Richard Perkins Sr., Tom Porter, Craig Primiani, Gayle S. Rose, Barry Rubin, Gigi Bechir Rudd, Nancy Sabin, Larry Sandman, Mark Sathe, Alfred Schwan, Jay Scruton, Mike Sime, Darrell Skramstad, Sandy Stein, Terry Tamminen, Skip Thaler, Jeff Thull, Kathy Tunheim, Bill Velin, Ken Volker, David Wagner, Bob Wahlstedt, and Tom Zosel.

Special thanks to our all-star reviewers, who answered beyond the call of duty: Vickie Abrahamson, Carl Baldassarre, Dave Cleveland, Allen Fahden, Shelly Fling, Andrea Luhtanen, Tom Macintosh, Jay Novak, Bink Semmer, and Sven Wehrwein.

A big thank-you to former colleagues who contributed their stories: George Argodale, Jim Bemis, Darrel Blomberg, Brad Burley, Mel Donnelly, Tom DuPont, Don Gullett, Gwen and Eric Heimer, John Hyduke, Chris Koepsell, John R. Leach, Mark Lessin, Gabe Lopez, Scott McPhee, Jim Pascale, Eric Randa, Wayne Shimer, Chris Speake, Trent Stoner, Dorie Thrall, Joe Thul, Dave Urspringer, Steve Varner, Dave Wilhelmi, and Jim Wolf.

Thanks to Genoveva Llosa, our editor at HarperCollins, who's as kind and patient as she is expert at the jigsaw work of assembling a book. Thanks to Arielle Ford and Brian Hilliard for always pointing me in the right direction; to Jack Caravela, Jay Monroe, and Sharron and Harry Stockhausen for their creative contributions; to Tita Gillespie, Joe Applegate, Denise Logeland, Mel Vork, and Mary McCarty for their editing prowess; and to Earnie Larsen, Brenda Schaeffer, and Barbara J. Winter for their inspiration.

Finally, immense gratitude goes to my Higher Power, the constant companion who's gifted me with an abundance of ideas and the drive to keep moving them forward.

INDEX

ABOUT THE AUTHORS

Tom Gegax, cofounder and chairman emeritus of the 500-store upscale Tires Plus store chain, served as chairman and CEO (head coach) for twenty-four years. By the time Tom sold the company to Bridgestone/Firestone in 2000, it had mushroomed from a napkin sketch to a market leader with 150 locations in ten states and $200 million in revenue. A pioneer of the tough-minded, warmhearted coaching style of management, Tom founded Gegax Management Systems in 2000 to coach growing companies. His ideas were featured in *The New York Times* and *Fast Company* magazine, and on CNN, CNBC, and PBS, and he has won numerous national and regional awards for his entrepreneurial leadership. Tom has served numerous corporate and nonprofit boards, including the Center for Ethical Business Cultures, and is also the author of *Winning in the Game of Life: Self-Coaching Secrets for Success* (Harmony Books). He and Mary Wescott live in Minneapolis and La Jolla. Visit him at www.gegax.com.

Phil Bolsta contributes to numerous business and general interest magazines. He also collaborates with a variety of firms to produce internal and external communications and marketing materials. He lives with his family in Minneapolis. Phil can be reached at pbolsta@yahoo.com.